TEXT IN THE EXHIBITION MEDIUM

Canadian Cataloguing in Publication Data

Main entry under title:

Text in the exhibition medium

(Collection Museo)
Translation of: L'écrit dans le média exposition.
Includes bibliographical references.
Co-published by: Musée de la civilisation.

ISBN 2-89172-024-5 (Société des musées québécois) – ISBN 2-551-13496-X (Musée de la civilisation)

1. Museum techniques. 2. Exhibition. 3. French language – Rhetoric. 4. Museum publications. I. Blais, Andrée, 1962- . II. Anctil, Roch. III. Société des musées québécois. IV. Musée de la civilisation (Québec). V. Series: Collection Muséo. English.

AM151.E3713 1995   069'.53   C95-940820-7

ISBN 2-89172-024-5/Société des musées québécois
ISBN 2-551-13496-X/Musée de la civilisation, Québec City
Legal deposit – 2nd quarter 1995
Bibliothèque nationale du Québec
National Library of Canada

PRINTED IN CANADA

The Musée de la civilisation is a government corporation that is subsidized by the ministère de la Culture et des Communications du Québec.

The Société des musées québécois is a non-profit agency that receives support from the Ministère de la Culture et des Communications du Québec and the Department of Canadian Heritage.

In the interest of stylistic clarity, the masculine form of pronouns is used and is taken to include the feminine.

TEXT IN THE EXHIBITION MEDIUM

Edited by Andrée Blais

Preface by
Chandler G. Screven

LA SOCIÉTÉ
DES MUSÉES
QUÉBÉCOIS

MUSÉE DE LA
CIVILISATION

CONTENTS

Contents

9

Foreword

Text in the Exhibition Medium, the latest addition to the *Muséo* collection, is intended to provide practitioners in the museum network at large with new theoretical considerations and practical advice on the presentation of text in the museum environment.

Scriptovisual materials present considerable challenges to museums of all types throughout the world. The nature and scope of these challenges are continually changing, yet certain matters of concern remain constant. In this unique book, specialists from a wide array of disciplines take stock of the question and share the findings of their research.

Works of art and objects – whether a modern sculpture, the prototype of a telescope, a shard of pottery or porcelain from an archeological site, or a naive painting – must be displayed; that is a museum's function. What should be said about them? What should the documentation offer the public? How and to whom should it be addressed? Visitors are not unique, but whether they are 6 or 87, literate or illiterate, native or tourist, they are always interested in learning. According to recent surveys, learning remains the main reason why people visit museums.

We would like to thank Andrée Blais of the Musée de la civilisation for acting as editor of this book, and Francine Lacroix of the same institution for coordinating its publication. We are also grateful to Catherine Franche and Carole Pageau of the Professional Development Service of the Société des musées québécois for their collaboration and support.

It is our hope that this book will be of use to the museum network as a whole and that it will offer the members of that network food for thought, now and in future.

Hélène Pagé
Director
Cultural Action and
Relations with Québec Museums
Musée de la civilisation

Sylvie Gagnon
Director General
Société des musées québécois

Acknowledgments

This book could not have been published without the support and collaboration of many people. We wish to express our gratitude to those people for their steadfast efforts and commitment.

We wish to extend our sincere thanks to the members of the scientific committee: Michel Allard, Faculty of Education, Université du Québec à Montréal; André Beauchesne, BOS Communications; Louise Boucher, LOCUS Loisirs et Culture; Frédéric Metz, Design Department, Université du Québec à Montréal; and Line Ouellet, Exhibition Services, Musée de la civilisation. These invaluable collaborators judiciously guided and advised us throughout the project.

We would also like to thank the contributors for spontaneously supporting this project from the outset, for their sustained interest and their unfailing rigour throughout this collective undertaking. We wish to acknowledge in particular Bernard Schiele of the Université du Québec à Montréal, Daniel Jacobi of the Université de Bourgogne, Marie Sylvie Poli of the Université Pierre Mendès-France, Chandler G. Screven of the University of Wisconsin-Milwaukee, Denis Samson of the Université du Québec à Montréal, Andrée Blais of the Musée de la civilisation, Anne Decrosse of the École des hautes études en sciences sociales et en muséologie des sciences et techniques, Jean-Paul Natali of the Cité des sciences et de l'industrie de La Villette, Hélène Lamarche of The Montreal

Museum of Fine Arts, Hélène Baños of the Université de Montréal, Laurent Marquart of GSM Design, Rock Anctil of Marinelli/Anctil Art & design, Antoine Del Busso of Les Éditions Fides, Dyane Plourde and Jean Michaud of Mauve design graphique, and Ghislaine Fiset, writer.

Finally, we would like to thank Christine Côté, Hana Gottesdiener, Martin Polczynski, Claire Simard and Marie-Thérèse Werra, who directly or indirectly assisted us in conducting the research and preparing the book for publication.

Preface

There has been impressive progress made in designing the scholarly, aesthetic and physical aspects of exhibition spaces – even in stimulating visitors to explore exhibits. For many museum settings, however, it does not appear that much substantive communication or cultural enrichment is taking place for the majority of unguided museum visitors. Certainly, some exhibits successfully stimulate and expand the horizons of some visitors. But, for many frequent as well as infrequent visitors, the meaningful content of exhibits and accompanying text often are misunderstood, oversimplified, and even distorted to fit pre-existing misconceptions. These visitors may be "enjoying" exhibit experiences, but may be receiving the wrong messages.

In this open environment, the unguided visitor's personal needs, attitudes, predispositions, misconceptions, time constraints and other characteristics play major roles in affecting what an how they attend to given exhibit content, how they interpret what they see and read, how they feel about the experience, what they tell their friends, and even how often they are likely to return. Their interpretations of exhibit objects and accompanying text are as much a product of "viewer psychology" as they are a product of the exhibit content and presentation formats of the objects and text that accompany them. Thus, useful and important text and graphics to help visitors understand and enjoy exhibit objects cannot help if they are not present, visible, or readable, and, if they are present, they have little value if visitors do not carefully attend to them, or if they distort the information they read.

One important question is the degree of control that exhibit planners and designers have over what visitors attend to and the distortions in communication that take place between the exhibit information and the "message" visitors receive. Can careful front-end analysis effective formatting and placement, type size, friendly language, formative evaluation, etc. improve communication effectiveness? Efforts to examine such possibilities in museum settings in recent years suggest that the answer to this question is *yes*. Without an effective "interpretive interface" between visitors and exhibit objects on display, it seems likely that the educational value of exhibit experiences will be very limited – i.e., unless viewers already have at least some background and experience with these objects. This book examines some of the important variables and results of labels research that provide the framework for how labels work and why.

It's about time. Historically, the use of interpretive text in public exhibitions has been resisted by curators and designers under the guise of arguments like *"the objects can speak for themselves," "exhibits are for those whose interests and backgrounds allow them to benefit," "museums are not for lay audiences," "too much text in and around exhibits distract from the visual properties of the objects," "labels are here for those who can benefit from them, not for the lay visitor,"* and *"people don't read labels anyway."*

Although the situation is changing, most museums in North America and Europe continue to resist the idea that interpretive text is a needed component in exhibition design, in spite of evidence to the contrary. Among other things, many exhibit designers and others appear to perceive the presence of labels as a kind of conflict of interest. Since interpretive text and graphics are not, themselves, artifacts or art, their presence often is perceived to be in conflict with acceptable exhibit "aesthetics," and/or the integrity of exhibition content. Therefore, text may be relegated to simple descriptive name-date tabs and made as unobtrusive as possible. When pressured to include text, it is formatted and often placed far from reference objects, high and out-of-the-way, printed in tiny type, "hidden" as take-home pamphlets, and so on. Too often, the text itself is written in "technospeak" by specialist who address conceptual, historical, and technical issues that bear little or no direct relationship to actual objects on display (which is an important negative feature for many visitors).

It is not surprising, therefore, that studies of label usage in museums generally show that few people are seen reading labels. Without real explanations whose style, format, and language have been adapted to be as understandable to targeted audiences, visitors not only do not learn from them, they learn to ignore them!

In recent years, with the advent of "visitors-centered" exhibit designs, concerted efforts have been made to plan and design text and other interpretive supports that give visitors better and more useful information for understanding what they are seeing. But, with important exceptions, these efforts have not been as productive as might be expected, for a variety of reasons: Typically, the formats and styles of this "new" educationally oriented text reflect a formal school-like framework, unsuited to the open settings. And there have been other deficiences – preparation of text formats and content often do not include input from the target visitors themselves, text style and language ignore the *informal* nature of museum settings in which reading must take place, and, usually, text design does not incorporate established principles of communication design.

Visitor usage of educationally oriented labels and their communication effectiveness have shown serious problems and, at the least, unpredictable results. Many visitors still do not use labels and, when they do, their primary messages often are misunderstood or distorted. Misconceptions about whales, food chains, plate tectonics, or abstract expressionist paintings still remain, except perhaps in different clothing. Visitors often do not (or cannot) follow instructions, they ignore important relationships, and attention appears more or less random and unfocused.

One lesson here has been that, when communicating to lay audiences, it is not just a matter of preparing labels in clear language and using snappy, attractive formats at more appropriate locations. When visitors view objects, paintings and read accompanying text and signs without benefit of teachers, documents or others, their interpretations depend not only on the text, graphics, and other features, but also on what visitors bring with them in the form of knowledge, pre-conceptions, interests, and attitudes. Because the museum is an environment in which visitor attention and effort are *voluntary*, visitors have no reasons to pay attention or invest time and effort on interpretive materials unless they have good personal reasons to do so. The "good reasons" include a host of personal and socially motivated agendas that affect the time and effort visitors may be willing to spend reading or relating exhibits to what they are reading. For example, spending time and effort are influenced by such things as how quickly visitors can find information that relates to their familiar, everyday world, can find answers to questions raised by exhibit content (*How did they make that! Why is the skin purple?*), recognize immediate uses of some exhibit information (*Where do I start? Which method will work best?*), and how they perceive their ability to understand the exhibit's content. All of these can be addressed in the design, layout, and wording of the labels themselves.

Given that print labels and graphics are important modes for delivering information can give meaning to exhibit objects, they can serve a variety of purposes. Labels can (a) provide specific *information* about the visual content of exhibits (names, dates, relationships, what an object does, why it is there); (b) *instruct* visitors on what to do or look for; (c) *personalize* topics (relate the unfamiliar to the more familiar); (d) *interpret* the content of an exhibit; and (e) *orient* visitors to what to expect, how things are organized, and how they might relate to exhibit content (from Screven, 1992, p. 185).

While many visitors resist reading labels, they *do* read them when they have reasons to read them: for example, to get an answer to a question (*How was that made? Why is it here?*), obtain information for taking and "action", and so on. The impact of different label and graphic formats vary depending on the purposes they are supposed to serve. Sometimes, traditional formats can work effectively (e.g., with high-interest objects) as *passive* two-dimensional text panels on walls, under

22

paintings, etc. If it is necessary to engage visitor attention to more subtle conceptual aspects of objects, an active voice and personal appeals may be needed such as the use of intriguing headlines or leading questions based on visitor interviews (Who *is the woman in Rembrandt's Nightwatch? Why are those temple figures painted blue?*) When discriminations or complex concepts need to be developed, this may require focusing attention to certain properties of objects, low tech "interactive" labels that present text/graphics in overlapping ("layered") layers often are helpful here (e.g., lifting hinged panel, sliding a door, or pulling a paddle to gain access to "hidden" information under or behind upper layers (Screven, 1992).

Some useful principles are evolving that are helping to predict what unguided visitors are likely to do or read, or attend to, during a visit, how they will move through exhibit spaces, how much time they will spend viewing a display, or remain in an exhibit hall. These have important implications for what and how text needs to be designed; for example, building personal connections and challenging tasks into text to provide positive reasons for giving time and attention to it, minimizing the perceived time to read text, and so on.

These characteristics, among others, form the context in which interpretive graphics and educational exhibits for the unguided general public must function. The density of objects, their organization, text-graphics formats, the ease of finding desired information, entrance-exit orientation, the communication efficiency of particular media, and active-passive formats affect both positive and negative impressions that can encourage or discourage visitor attention and, ultimately, what viewers take away with them from museum experiences.

This book is a welcome step in addressing the underlying elements of label/text presentations and the important roles that labels can play in making exhibitions meaningful to the nonexpert. The book addresses the variables that can affect the communication properties of labels and their ability to "bridge the gap" between exhibition objects and the visitors who view them.

In future competition for leisure publics, museums and other cultural institutions face stiff competition from the many alternatives that leisure-time audiences will have in the future when choosing how to spend limited discretionary time. To provide the memorable and enjoyable experiences that can effectively compete with these alternatives, museums must become more sensitive to the motivational conditions that can hold current audiences and attract new ones. While learning new things and new meanings of things can be memorable and rewarding it cannot be assumed that simply seeing exhibit content will be enjoyable by itself without help from interpretive supports such as well designed labels. For this to happen, museums must learn how to motivate visitors to give more than casual time and attention to the important ideas and resources in their exhibitions. Explanatory text is crucial to this process because it can provide much of the meaning to the objects visitors are seeing and discovering. If museums ignore the role of explanatory text and other supporting interpretive media, they will be doing so at great risk.

The importance of this book is that it addresses this task and can help museums meet this challenge through its careful analysis and research on motivating visitors to read text and the conditions under which text can enhance museum experiences for traditional and nontraditional publics.

Chandler G. Screven, Ph.D.

Emeritus Professor
Department of Psychology
University of Wisconsin-Milwaukee
Principal, Screven & Associates, Chicago

Introduction

The question of the exhibition text has been raised over and over again in recent years. This question is not whether text should be used: the importance of the written word is well recognized in museum practice. However, the text is a source of concern, as many books, articles and seminars have clearly shown. Despite all the discussion the exhibition text has fuelled, there are few broad surveys on the subject, a gap this publication is intended to fill.

Text in the Exhibition Medium challenges the foundations of museum-related writing at a time when museums are focusing more and more on the dissemination of information and text is being used to structure the message conveyed. Art museums, history museums, science museums and interpretation centres all use text for different purposes and in different forms. However, the widespread use of texts does not mean that the rules of the art are known or understood, as the need for training expressed by numerous museum officials indicates. While the ample use of text is beyond debate, the forms it takes are regularly discussed from the standpoint of museum practice and the effect on visitors.

How could we meet so many different needs? How could we cover all aspects of text as it is used in exhibitions and still find a unifying thread? The solution was to pause and look for common ground, a general theme that could be of interest and value to a broad range of institutions. After a great deal of thought and discussion, we chose the text in its scriptovisual form as the main subject of this book and the audio text as the secondary theme.

Text in the Exhibition Medium focuses on the rhetoric of the text, its reception and its production. It is precisely these three points that distinguish this book and its contribution to the general debate on text in the exhibition medium.

The book is divided into two main sections. The first is largely theoretical and contains three chapters: "Defining", "Reading" and "Hearing". The second, which is more practical in nature, also consists of three chapters: "Writing", "Showing" and "Evaluating".

The variety of subjects discussed naturally required a collective effort. The authors have focused their expert eye on analyzing scriptovisual text as it is used in exhibitions. The authors have their own particular area of expertise, which they have applied to museum practice. Each essay is self-contained and reflects the viewpoint of the author. However, their placement clearly reflects the complementary nature of the various viewpoints and their combination provides an exhaustive treatment of the subject.

This book does not offer a series of recipes and ingredients obligingly revealed by the authors. All of the authors agree that empiricism in the area of the exhibition text is essential. Standards, rules and trends do exist, of course, but they must be tempered by experience and experimentation.

Defining

This chapter presents the theoretical parameters needed to analyze text in the exhibition medium. Bernard Schiele introduces the notion of the repeated resurgence of the text at all stages of an exhibition and demonstrates its role in organizing the exhibition. He also surveys substitute and complementary forms of text. He categorizes different institutions according to the use they make of text in conjunction with exhibitions. Daniel Jacobi and Marie Sylvie Poli define the text by its linguistic components, its various semiotic registers and its communication roles and functions.

Reading

The second chapter focuses on the question of text reception by examining the reading process. Andrée Blais provides a general description of the act of reading and establishes links between this act and the production of exhibition texts. Denis Samson specifically analyzes the reading strategies of exhibition visitors. He identifies the basic elements of such strategies, i.e. the selection of information, conceptual orientation and assimilation of content.

Hearing

The third and final chapter of the theoretical section of the book presents two cases in which text is heard rather than seen. These cases indicate the numerous forms a text can take, whether complementary or substitute. Anne Decrosse and Jean-Paul Natali question the notion of text used in conjunction with a scientific exhibition, with a conceptual bias that favours text presented orally. Hélène Lamarche offers the viewpoint of an art museum through the audioguide, which is perceived as an educational aid.

Writing

Chapter 4, which begins the second part of the book, examines practical questions aimed at text writers. Andrée Blais describes the critical process of writing, in the form of a guide that systematically covers the essential phases required in the writing and displaying of exhibition text. Hélène Baños examines the linguistic standards to be observed, and the importance of readability and intelligibility.

Showing

Chapter 5 looks at the format of texts. Laurent Marquart takes a critical look at the use of text and encourages readers to reflect on the location of scriptovisual messages along the exhibition itinerary. Rock Anctil focuses on typography and page layout, using legibility and information structuring criteria. Antoine Del Busso delves into the area of revision, and stresses how the reviser establishes connections between the verification of linguistic signs and the verification of the typographic code. Dyane Plourde and Jean Michaud describe the various printing processes, ranging from photocopying to silkscreen printing, and emphasize the strengths and weaknesses of each.

Evaluating

The sixth and final chapter is intended to be a practical evaluation tool. It contains a checklist of the points to be considered when a scriptovisual text is evaluated.

Andrée Blais
Editor

PART 1

THEORETICAL CONSIDERATIONS

CHAPTER 1

DEFINING

Text in the Exhibition Medium

Using the Cités-Cinés exhibition as a concrete example, the author seeks to show the formative nature of text. He starts by defining the exhibition medium, which consists of a complex whole made up of different registers and media, of which text is one component. Text may be essentially absent from the exhibition, as is the case in Ciné-Cités, provided visitors can decipher the content from what they already know. Through language, which structurally precedes the written document, visitors can name the things they see. Text helps make explicit the structural role that language plays in anchoring meanings. The author then turns to another aspect of text, the genesis of the exhibition. He explains how the written word governs the organization of the program, of which it is the initial form, and how the text contributes as organizer to the construction of the promotional discourse. Even outside the exhibition, text reflects the program and influences visitors' perception. While there is a tendency today to replace text with more contemporary means of communication such as the audioguide and multimedia presentations, these means do not obviate the need for the written word. In fact, text is integrated into the exhibition more than ever in the form of accompanying documents, catalogues, guides and brochures that complement and enrich it. Text is the very foundation of the exhibition and is present from the genesis of the exhibition to the promotional discourse. The second article in this chapter, by Daniel Jacobi and Marie Sylvie Poli, examines the scriptovisual document, one of the most commonly used forms of text.

Text in the Exhibition Medium

Bernard Schiele

Professor in the Department
of Communications, Université
du Québec à Montréal (UQAM),
and in the joint Université
de Montréal-UQAM
museology program

This article focuses on the formative role that text plays in an exhibition. To illustrate this role, I have chosen to examine the *Cités-Cinés* exhibition, designed by the Cité des sciences et de l'industrie (CSI) La Villette and presented first in Paris, then in Montréal for two consecutive years.

This exhibition was remarkable in many ways. It featured a number of celebrated film settings such as the roofs of Paris, the tunnels of the New York subway, and English pubs. These settings are well known to us because the film industry, since its inception, has used them as a backdrop for its stories. The metaphor of the city organized and linked the various components of the exhibition. It was an imaginary city, at once strange and familiar, made up of heterogeneous fragments, juxtaposed in much the same way as memory associates separate recollections that are remote in time and space. In Montréal, the exhibition was mounted in the Palais de la Civilisation, where it occupied all of the floors and made use of the passages and stairways in the building. Visitors were encouraged to criss-cross the city, from the roofs, installed on the uppermost floor, to the sewers, located below the ground floor. In each of the settings, film clips were continually projected.

Visitors were expected to recognize and react to these celebrated moments as they appeared on the screen.

The most remarkable feature of this exhibition was not the intrusion of the real into the virtual, imaginary universe being exhibited, but the apparent absence of any trace of the written word.

How did the exhibition function? To answer this question, let us take a brief look at the exhibition as a medium.

THE EXHIBITION, A COHERENT, MEANINGFUL WHOLE

Without assembled objects, there can be no assessment, and without an assessment, there is no exhibition. To exhibit means, first and foremost, to select what is worthy of attention or representative of a whole.[1] This is what *Cités-Cinés* did. It assembled in a given time and place what were deemed significant elements of film in order to draw them to the attention of visitors.

Was the exhibition an attempt to display everything noteworthy in film? By no means. The exhibition's designers had to pick and choose. From the standpoint of the designers, not showing everything, or from the viewpoint of visitors, not seeing everything, was of secondary importance: the exhibiting process took precedence over the elements displayed.[2] It is an exhibition's theme, the principles guiding the decision to include or exclude an object, and the manner in which it is arranged that reveal the internal logic of its discourse. The logic of visiting practices is made manifest by the itinerary followed, and the understanding, interest, pleasure or boredom experienced by visitors.

Thus, the only acts of importance are the act of putting on the exhibition and the reciprocal act of visitors who, turning toward the designated objects,[3] become a party to the discourse addressed to them.[4] An exhibition depends on the conjunction at a given time and in a given

---

1. J. Davallon, "Gestes de mise en exposition" in *Claquemurer pour ainsi dire tout l'univers* (Paris: Éditions du Centre Georges-Pompidou, CCI, 1986), pp. 241-266.
2. The notion of totality is drawn from structuralism and Gestalt theory.
3. The term "object" is used here in its usual meaning. It is not solely a question of art objects, but of anything that is included and worthy of attention in the exhibition.
4. J. Davallon, "Avant-propos" in *op. cit.*, pp. 7-16.

setting, of the packaging of content through the mobilization of different registers of iconic, verbal, gestural, spatial, stylistic, ideological and other codes, and the shaping of a materiality and the objects, artifacts, panels, space, colours and other components that underlie this materiality.[5] The relationships established among these constituent elements regulate the workings of the exhibition. It is for this reason that an exhibition is defined by its underlying components and the manner in which they are organized in space:[6] the whole is greater than the sum of its parts.[7]

This leads us to a **first observation: text in an exhibition is only one of several media, a possible component and nothing more**. The designers of the *Cités-Cinés* exhibition decided not to use it.

COROLLARY:
To dissociate text from the other constituents in order to consider it separately is impossible without affecting understanding of the system of meanings inherent in an exhibition. However, it is possible to scrutinize the role of text in order to better ascertain its particular contribution by temporarily considering it in and of itself, but it is essential to bear in mind that only when text is set against the other constituents does its formative effect contribute to the overall meaning of the exhibition, as visitors reconstruct it.

Without text, how could visitors to the *Cités-Cinés* exhibition organize all of the signals they perceived and attribute meaning to the exhibition?

THE EXHIBITION, A REBUS TO BE DECIPHERED

For the designer, the overall scheme of the exhibition must reflect the objectives adopted, i.e. the units of meaning that visitors must absorb and interpret as they receive information. For visitors, the perspective is

---

5. U. Eco, *La structure absente* (Paris: Mercure de France, 1972).

6. Strictly speaking, there is no difference between objects and aids; both are components of the exhibition, just as the spatial arrangement is. Here, I am maintaining an artificial distinction for the sake of clarity.

7. J.-F. Barbier-Bouvet, "Le système de l'exposition" in *Histoire d'expo* (Paris, *Peuple et Culture*, Centre Georges-Pompidou, CCI, 1983), pp. 13-17.

different, in that the exhibition is a rebus to be deciphered. The meaning of the exhibition does not exist prior to the visit. To enter the exhibition is, for visitors, to penetrate a labyrinth that invites them to follow a multitude of paths and confronts them with a multitude of stimuli.[8] Visitors must go forward, turn right or left, go back, branch off, retrace their steps or come up against an obstacle to discover the sections of the exhibition and visualize its layout. They must orient themselves in and through the process of discovering the exhibition.[9]

At the same time, visitors must understand what is expected of them, i.e. to decode what is being shown them and what is being said about what is being shown them. Thus, visitors look, observe, read, manipulate, associate, compare, dissociate, and regroup. They constantly try to sort, select and integrate information in order to ascribe meaning to what is being offered. From focusing and refocusing, they engage in a cognitive shuttling back and forth in order to understand the spatial organization of the exhibition and its content.

Cités-Cinés was effective because each visitor could ascribe a meaning to it, although not just any meaning, because the visitors were familiar with what was being presented. The exhibition was based on a film culture shared by most, if not all, of the visitors. This did not necessarily mean a detailed knowledge of each of the films illustrated by a sequence, although such knowledge was not excluded, but instead a knowledge of the situations and the settings in which they took place. In other words, visitors had an intuitive knowledge of the functional structure of film, which enabled them to recognize a narrative structure because they have learned how to follow a plot and anticipate the events that will take place. The art of staging is, of course, to orchestrate surprises so as to foil expectations. The visitors, limited to what they have already seen and know through previous experience, projected that experience onto *Cités-Cinés* and thus decoded the exhibition and reconstituted its messages. They were able to name the settings through

---

8. A. Moles, "Vue générale de l'exposition" in *L'écrit dans l'exposition* (Paris, Peuple et Culture, 1983), pp. 23-33.

9. Obviously, the question of choosing an itinerary at the time of the second visit is posed in an entirely different manner.

which they moved and to identify the film excerpts projected. In the process, they structured their relationship with the exhibition, where, as noted earlier, turning to the designated objects, they became a party to the discourse addressed to them.

This leads us to a **second observation: it is because the visitors could name the settings and the films and recognize them that *Cités-Cinés*, which might otherwise have remained a formless space, became coherent. Stated more simply, the shaping of objects is based on the mediation of language.**[10] **Structurally, language precedes text.**

CROLLARY:
Text can be excluded only when everyone is familiar with it. Conversely, it can be said that text is the very foundation of the exhibition, even when an exhibition such as *Cités-Cinés* forgoes its overt expression.

However, visitors seemed even freer to reconstruct the meaning because almost nothing hindered their spontaneous evocations and associations or distracted them from the object itself and what they knew about it. The exhibition's objective was certainly not to wrench the visitor from his representations and cause him to distance himself from them. Does this mean that, by excluding text, *Cités-Cinés* also excluded the possibility of guiding the manner in which the visitor received what was being shown? Nothing could be further from the truth.

THE EXHIBITION, A MEANS OF INTERACTING WITH THE VISITOR

Exhibitions can be classified in different ways. They can be called documentary when they enable the public to discover and assimilate a certain amount of information on a given topic,[11] in contrast to exhibitions that present primarily a body of work, the art exhibition

---

10. E. Cassirer, *The Philosophy of Symbolic Forms* (New Haven and London: Yale University Press), 1966.

11. J. Davallon, "Exposition scientifique, espace, ostension" in *Protée*, 1988, Vol. 16, No. 3, pp. 5-16.

being the prototype. Between these two extremes, the divisions and categories vary and overlap: scientific, cultural, historical or ethnological exhibitions; thematic, didactic, discovery or awareness exhibitions; and so on.[12] It should be noted, in passing, that treatment of text is also affected by the traditions prevailing in different institutions, which establish a reference framework. Text occupies a space delimited by the institution's history and the rules it has developed. To classify exhibitions also means differentiating them in terms of how they treat text. Let us now turn to what they have in common.

Whatever their genre, all exhibitions use a huge assortment of processes, such as evocations, spectacular elements, artifacts, demonstrations, multimedia presentations and so on to captivate, convince, sensitize or inform the visitor. Above all, they present in order to establish contact, show in order to foster recognition or discovery, and explain in order to make viewers understand. The exhibition, through what it presents and the manner in which its content is presented, guides the way visitors perceive what is being shown and receive the information that is provided on what is being shown. In other words, all exhibitions, to varying degrees, strive to alter visitors' perception or vision of things, aesthetic sensibility and knowledge. Indeed, they all seek to influence viewers' behaviour.

Third observation: text is only one component of a complex guidance system elaborated to orient the interpretation of the exhibition, whose operationality only reveals itself during the mental reconstruction that visitors perform during the visit.

In this respect, the text controls the decoding of the exhibition, in order to limit the latter's polysemy, in at least three ways: it presents the objects it wishes to bring to visitors' attention; it transmits information about the objects; and it reveals the writer's or the designer's bias.[13]

---

12. A categorization by topic would be endless, i.e. architectural, botanical, photographic and other exhibitions.

13. M.S. Poli has shown that labels, despite the constraints on the writing of them, combine the three registers. See M.S. Poli, "Le parti pris des mots dans l'étiquette: une approche linguistique", *Publics & Musées*, 1992, No. 1, pp. 91-111. In the same issue, see the article by J. Desjardins and D. Jacobi.

From a conceptual standpoint, while the use of text makes explicit the structural role of language in the process of anchoring meaning, the form it takes demonstrates an economy specific to the exhibition medium. It is from this perspective that we must interpret all discussion about text in the exhibition medium, whether to make it more effective and efficient,[14] or, in a more pragmatic sense, to justify its use.[15] In other words, the structural relation of text to the meanings of the exhibition is actualized in and through a functional relationship. The meaning of a text is always thought out in a concrete situation: the work of language, since what is at work in a written text is at least language, occurs within social reality, never outside it.

Its role in the genesis of the exhibition is another facet of text that warrants mention.

EXTRAMURAL TEXTS: THE SUPRATEXT[16] PRECEDES THE EXHIBITION

An exhibition usually starts out as a preliminary proposal, followed by another proposal in which the subject, objective, themes and an initial conceptual breakdown of the content are indicated. Next come the scenario and the design describing each exhibition area in detail. This preliminary conception constitutes the program of the exhibition. In the example at hand, *Cités-Cinés*, it is concealed in and by means of the elaboration of non-textual aids that contain no trace of text. It regulates the intentional combination of elements, i.e. the organization of the whole, the choice of the settings to be reconstituted, the choice of sequences, and so on. Moreover, it governs the implementation of the plan of action producing signs and determines the strategy chosen to capture and hold visitors' attention. The objectives are transformed into

---

14. B. Serrell, *Making Exhibit Labels. A Step-by-Step Guide* (Nashville: American Association for State and Local History, 1983).

15. P. McManus, "Oh Yes They Do: How Museum Visitors Read Labels and Interact with Exhibit Texts" in *Curator*, 1989, Vol. 32, No. 3, p. 174-189. M. Borun and M. Miller, *What's in a Name? A Study of the Effectiveness of Explanatory Labels in a Science Museum*. Philadelphia: Franklin Institute and Science Museum, 1980.

16. Through the neologism supratext – "supra" means before, prior to – I wish to designate the preliminary work from which the exhibition develops.

operators. Ideally, visitors will perceive them at the time of reception and decode them as units of meaning. This is true to such an extent that, when an evaluation is carried out, the process, regardless of its specific variations, compares the initial objectives with the behaviour observed, the components perceived and the concepts understood and retained.

Fourth observation: text governs the genesis of the exhibition and establishes the exhibition program. However, it is readily apparent that its realization and transformation into a concrete object is a matter of finding a way to incorporate constraints, while the realization of the program, which is more analytical in nature, is aimed at the finest possible breakdown of the constituent elements.

THE EXHIBIT TEXT: THE CONSTRUCTION OF A DISTINCTIVE IMAGE

The reader may well object that visitors may have heard about the exhibition, listened to comments or criticism on radio or television or seen posters or advertisements, in other words, that they already have in mind a representation of the exhibition, which serves as an analytical framework for the stimuli they perceive when visiting it. It is possible, then, that visitors already know how to orient their reading of the exhibition. The text that underlies the program actually operates at a second level, that of the promotional discourse whose purpose is to give the exhibition an existence as an event in the social arena. The objective is, of course, to encourage and motivate the visit but, in so doing, it contributes more or less explicitly to constructing a framework to receive what viewers perceive.

Everything that accompanies an exhibition contributes to the production of its meaning. Advertisements in the print media and on television,[17] posters and news reports all rely on text in one form or

---

17. Television is said to be the medium par excellence of the image. In one sense, this is true. The image is omnipresent on the small screen. However, it is rarely sufficient in itself. Indeed, television is often little more than illustrated radio, where the accompanying text anchors and sustains, in a coherent discursive framework, the meaning to be attributed to a series of shots that would otherwise remain merely juxtaposed to each other.

another. The attention-getting function is undeniable, i.e. stimulating potential visitors' curiosity and attracting them to the exhibition. The objective is to make the exhibition exist in the minds of potential visitors and create a social event. Other occurrences contribute to this end. The vernissage, for example, with its pomp, invitations, press releases, media coverage and the inevitable comments, criticism and gossip that accompany it, also emphasizes the social nature of the event.

Fifth observation: the promotional discourse and the procedures that emphasize the social nature of the exhibition also reflect the program. Indeed, they are derived or transposed forms of the program. When text is presented to visitors in the form of slogans or snatches of conversation, even outside the exhibition, it remains the very foundation of the exhibition.

COROLLARY:

The exhibition is a form of intertextuality[18] given weight by its social aspect: the legitimacy of whoever speaks or writes about it ensures its fame and influence, makes an event of it, compels choices to be made, and so on.

ALTERNATE FORMS OF THE TEXT

Debate over the text continues. Some observers feel that labels and panels have had their day and now belong to the past. They should be replaced by more contemporary, user-friendly forms such as *in situ* animation, audioguides, audiovisual materials, computers, multimedia presentations and so on, in other words, an array of devices that alleviate the effort the visit requires, whether to satisfy the visitors' momentary need for information, as is the case with animation, or to contextualize the visit and thereby provide a key to it through demonstrations or shows.

In fact, none of these substitutes excludes text and, even less so, language, for the reasons mentioned earlier. They are intended as

---

18. The term "intertextuality", introduced by Bakhtine, is widely used in semiotics. It refers to the influences that discourses exercise on each other and, consequently, the constant borrowing that goes on between them. A discourse is never independent. Rather, it represents a transformation or reproduction of more or less implicit models.

contemporary solutions to historic forms of text. Consequently, debate surrounding text must not be confused with repudiation of text. As exhibitions have become recognized as a medium and museums have become transformed, the forms taken by text have changed considerably. For example, the rise of the thematic exhibition and its typical device, the narrative framework, has certainly contributed to a rethinking of the role hitherto attributed to text. In this type of exhibition, which is explicitly designed to alter the visitors' behaviour, text is undoubtedly the preferred instrument. In this perspective, it is noteworthy that the question of text did not arise alone, but was accompanied by the question of the audience, with which it is inextricably linked.[19] Similarly, the educational upsurge in the early 1970s also helped transform text in exhibitions, by attaching, more than ever before, a crucial importance to the objectives pursued.[20] As this movement intensified, the reading of text was subjected to questioning. Since meaning is transmitted above all by text, this is entirely understandable. Scores of studies focused on the relationship between text and its interpretation in order to optimize it.

Sixth observation: current debate on text is less a rejection of it than a transformation of its role and of the visibility accorded to it. We must examine this transformation in relation to the transformation of the exhibition medium itself in light of the new social functions assigned to the latter.

If text precedes the exhibition, it also ensures it some degree of durability once it has ended. Before concluding, let us examine several forms of text which, in parallel with or outside the exhibition, facilitate an understanding of and confirm its new role discussed above.

---

19. For the background of the relationship between the exhibition and problems inherent in communications, see B. Schiele, "L'invention simultanée du visiteur et de l'exposition", *Publics & Musées*, 1992, Vol. 2, pp. 71-95.

20. Screven's name dominates this entire period. For a selection of his writings, see D. Samson and B. Schiele, *L'évaluation muséale. Publics et expositions. Bibliographie raisonnée* (Paris: Expo Media, 1989).

COMPLEMENTARY FORMS OF TEXT

Catalogues, guides, brochures and other materials make it easier to visit the exhibition and serve to complement and enrich it. Such documents, while they remain independent, become an organic part of the exhibition, completing it and superimposing themselves on it. While catalogues are intended to provide a durable record of a temporary gesture, other, more utilitarian materials are meant to facilitate the visit. The latter documents usually contain a simple text, frequently illustrated or enhanced with graphics, which gives visitors a sense of direction and emphasizes what the organizers are endeavouring to call to their attention, in order to ensure that when the visit is over visitors have seen what they were intended to see. In recent years, accompanying documents have developed considerably, no doubt as a result of the development of the market for spin-off products. From the standpoint of this essay, this point is secondary. What I wish to stress is that the catalogue, for example, adds an additional register to the forms of text that accompany the exhibition.

The concept of the catalogue has changed in recent years. It has become a document separate from the exhibition, by elaborating on the exhibition's theme or presenting discussion about it. *The 1920s: The Age of the Metropolis*, a catalogue that accompanied the exhibition of the same name mounted by the Montreal Museum of Fine Arts, contained reproductions of the works exhibited, historic and interpretative essays on each of the themes the exhibition examined, and a brief biography of each of the artists whose work was on display. The catalogue, which closely followed the exhibition, discussed the entire period covered. Indeed, it was a veritable self-contained monograph whose encyclopaedic nature invited the reader to examine a presentation of the cultural flux that has moulded contemporary urban space. The catalogue may even have delved more deeply into the subject than did the exhibition. One thing is certain. Such a document, while it may enable visitors to deepen their knowledge, cannot be consulted during the visit. In fact, a concise document, in the form of a handout given to visitors at the entrance to the exhibition, guided the viewers through the exhibits, thus satisfying two conflicting needs to put the objects presented in context and to keep their presentation as simple as possible.

Another example, *Mémoires d'Égypte*, a catalogue produced by the Bibliothèque Nationale de France, followed the exhibition step by step, examining each of the themes in the order in which they were presented in the exhibition. To read this catalogue, if the term still has meaning, is to retrace the established exhibition itinerary, dwelling on each theme and delving deeper into it. Thus, the history of the rediscovery of Egypt is, for the reader, the history of those who participated in Bonaparte's campaign, then the Champollion years and the deciphering of the hieroglyphs, and finally, Egypt's entry into the Louvre. Pointe-à-Callière, an archeological and historical museum in Montréal, has opted for another approach. The visitor-reader is encouraged to read a subtle, detailed presentation on the history and archeology of the site on which the museum was built. In this way, the history of Montréal is related to a real place that holds meaning. Instead of giving more examples, let us establish what these three catalogues illustrate. Since they can be consulted prior to or after the visit, or even without visiting the exhibition, they dissociate the object exhibited from the discourse the object addresses to visitors. Consequently, the visit and the assimilation of information occur at two different stages.

It is worth noting the form taken by text within these three exhibitions: *The 1920s: The Age of the Metropolis*, labels; *Mémoires d'Égypte*, an infrared audioguide; and *La mise en valeur du site de Pointe-à-Callière*, a multimedia presentation and a guide-animator. In all three instances, text provides a minimal anchor. The latter two exhibitions rely extensively on oral communication and direct contact with visitors.

Seventh observation: contrary to appearances, text is more pervasive than ever in the exhibition. However, with the development of accompanying documents and various aids to facilitate the visit, text's focal point is shifting. Text, at least in the most contemporary forms of exhibition, is tending toward permanent documents, a change that reinforces the presence and significance of text in reconstituting the message addressed to the visitor.

This trend is apparent even in scientific exhibitions, which have traditionally reserved an important place for text by making extensive use of panels containing descriptive or explanatory material, to the extent of being described as veritable illustrated books. To give one last, recent example, the *On a marché sur la Terre* exhibition at the Muséum national d'histoire naturelle in Paris, which focused on the conquest of the land environment by plants and animals, broke with this tradition. Text in the exhibition, for text was indeed present, consisted mainly of scriptovisual panels presenting the ideas deemed essential to an understanding of the physical and physiological conditions that enabled species to leave the water and thrive on the land. In keeping with current trends, the catalogue was a composite document with respect to its content and iconography, which were largely distinct from those presented in the exhibition. It reviewed the question of evolution by means of scientific essays, popularized texts and historical background and successively indicated the scientific and social impact of the theory of evolution. At the same time, it offered a parallel reading of the exhibition.

Text cuts across all levels of the exhibition. It is a part of all key aspects, from the program to the accompanying documents, not to mention the promotional discourse and substitute and complementary forms. Text, a mode of discourse, is the veritable foundation of the exhibition. Its pervasiveness is a reminder that, in the background, language is at work. If an exhibition excludes language, it runs a risk of sacrificing its most salient function: indicating what it has to show the visitor.

Bibliography

Barbier-Bouvet, J.-F. "Le système de l'exposition" in *Histoire d'expo*. Paris: Peuple et Culture, Centre Georges-Pompidou, 1983, pp. 13-17.

Borun, M.; Miller, M. *What's in a Name? A Study of the Effectiveness of Explanatory Labels in a Science Museum*. Philadelphia: Franklin Institute and Science Museum, 1980.

Cassirer, E. *The Philosophy of Symbolic Forms*. New Haven: Yale University Press, 1966.

Davallon, J. *Claquemurer pour ainsi dire tout l'univers*. Paris: Éditions du Centre Georges-Pompidou, 1986.

_____. "Exposition scientifique, espace, ostension" in *Protée*, Vol. 16, No. 3, 1988, pp. 5-16.

Eco, U. *La structure absente*. Paris: Mercure de France, 1972.

McManus, P. "Oh Yes They Do: How Museum Visitors Read Labels and Interact with Exhibit Texts", *Curator*, 1989, Vol. 32, No. 3, pp. 174-189.

Moles, A. "Vue générale de l'exposition", *L'écrit dans l'exposition*. Paris: People and Culture, 1983, pp. 23-33.

Poli, M.S. "Le parti pris des mots dans l'étiquette: une approche linguistique", *Publics & Musées*. Presses universitaires de Lyon, No. 1, 1992, pp. 91-111.

Samson, D.; Schiele, B. *L'évaluation muséale. Publics et expositions. Bibliographie raisonnée*. Paris: Expo Media, 1989.

Schiele, B. "L'invention simultanée du visiteur et de l'exposition", *Publics & Musées*. Presses universitaires de Lyon, No. 2, 1992, pp. 71-95.

Serrell, B. *Making Exhibit Labels. A Step-by-Step Guide*. Nashville: American Association for State and Local History, 1983.

Summary   Daniel Jacobi
                                          Marie Sylvie Poli

Scriptovisual Documents in Exhibitions: Some Theoretical Guidelines

This essay proposes a definition of the exhibition text and describes the role it plays with respect to the discourse on which it depends. It shows how displayed text becomes a scriptovisual document, which depends both on linguistic and on paralinguistic and visual signs: text is intended to be read but also to be seen. The authors then focus on the characteristics of the scriptovisual document, with particular emphasis on its different forms, first as a visual object incorporated into the exhibition, then as a system designed to inform. An image can, of course, transmit information in all of its aspects. What is its role in relation to the text? Can it replace the statement? These are the questions that the authors raise before turning their attention to the forms and functions of the text itself. Speaking from the standpoint of the producer, they emphasize the importance of the written document in expressing the exhibition's content, organizing the itinerary followed and ensuring that it is both cohesive and adequately segmented. The text is an ideal vehicle for transmitting meaning. It gives viewers a grasp of the objects and serves as a place where visitors can stop and get their bearings. However, to fulfil this role, it must satisfy certain criteria. Within these constraints, the writer is free to use the abundant resources of the language and an exhaustive typology of the written word to reveal the narrative framework and suggest reference points to viewers that will help them interpret the exhibition. The next essay, by Andrée Blais, explores the complex mechanisms of this reading and interpretation process.

Scriptovisual Documents in Exhibitions: Some Theoretical Guidelines

Daniel Jacobi

Professor, Université de
Bourgogne, Dijon, and Director
of the Centre de recherche sur la
culture et les musées, Dijon

Marie Sylvie Poli

Assistant Professor, Université
Pierre Mendès-France, Grenoble

When visitors enter a museum or an exhibition, they are explorers of an architecturally defined space, observers of everything presented there, and readers of the texts displayed. Yes, they are almost always readers, and occasionally without being aware of it. Of course, these readers are curious and they seek, learn and criticize. Their reading is of a special kind: the visitors' attention is constantly captured by new things to look at; they move around, rarely staying in one place for long; and they do not usually go to exhibitions alone. So designers of exhibitions attempt to create visible, readable, comprehensible, attractive texts, often combined with images.

A study of the texts displayed in exhibitions must necessarily look at two complementary dimensions. The first involves what is readable, i.e. an analysis of the text as a linguistic entity, generally expressed by the written word. The second pertains to what is visible, since the displayed text is a scriptovisual document that is looked at and seen before it is read.

This article will examine these two facets of the exhibition text. It will first present a number of definitions, then focus on the text as an image, with particular emphasis on the visual grammars inherent in it. Texts function as linguistic communication tools, elements of a dialogue between the person who writes them and the person who reads them. The second part of the article will examine various linguistic forms and the functions of the exhibition text.

TEXT AND DISCOURSE OF THE EXHIBITION

Text or discourse? Is it possible to speak interchangeably of the text and the discourse of an exhibition? The interplay of definitions is inescapable. An exhibition text can encompass all statements designed and organized to communicate meaning or any single text that is part of the whole.

Language is the sole raw material of the text. As is the case in any communication, language, in an exhibition, equally relies on two distinct levels, i.e. the oral (spoken language) and the textual (written language). Because the exhibition exists in a physical space, it emphasizes the graphic signs or graphemes of written language. The exhibition text is by and large textual in nature.

The expression "exhibition text" is used to designate all of the linguistic components organized into a meaningful system at an exhibition.[1] A text is also any unit, such as a title, a panel, a notice or a label, that provides specific information.

The (exhibition) text does not correspond exactly to the (exhibition) discourse. The exhibition discourse is a composite. It includes a number of semiotic codes, e.g. symbols, drawings and photographs, which combine with the linguistic signs: the exhibition discourse is a multi-coded message constructed for a specific communication context, called

---

1. *Signifier system* refers to the entire range of interdependent elements that a text uses to elaborate its different physical aspects, e.g. words, sentences, punctuation, lines, typography, surface marks and so on.

the exhibition. This context is well defined for both the production and the reception of the message.

All exhibition discourse constitutes a broad message that is strictly language-based, but that uses all of the different museographic registers, including the spatiovisual, temporal, iconic, sound, object, architectural and symbolic.

The text does not form an independent part of the exhibition discourse. On the contrary, it is a product that depends on its context, integrated into a process of mediating meaning, whose characteristics must be assimilated. Who issues it and who receives it? What rules and what constraints are inherent in the exhibition?

Text, because it is an act of language, is also an original, essential component: any act of language is a manifestation of intelligence. Text is the primary aid to interpretation. In an exhibition, it establishes a unique link between what is exhibited and what the visitor thinks. Text makes the exhibition intelligible and communicable.

THE TEXT BECOMES A SCRIPTOVISUAL DOCUMENT IN AN EXHIBITION

Recourse to language reveals itself by and large at the textual level. An exhibition text appears, first and foremost, in the form of a written text. What is a text? The answer is deceptively simple. A text is a series of linguistic signs that can be assembled to make words. Words, in turn, are organized in sentences, and sentences are joined to form paragraphs. Thus, a text is a long structured chain of linguistic signs. To obtain information, it is sufficient to read, i.e. to mobilize a largely automatic cognitive activity. Generally speaking, a text is made to be read.

In a museum or exhibition, however, this is not entirely true. The text, while meant to be read, is also characterized by its spatiovisual organization in the space that it occupies. Thus, an exhibition text is also made to be seen. Texts displayed in museums differ from the texts or printed material we usually read. Reading/seeing, seeing/reading: in a museum, these two cognitive activities are permanently intertwined. Consequently, it is preferable to call the written component of the exhibition discourse "scriptovisual".

There are other reasons for doing so as well. The text is scriptovisual because paralinguistic[2] and visual signs are interwoven very often among the linguistic signs organized into homogeneous areas, i.e. the columns of text. These visual areas make up a system distinct from text, called "paratext".

Text and paratext are usually linked: a visual area of the paratext may include a brief, independent text called a legend. Conversely, the text may specifically refer the reader to a visual figure.

We will discuss this dual textual and visual system before we focus specifically on the text, i.e. on the linguistic component alone.

DISPLAYED TEXT IS AN IMAGE

Text is included in two ways in an exhibition: as an object integrated into the exhibition and as a two-dimensional system that informs about or comments on the exhibition.

First, text can be a component of the exhibition, e.g. a parchment, manuscript, book, poster, or register, all of which are printed or handwritten documents that can be put on display. However, for fear that they will deteriorate, museums often replace authentic documents with facsimiles. The two-dimensional photocopy, by depriving the document of its materiality, denatures it and occasionally tends to make it merge with the second system, that of the interpretative text.

Second, the text is a homogeneous system for presenting the exhibition. It is the primary (and essential) aid to interpretation. To describe the displayed exhibition text, we will focus on five characteristics: spatial location, structuring, degree of independence, materiality and visual aspect.

Scriptovisual location in space

The visitors locates text as soon as he sets foot in the exhibition. Text is intended not only to be *read* but, first of all, to be *seen*. The location of

---

2. Paralinguistic elements are not part of the alphabet of linguistic signs but frequently accompany them. Punctuation, figures and mathematical symbols are examples of paralinguistic signs.

texts is therefore of great importance. Texts are hung in the exhibition somewhat like paintings, i.e. spotlit on separate panels, or discreetly in passageways. They may also be hung from the ceiling, written directly on the floor or spray-painted on the support.

Texts are intended to be read and will be more widely read if they are located at a convenient height or on tilted supports that offer visitors the best viewing angle. Placing texts in certain strategic locations, e.g. at the beginning or end of an itinerary or at the entrance to exhibition rooms, helps organize and structure the visit: text signals, communicates, introduces, emphasizes, concludes and so on.

Typographic structuring

A text is, admittedly, only a series of words and sentences, a simple assemblage of lines. However, the author of the text organizes this assemblage. The text is divided clearly into paragraphs, structured by subheadings. The visitor-reader quickly assimilates this structuring, if it is consistent: heading, summary lead, concluding sentence and so on. The visitor uses this structure to organize the assimilation of information.

Moreover, the surface organization, e.g. the arrangement of the lines, changes in typography or style of character (bold, italic), underscoring or highlighting, can reinforce and emphasize this structuring. Text marking can make key words, proper names, dates and concepts stand out.

Independence or interrelation?

There are two broad categories of exhibition text. The first is the independent textual system, which includes independent units such as panels. For example, a panel can present the biography of a famous person through texts and photographs, or briefly describe a discovery or invention. It can inform the public about the operating principle behind a technological process.

Beside the independent panel there exists a second type of text, which interrelates with the objects, items and artifacts in the exhibition. This type of text may introduce an exhibit case or label objects. It may explain how to use an interactive terminal, ask questions or encourage the visitor to do something.

These categories, i.e. the independent scriptovisual panel and the interpretative text linked to one or more items, and more generally any text used in an exhibition (the title of the exhibition or of a section of it, an introductory text or a notice, production credits and so on) complies with the constraints inherent in its genre.

Bearing in mind these three variables (location, structuring and degree of independence), the museographer can produce an infinite number of texts, all of them different. However, each of the texts is created for a specific purpose. Each of the units of discourse, by its location, structuring, typography, and possible relation to the item exhibited, becomes a specific category, i.e. title, heading, introductory text, legend, label, detailed notice, scriptovisual panel and so on. This controlled, organized structuring is an essential means of communication between the museographer-writer and the visitor-reader.[3]

Materiality of the message

A text is a physical object: for example, black letters written or printed on or transferred to a white support. In order to contrast the text, linguistic signs may be written in white on a black or coloured background.

The support may be opaque or transparent, white, neutral or vividly coloured. The letters, too, can change shape, value (from light grey to deep black) or colour. The play of the alphabets on the supports is infinite.[4]

---

3. We prefer *writer* to other possible synonyms. By calling the museographer or exhibition designer a writer, we wish to emphasize the written as opposed to the spoken text.

4. The support is the surface or material underlying a painting, a setting and, by extension, a displayed text.

Zoology gallery, Muséum d'histoire naturelle, Dijon

A beak, a tool

The theme of this exhibit case is the relationship between the shape of the bird's beak and its diet. The analogy type of beak and tool from everyday life is emphasized by the title of the exhibit case and the title of each label, which refers to two things: a bird perched on a pedestal, on which is mounted the object-tool (in this instance an oyster knife) and the text of the label. The text, in white letters on a dark grey matte background, is clearly legible. Capital letters discreetly emphasize the key words OYSTER KNIFE and OYSTER CATCHER. The message is simple, displayed clearly and easy to read.

However, in an exhibition, text is found in an increasing variety of physical forms, from a loose-leaf sheet to a catalogue. It is increasingly becoming non-material. A non-material text is one that is directly projected using an optical device, or displayed on a TV or videotex screen. The latter type of text is an electronic text. The flicker and vibration of the light signal interfere with the reading of the text and give it a special character, appreciated by some and criticized by others.

Visual aspect of the text

The exhibition text is intended to be seen. Aside from its structuring, which, as we noted earlier, fosters communication through its consistency, it is also a physical object. The typography, the length of the lines, the line spacing, the absence or presence of justification, surface markings (bold, italic, underlining), the colour of the background or the letters are all parameters that enable the designer or the scenic artist to design an attractive, eye-catching visual system that may be discreet or, on the contrary, conspicuous.

To illustrate this dimension, here is a brief example,[5] deliberately simplified, inspired by a work of the surrealist poet Goemans. The same text is presented as three images or variants, i.e. the text in a line, the text in a block and the text composed and edited by the poet.

> ## write to me milky way swallow the eye
> ## before the oar chains I stay

The text in a line

Visually, the text appears as a long line accentuated by the absence of punctuation marks and the uniformity of the lower case letters. The text string envelops the reader. The words "I stay", placed at the end, sound like a challenge.

---

5. This example is based on the curious exhibition *Tire la langue ou les irréguliers du langage* – Centre culturel de Wallonie, Paris, 1990. The poem by Camille Goemans, excerpted from the catalogue (p. 78), was published in Camille Goemans, *Œuvre 1922-1957* (Brussels: De Rache, 1970), p. 29.

```
write to me
milky    way
s w a l l o w
the      eye
b e f o r e
the oar chains
I   s   t   a   y
```

The text in a block

The text is justified on the left and on the right. The length of short lines is equal to the height of the block of text. The cesura, which is excessive but respects the principle, allows a strictly square shape. The text is hard to read, but its stable form is reassuring.

```
WRITE TO ME MI
LKY WAY S
WALLOW THE E
YE BEFORE TH
E OAR CH
AINS I STAY
```

Goemans' unorthodox text

The text is justified at the left and the line spacing has been reduced. The poet has chosen the capitals and the unpredictable cesuras. With very limited means, this surrealist poet has succeeded in destabilizing common sense. Not only are there changes in our perception which produce visual effects but – and this is what draws our attention – we note that semantically the text moves and changes.

To summarize briefly, in an exhibition, we find different types of texts: printed or handwritten documents, which are exhibition objects, and the textual system that interprets and explains the exhibition and its different objects. For example, an open book, whose double page the visitor can skim through, will be presented and commented upon in the same manner as a statuette or the rendering of a landscape. The textual system can be divided into two main categories: the independent panel and the interpretative text. These texts do not form a homogeneous whole.

Musée de la vie bourguignonne Perrin-de-Puycousin, Dijon.

The text as a visual form

In a recently renovated part of the exhibition rooms of the Musée de la vie bourguignonne Perrin-de-Puycousin, the texts, rather like calligrams, interact with the objects exhibited. The text escapes, like a bubble, from a glazed earthenware pot with a lifted lid; it undulates from the neck of a flask on which encouragements to drink are written; or, as in this example, a measure pours the text into a milk-can. The text is hand-painted in white on a transparent background. The handwritten form gives the lettering an intimate quality, although its legibility is lessened by this effect.

PARATEXT AND VISUAL GRAMMARS

A displayed text represents a whole that is intended to be perceived in space. In other words, in the exhibition, it is impossible to see a text independently of its background, just as a painting in an art exhibition in some sense cannot exist without the support and frame that delimit it. This habit of viewing is so inevitable that certain artists, such as the

Support-Surface group, have made a point of trying – possibly in vain – to rebel against the physical limits of the painted work.

Demarcation of the text

The same system of constraints applies to displayed texts, which do not form a continuous, uncontrasted, homogeneous whole. They break up space and organize themselves into isolated, independent entities that are often scriptovisual, as we noted earlier.

Regardless of the nature of the support, it can support both textual stimuli (the linguistic signs that make up words and sentences) and visual stimuli (iconic signs or areas that combine iconic and linguistic signs). A scriptovisual document is intended to be read and seen.

A text, as it is presented on its support, is intended to be read.[6] However, the text leaves free part of the surface of the support that delimits it in an exhibition. It is not unusual for one-third of the area to be left. In the available space around the text, the writer can arrange so-called paratextual components, which are designed to be seen or viewed. Unlike the texts, the visual areas, intended to be consulted, demand another kind of cognitive activity of visitors.

The process of deciphering a visual area is probably more complex and heterogeneous than the act of reading, which, as we know, is largely automatic. We do not look in the same way at a photograph of a landscape and a geographic map, or a graph and a comic strip. Moreover, visual areas are syncretic. They are seen globally. As Bresson has emphasized, they contain much less information – and occasionally no information at all – on the rules that the visitor must use to decode them.

A text is always read in the same way, but how does a viewer approach a visual area? Is the centre more important that the periphery? Do the colours represent a stable code, or do they reflect a simple whim on the part of the illustrator?

---

6. This is true because, from the outset, visitors knows that they are looking at a written whole, i.e. a series of interrelated signs that unfold in one direction only. A text always, unequivocally implies perception and motor activities that the reader must initiate in order to grasp the meaning, which is the purpose of any recognition activity.

Text, paratext and infratext

Faced with scriptovisual text, the visitor is compelled to set in motion a complex series of cognitive operations. From the standpoint of production, we have proposed distinguishing three such series: text, paratext and infratext.

Paratext consists of the visual areas (paralinguistic and visual signs) that occupy the free space on the support. Some authors maintain that, in the case of scriptovisual panels, the title, headings and introductory paragraphs, although they are made up of linguistic signs, already belong to the paratextual space. They stand out very clearly from the body of the text: typographical characters in bigger point sizes, position on the page, and different kinds of boldface and justification. They are fragments of text, set apart and intended to be read, but in an independent manner.

The paratextual system includes visual areas, occupied by photographs, drawings, diagrams, maps, curves, histograms, structural formulas, bioelectrical recordings and so on. The list goes on and on, an indication that calling the content of such visual areas images or illustrations is an oversimplification.

These visual areas are always accompanied by a brief linguistic statement, which in turn may be preceded by a short title, called a legend. While these legends are also made up of linguistic signs, they are not read like text, or at least, not at the same time. Visitors read them when they look at and consult the visual area on which they comment or which they explain.

There is another special paratextual component called an "insert" or "box", which is a bit of text set off from the main text. It is separated by surrounding lines, set in a different font and often written in a different style. The reader perceives that the insert is peripheral, that it has been added to the text and that the reading of it is optional. In any event, it is accompanied by a series of visual signs that set it off from the rest of the text.

In practice, the status of the insert can vary widely. It can recall basic knowledge or develop a secondary concept; it can provide examples that illustrate or present a different viewpoint from the one presented elsewhere in the exhibition.

Other tiny but essential components are found in the paratext, i.e. very brief indications that appear in the margin, below the text, or sometimes vertically alongside the visual areas. These components are also linguistic in nature, but so small that the observer may well ask himself whether they are intended to be read and, in any case, if so, by whom. We suggest calling them infratext. They include bibliographic references, the names of institutions and laboratories, and sponsoring agencies or firms, all indicators of the source of the information.

Professionals always read and take note of the infratext, which is one of the visible manifestations of the social nature of the act of exhibiting. For example, the (compulsory) mention of the source (or the origin) of an illustration enables a specialist to establish at a glance the source document to which the museographer has referred.

Scriptovisual transitions

Do a map, a histogram, a structural formula, an electronic photomicrograph and a reproduction of a Daumier lithograph have anything in common? All of these items are jumbled together under the generic name "illustration" or "image".

The distinction between text and image is based on a functional categorization that is generally accepted but inadequate for a sophisticated analysis of the relationship between text and paratext. In the case of scientific and technical exhibitions, this distinction is entirely inoperative.

Is a structural formula an image or an illustration? What is a map? In response to such questions, some researchers have proposed another pair of categories: linguistic and paralinguistic. The paralinguistic is a catch-all category that can encompass everything that does not belong to the realm of linguistic signs in the strict sense, which is not ambiguous. This typology is functional and makes it possible, for example, to distinguish between the **Cl** in **Claude** and the **Cl** representing the chlorine atom in chemistry. **Cl** is linguistic in **Claude**, **Clef** and **Clap**, but paralinguistic in **HCl** (hydrochloric acid).

Chemical formulas, the genetic code and other alphabetic symbols creep into the text but they cannot be decoded as words. In order for paralinguistic signs to be interpreted, it is assumed that visitors are already familiar with chemical, genetic, mathematical or other semiology.

Visual grammars

The visual areas of the paratext amplify or reinforce the main text or serve as a counterpoint to it. They are sometimes accompanied by a legend that enables visitors to select a reading itinerary. Instead of glancing through the text string, visitors can first look at a visual area that attracts their attention, then refer to the linguistic statement in the legend.

If this statement is independent, i.e. if it does not refer to the main text, information can be obtained through this channel, provided the iconic information is decipherable, either spontaneously or by means of the legend. This description of the combination of visual area and legend raises a question of concern to all museographers: can iconic information replace lengthy textual development?

Can visual areas become independent, and under what conditions? It should first be emphasized that in the visual register, only a limited number of grammars can be recognized directly. It is a question of analog images, e.g. photographs or drawings, which reflect, as a mirror does, a referent, in exactly the same way that we could perceive it through sight.

In the scientific and technical fields, an increasingly complex instrumentation has imposed itself between what is to be shown and emphasized and the eye of the observer. Whether in the realm of exploration of the extremely small (electron microscope) or the immensely remote (radio telescope), current techniques enable the viewer to see the invisible, to the extent that some of these images cannot be interpreted for want of a theoretical model on which to base the interpretation.

In recent years, research on iconic repertories has led to the establishment of several families of visual areas, such as the repertory of graphic semiology, the field of scientific imagery, and attempts to present and explain knowledge figuratively.

Graphic semiology seeks to visually transpose information according to rules that are at least stable and univocal, if not universal. In addition to visually representing data or information, this transposition is also a powerful means of processing information. Curves, pie charts, histograms and factorial analysis graphs can now be easily generated by computers.

We call scientific imagery the visual areas produced by researchers as research instruments, i.e. to produce knowledge. These visual areas, while sometimes striking, are almost never spontaneously decodable. They have been produced to demonstrate and prove. They are the hard core of scientific information, not an ornamental but dispensable illustration.

One last major family groups together visual areas intended to present, explain, and help retain information, the diagram being the prototype. A diagram, in constructing a visible image, simplifies and emphasizes the essential. While it is concrete, a diagram generalizes and makes it possible to represent an entire class of events or individuals. Through its form and simplicity, a diagram codifies complex reality facilitating its retention in memory.

Images of the geosphere

The easiest way to show both the appeal of visual areas and the problems engendered by them is to zoom in, like a filmmaker, on a number of them. With the widespread acceptance of the geological model of plate tectonics, all exhibitions devoted to volcanoes, earthquakes, continental drift and so on must explain complex notions to visitors, e.g. the nature of the movements that occur at great depths in the lithosphere, the structure of the earth's crust, proof of the existence of reversals of the earth's magnetic field, gravitational anomalies and so on.

In order to produce the proof and confirm the explanatory strength of this model, specialists such as geophysicians and geochemists from around the world use sophisticated instrumentation. They sail all over the oceans in specially equipped ships. They use satellite measurements taken from space. Their instruments and automated techniques produce maps and images of the planet that increasingly turn up in popular science and general magazines and in museums.

FORMS AND FUNCTIONS OF TEXTS

Imagine an attentive, scrupulous visitor who, as he proceeds through an exhibition, reads all the texts displayed. He does not need to be a great expert to perceive the numerous differences between the exhibition texts. These differences result from their production and their reading, which we will now examine.

Genesis of the text

When a designer starts to work on a project, the content he wishes to express is still not clearly defined. Even before he puts down his ideas on paper in the form of a broad plan intended for his fellow workers, he has the exhibition concept in mind, thinks of certain key objects, and adopts a tone and a point of view. While the designer has a sense of the general content of the exhibition, the discourse to express it has yet to be articulated.

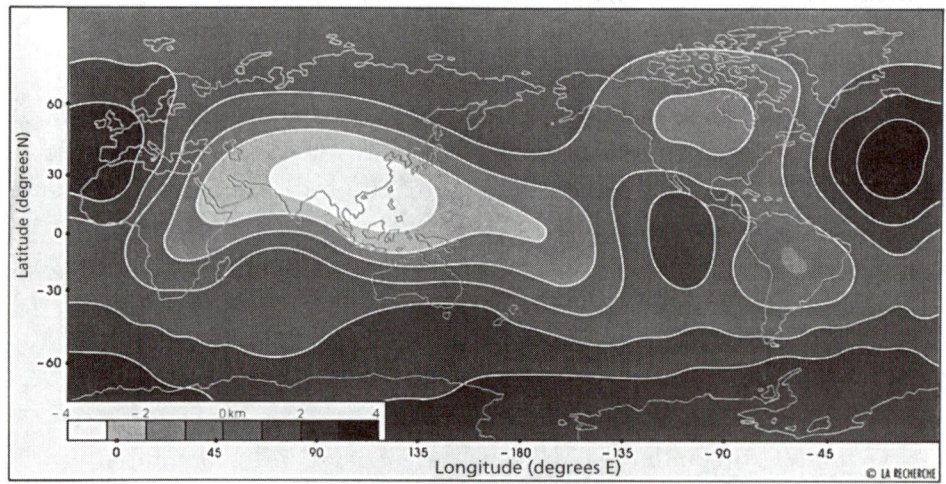

Source: J. Hinderer, H. Legros and A. Souriau-Thévenard, "Le noyau terrestre", *La Recherche*, No. 233, June 1991, p. 763.

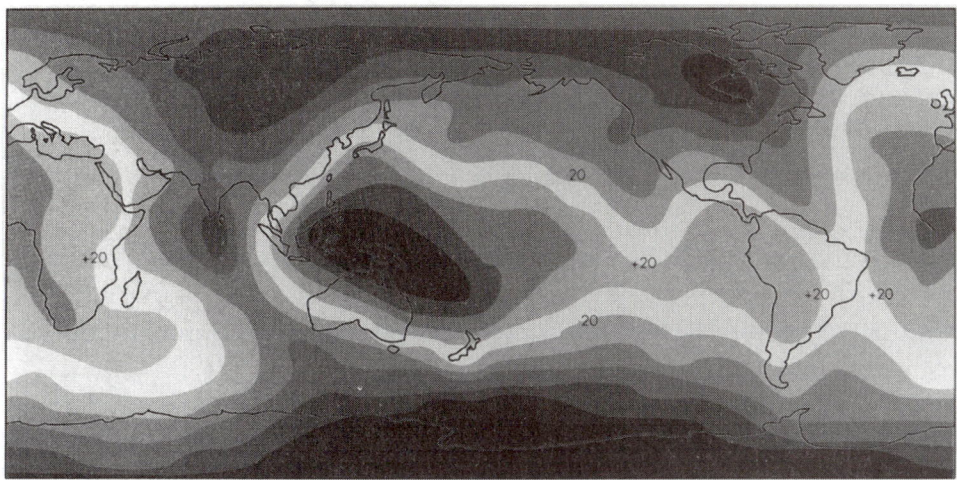

Source: A. Nicolas, *Les montagnes sous la mer: expansion des océans et tectonique des plaques.* Orléans, France: Éditions du BRGM, 1990, p. 54.

Two ways of looking at the geosphere

The juxtaposition of these two maps of the earth is deliberate. At first glance, the two maps resemble each other: without regard for the contours of seas, oceans or the continents, sweeping curves outline shapes that are coloured with different hues and values (only the latter are visible on the black-and-white reproductions). However, from one map to the next, neither the colours nor the shapes of the curves can be superimposed. Using the results of seismological tomography, a measuring technique that cannot be described in a few words, the first map reveals the bumps and troughs at the surface of the core that cause a linkage between the movements of the liquid core and the mantle of the geosphere. On the second map, these troughs and bumps are also revealed using another technique, which relies on a laser-equipped satellite to measure altitude above the ocean.

Removed from their scientific context, i.e. plate tectonics, and without the necessarily long explanation of the equipment that makes it possible to draw them, can these maps be consulted and interpreted?

This content resembles a nebula of objects and ideas more than an organized system. The designer must quickly transform this nebula into a coherent content. Consequently, he must choose, sort, eliminate, segment, conceal, emphasize, qualify, evoke and stress.

To some extent, it is as though the designer invents the exhibition by giving it a content. The museological expression of this content must be created for each exhibition. In other words, what the designer must imagine is an appropriate mode of expression that relates the meaning of the content to the expression of this content. Numerous comments from museographers indicate that words and writing are the preeminent instruments of this veritable act of creation.

As is the case in any creative act, form and meaning adapt themselves to the exhibition's entire array of registers of signs and are stimulated by such signs. The written text is one of the principal semiotic registers, but obviously not the only one. The objects presented, or *expôts*, according to Rivière's terminology, images (drawings, photographs) and interactive devices also act as stimuli and constraints.

Turning back to the question at hand, this means that text in an exhibition is not given in advance in dictionaries or grammars. In each instance, the system must be invented and implemented, in compliance with a code, in order to express the exhibition's content.

The text and its closure

The structural organization of an exhibition text, as with any text, produces a closure that individualizes it and constructs it as a fairly independent entity. Whenever visitors read a text, they seek such closure: the beginning of the reading is stimulated by the foreseeable end. Moreover, any exit from an exhibition text implies, in a symmetrical fashion, an entrance. A concise, visible structure fosters congruence between the recognition and production processes.

Even if visitors do not read all of the texts thoroughly from start to finish, their reading has a provisional beginning and end, wherever they may occur, without necessarily respecting the linear nature of the text. Writers make full use of this closed circuit, especially with respect to statements marking the beginning and the end of the exhibition discourse.

> **A HIGHLY READABLE INTRODUCTORY TEXT**
>
> From the armistice to the Liberation,
> from June 1940 to August 1944,
> three kinds of logic were at work simultaneously.
> The German occupier was seeking to derive the greatest
> benefit from its victory.
> The French government in Vichy had come to terms
> and was collaborating with Germany.
> However, some people, at first isolated,
> rejected the defeat and the Vichy government.
> Confrontations became more widespread.
> The greater the disorder, the harsher the repression.
> This was the chain of events in which the French were
> caught.
> What about the residents of Grenoble?
> How did they live through these **bleak years**?

Les années noires exhibition, Musée dauphinois de Grenoble.

The foregoing is an example of a highly readable introductory text designed to establish from the outset the exhibition concept and announce the themes dealt with by the exhibition. The text concludes with a question that invites visitors to explore the bleak years. The statement closes on the key words of the exhibition title, which are emphasized by surface marking.

From text to texts

When these text types are examined and compared, it is easy to show that we are not looking at a homogeneous whole. The exhibition text, as is the case with any text, displays a broad range of registers, i.e. the lexicon, syntax, type of enunciation and style, which enable the museographer to produce a vast range of text types.

The writing of an exhibition text requires a series of choices: a choice of words; a choice of sentence structure and location of data; a choice of verb tenses and personal pronouns. Who is talking to whom? At what time and in what place(s)? The diversity of texts produced also depends on the writer of the exhibition texts.

The literature on exhibition texts often describes a recurring theme: What are the different forms and functions of exhibition texts? The typologies involved are based on two approaches: the hierarchical arrangement of the texts and the role of the text in construction of the exhibition discourse.

However, there is no point in reexamining the distinction between title, heading, main text, secondary text, notice or peripheral text (hierarchical classification), nor the distinction between explanatory, demonstrative, descriptive, interpretative and injunctive texts (the so-called functional classification). Why?

First, there is no hierarchical, functional classification that is sufficiently precise, operational and, above all, generally agreed on by professionals and specialists. Among the 20 or so classifications that have been proposed over the past 20 years, no consensus has been reached on the number or nature of the components.

These classifications have another shortcoming. Professionals find it very hard to submit to their constraints, even when they adopt *a priori* a certain number of rules on the production of exhibition texts. Moreover, an observer who consults the texts produced finds it very hard to perceive the system of rules that has, in principle, governed the entire production process.

In fact, the classifications have either been simplified to such an extent that they no longer reflect heterogeneity and complexity, or refined but of necessity context-limited. They are appropriate for one type of exhibition or museum and relate to only a small portion of the texts used in exhibition discourse. In our opinion, only a linguistic approach, derived from a modern theory of language, can result in a satisfactory analysis of exhibition texts.

Inventorying and anchoring

Exhibit labels are among the most rudimentary texts in any exhibition. It is often said that an exhibition involves, above all, the task of inventorying. However, an inventory always satisfies a logic and an intention. To inventory, classify and organize is to give meaning to the world. Behind any inventory lies a person who puts a stamp of approval on the meaning. The text of the exhibit label shows the fundamental place that language occupies in communicating this ordering and in facilitating the reading of the label.

As Roland Barthes has noted, any inventory comes down to proposing an act of possession, not just managing the contents by fragmenting and enumerating them. He adds that inventorying means not only observing, as it appears at first glance, but also appropriating. The specialist assembles a series of objects that have at least one trait in common. He separates the objects chosen according to distinctive criteria. Then he names the series, sub-series and units assembled in this manner. Finally, he classifies all the items chosen according to a personal organizational framework.

When he writes his labels, the writer partitions the universe at the same time as he names the objects. These objects, retrieved from the anonymity of the indeterminate, are transformed into the displayed objects and may be included in an exhibition discourse. Through the process of naming, the writer describes, designates and thus encourages visitors, as Goody has noted, to take possession of the objects by accepting and assimilating the designations.

Interpretative anchoring

Almost immediately, the text shifts to another function that Barthes calls anchoring. At the same time as text designates, it serves as a guide to interpretation. The writer constantly seeks to control the proliferation of meaning, i.e. to maintain the meaning within the semantic limits of his discourse.

How are designation and anchoring implemented in the exhibition? Through sparing use of words and brief forms, but according to two different writing strategies, one autonymous, the other predicative. Autonymous labels have a minimal text made up of a few words, but not sentences. Such labels make is possible to at least name the object and occasionally say a bit more about it. Sartre has noted that through the very act that gives the thing its name, the idea becomes a thing and enters the realm of the objective mind.

AN AUTONYMOUS LABEL	
Scientific name:	Rhinecanthus acuelatus
Common name:	Picasso fish
French name:	Baliste picasso
Maximum length:	30 cm
Distribution:	Indo-Pacific Ocean

Sequarium, Palais de la mer, Le grau du roi.

An autonymous label using individual words rather than sentences to name and describe an object.

A PREDICATIVE LABEL

The ALPINE CHAMOIS (ALPENGEMSE – CHAMOIS)
The male and female can be distinguished by the overall shape of the head and the smaller, less curved horns of the female.
In summer, the chamois has a reddish brown coat, which becomes much darker and thicker in winter.
The feet of the chamois are adapted to rugged mountain conditions. The shape and structure of the animal's hooves enable it to hug the rough ground and prevent it from sliding on bare rocks and névés.
The animal feeds mainly on herbaceous plants, leaves and shrub shoots.
Rutting occurs in November and December and one or two kids are born in May or June.

Salle Montagne vivante, Muséum d'histoire naturelle de Grenoble.

A predicative label contains complete sentences, carefully written to explain and inform. It is an interpretative aid that guides the acquisition of information.

Occasionally, as is the case in the preceding example, the text of a label consists of one or more basic sentences. These statements are called predicative texts. Assembled into a coherent text, the statements present complex mechanisms, or scholarly, humorous or astonishing ideas in a few sentences.

By dictating a meaning, the writer settles on a semantic option. He chooses among several other meanings, all of them relevant and potentially usable. In this respect, he acts as a barrier against rash, erroneous (for a scientist) interpretations that a non-specialist visitor might build up around this object. The text limits the proliferation of representations. It weaves a network of links made up of sentences. By selecting the concepts, the writer imposes his own version or vision of the world. The text contains and channels the profusion of meaning.

Text and narrative framework

The exhibition is not just the accidental juxtaposition of a series of objects and texts that name or comment on them. It is a whole organized according to an itinerary whose continuity must be structured and controlled. Text is also the vital thread that links the objects presented or segments the exhibition space.

Titles, headings, labels, panels, legends and so on make up a single text which, by linking the parts to a whole and the whole to the parts, constructs the overall meaning of the exhibition. The text assumes a macrodiscursive function of linking the whole, which confers coherence and ensures cohesiveness. Through the textual network, the unity of the message occurs at a higher level, that of the story, the concept and the theme.

Text makes it possible not only to shift from the object to the word, but also from the word to the discourse. Beyond that, text serves to assemble meanings and acts as a tool for semantic cohesiveness (discourse) and syntactic structuring (itinerary to be followed). As Cameron has noted, even the best text can never make up for a lack of what he calls a museographic *gestalt*, i.e. a model or structure that is perceptible from the outset, while if the *gestalt* is effectively constructed, the text can efficiently emphasize and bolster it. The text enables visitors to assemble fragments of meaning into a coherent whole.

The exhibition text can, in this way, be segmented, i.e. divided into a finite number of statements or sequences, which are linked according to certain rules. These rules obviously depend on the exhibition program and support its narrative framework. The writer writes at the same time for each object presented and for the exhibition overall. Each text, from labels to panels, from titles to headings, is written as a sentence or a paragraph encompassing a homogeneous textual entity.

Text and enunciation

When the writer assembles his text according to particular structural and communications criteria, he produces a whole that presents expressive, formal characteristics of such great diversity that it seems illusory and, indeed, of no interest, to seek to construct a general and theoretical typology of the texts in the exhibition.

In fact, it is more interesting, and theoretically more coherent, to distinguish the texts according to the production process and not solely according to their finished state. To some extent, it is necessary to endeavour to understand the texts being created rather than to analyze the finished texts, in order to recognize possible correlations among all of the text production processes. Based on this principle, it is preferable to focus on living language, since to mount an exhibition is also to mount the text. These, then, presented in abbreviated form, are some of the enunciative marks that say more about texts than an artificial classification into titles, headings, panels, labels and so on.

The writer also attempts to make the text a product or tool of visual communication. To this end, he complies with a number of recommendations to ensure that it is seen and perhaps read: there is a contrast between the lettering and the background; the text is located at eye level; and the page format and typography facilitate reading and avoid visual fatigue. Less well known but equally important is the recurrence of scriptovisual forms that structure and make automatic the acquisition of information.

The writer tries to facilitate the absorption of knowledge. He uses the text as a tool to disseminate and popularize information. Consequently, the text has an educational function, and the writer seeks to produce statements that the public can understand. Several linguistic traits facilitate such understanding: the texts are short and divided up so as to facilitate reading; the most important information appears at the beginning of the sequence; and scientific concepts and specialized terms are reformulated by means of synonyms and redefinition.

> ### AN EXAMPLE OF REFORMULATION
>
> **Desertification**
>
> Desertification is a loss of biological activity resulting from a combination of drought and human intervention in the environment.

Îlot Environnement, Explora, CSI La Villette, Paris.

This brief text is an example of reformulation. The concept of desertification is explicitly defined using everyday vocabulary.

The writer commits himself in one way or another because even an objective, neutral scientific text displays a viewpoint through its very rejection of subjectivity or political bias. However, life is made up of pleasure and emotions. So that the text will elicit a reaction in visitors, the writer may take a stand, as numerous linguistic marks attest with respect to the macrostructure (recourse to narration, to cite the best known mark) as well as the sentence.

Sentence marking occurs more frequently, e.g. the use of figures of speech such as imagery and metaphors, model expressions in the register of doubt or perplexity (see the example of the vulture on the next page, as well as subjective or even polemical assertions such as: *5 million tonnes of sewage sludge, 55 million tonnes of dredging materials [...] plus 100 000 tonnes of toxic industrial wastes incinerated off Friesland. This is a partial list of waste dumped or processed in the North Sea in 1988* (CSI, La Villette, Explora).

The writer can become an author in his own right, provided he is capable of adapting to the special circumstances surrounding the exhibition discourse.

ENUNCIATION MARKS

THE GRIFFON VULTURE

The literature contains little reliable information on the actual presence of the vulture in the Alps.

It seems that the species was found there until the 18th century, then apparently disappeared as a result of poisoning, shooting and removal of the young from the nest.

Following the spectacular, successful introduction of the species into the Cévennes, a study is under way concerning the vulture's reintroduction into the southern zone of the Alps.

Salle Montagne vivante, Muséum d'histoire naturelle de Grenoble.

This statement contains numerous enunciation marks, such as qualifying adjectives (reliable, spectacular, successful) and adverbs, and expressions indicating uncertainty (it seems, apparently).

ONGOING READINGS

Because its raw material is the system of words and sentences, the exhibition text presents in black and white the other museographic registers that bind together the exhibition discourse. In this respect, the text occupies a special place in the exhibition discourse.

A displayed text becomes a semantically rich scriptovisual document, one that is easy to integrate physically into the exhibition scenography. It is an object intended to be viewed and read, and is a significant locus of communication between designer and visitor. First, its role as an image to be viewed bolsters its status as a point of contact between blocks of text and the eyes of visitors. Next, its linguistic nature defines its twofold function in the context of the exhibition, i.e. to appropriate the objects named and to make a judicious selection of the intellectual and affective memories associated with the objects presented.

Text is the key aid to interpretation. It is subject to an ongoing reading that demands, on the one hand, a strong structuring of the text units, including their closure and, on the other, their inclusion in the narrative framework of the exhibition.

If, as we have tried to do, we attempt to determine what it is that makes a text a scriptovisual exhibition document, we conclude that there are two ways to answer this question. The first is to adopt the system used so far, of text typologies defined according to the place, typography and function of statements in the overall framework of the exhibition: introduction, conclusion, titling, panel, notice, legend, label and so on.

However, texts are as many and various as exhibitions. A typology of text grammars enables us to pinpoint all the known genres. In descriptive, informative-explanatory, synoptic, narrative and injunctive texts, forms follow or overlay one another in the same unit. We would have to inventory all the genres and structures of sentences (affirmative, interrogative, exclamatory), all turns of phrase (attributive, impersonal, nominal); all anticipated constructions, of course, but all figures of speech as well (analogy, metaphor, comparison, metonymy, ellipsis and so on).

Any normative, exhaustive classification is doomed to fail: the creative matter of texts cannot be reduced to the classification processes of scientists. Because we are aware of the limitations of a functional approach that operates by fixed categories without taking account of the expressive and enunciative criteria of the exhibition texts, we have decided to take into consideration all of the semiolinguistic variables that occur when texts are produced.

Only an approach that does not separate the textual product (expression of content) from the production system (context, writer) and recognition system (receiver, meaning-related effects) can sustain a theoretical analysis of the exhibition text.

*

Acknowledgments:

M. Blondel (Musée de la vie bourguignonne Perrin-de-Puycousin, Dijon) and G. Ferrière (Muséum d'histoire naturelle, Dijon) provided the photographs reproduced in this chapter.

J.C. Duclos (Musée Dauphinois, Grenoble), A. Fayard (Muséum d'histoire naturelle, Grenoble), J. Le Marec (CSI-La Villette, Paris), the journal *La Recherche*, A. Nicolas and GRGM granted us permission to use the texts and maps.

Bibliography

Barthes, R. "Les planches de l'encyclopédie" in *Nouveaux essais critiques*, Seuil, 1964.

_____. "Rhétorique de l'image" in *L'obvie et l'obtus*, Seuil, 1964.

Bertin, J. *Sémiologie graphique*, Mouton, 1967.

Bitgood, S. "Deadly Sins Revisited; A Review of the Exhibit Labels Literature", *Visitor Behavior*, Vol. 4, No. 3, pp. 4-13, 1989.

Bresson, F. "Compétence iconique et compétence linguistique", *Communications*, No. 33, 1981, pp. 185-196.

Cameron, D. "Problèmes de langage en interprétation muséale (1971)" in Desvallées, A., editor, *Vagues: une anthologie de la nouvelle muséologie*. Macon: Éditions W-MNES, 1992, pp. 271-288.

Desjardins, J.; Jacobi, D. "Les étiquettes dans les musées et les expositions scientifiques", *Publics & Musées*, 1, 1992, pp. 13-32.

Floch, J.-M. *Sémiotique, marketing et communication*, PUF, 1990.

Freud, S. *L'Interprétation des rêves*, PUF, 1967 edition.

Goody, J. *La Raison graphique*, Seuil, 1985.

Jacobi, D. *Textes et images de la vulgarisation scientifique*. Berne: Peter Lang, 1987.

Jacobi, D.; Poli, M.S. "Écrire/lire les étiquettes dans les musées et expositions scientifiques", *La Muséologie des sciences et des techniques*, Actes REMUS, 1993, pp. 66-75.

Latour, B. "Les vues de l'esprit", *Culture technique*, No. 14, 1985.

McManus, P. "Watch Your Language! People Do Read Labels", *ILVS Review*, Vol. 1, No. 2, 1990, pp. 125-127.

Metz. C. "Au-delà de l'analogie, l'image", *Communications*, No. 15, 1970, pp. 1-11.

Panofsky, E. *L'œuvre d'art et ses significations: essais sur les arts visuels*, Gallimard, 1969.

Poli, M.S. "Le Parti pris des mots dans l'étiquette; une approche linguistique", *Publics & Musées*, No. 1, 1992, pp. 95-106.

Quaghebeur, M. *et al. Un pays d'irréguliers*. Brussels: Archives du Futur-Labor, 1990.

Sartre, J.-P. *L'Homme et les choses*, Gallimard, 1947.

Schiele, B. *Faire voir, faire savoir. La muséologie scientifique au présent*. Québec City: Musée de la civilisation, 1989.

Screven, C. "Comment motiver les visiteurs à la lecture des étiquettes", *Publics & Musées*, No. 1, 1992, pp. 33-56.

Serrell, B. *Making Exhibit Labels. A Step-by-Step Guide*. Nashville: AASLH, 1983.

CHAPTER 2

READING

Summary Andrée Blais

What factors make it possible to read a text easily and, consequently, to retain it? To answer this question, the author briefly examines the physiological functioning of the visual system. She explains that, in the reading process, the unit of perception is not the letter but the word, and that the word is the key to meaning, which calls upon memory. Reading necessarily involves a number of phases before the reader succeeds, through the formation of assumptions and the assimilation of clues, in discerning the meaning of what he sees. It is easier for a museum visitor to understand and retain a message when everyday vocabulary and simple sentences are used. Conversely, complex terms and sentences, which can require backtracking and rereading, hinder a quick understanding of the content and lessen the reader's motivation. Readers use different reading methods, depending on their particular objectives and circumstances. The author identifies two main types of reading: full reading and selective reading. A visitor to an exhibition appears to be a very special breed of reader. In this singular environment, the visitor, whose attention is solicited from all quarters, establishes his own reading methods in order to select the information he wishes. These different reading strategies, as we will see in the essay by Denis Samson, affect communication of the message in the museum setting.

The Reading Process

Andrée Blais

Project Manager and Production
Assistant, Exhibition Services,
Musée de la civilisation,
Québec City

Reading opens a window onto reality and offers access to knowledge, different sensibilities and numerous pleasures. Through reading, an individual broadens his knowledge of the world and is prompted to engage in reflection.

Reading is an organized social activity. It requires a network of producers, distributors and consumers. From author to publisher, bookseller to reader, reading plays a socioeconomic role in the dissemination of messages. It brings individuals, groups and institutions into contact. It is a nonspontaneous act of communication in that the emitter and the receiver do not interact directly. This significantly affects the manner in which the message, to be perceived later, is presented.

The museum is part of this reading culture and acts as both producer and distributor of the written word. It targets a vast audience and different types of visitors, all of whom look around, ask questions and read.

An understanding of the reading process can help clarify the complex relationship between physiological reactions to text, cognitive structures and the structural properties of a text. The primary objective of this essay is to zero in on the various types of knowledge required to design and produce a text. It focuses on reading efficiency and investigates the factors that enable a text to be easily read and, consequently, largely retained.

THE ACT OF READING

Reading consists in extracting meaning from what is written. Readers freely read a message at their own pace and for their own purposes in order to discern a singular meaning. According to Paul Valéry, the author does not exercise any authority: a text is like a device that individuals can use as they see fit and according to their skills.[1]

Readers remain active during the reading process, which is no longer considered a simple decoding exercise that consists in deciphering the letters of each word to transform them into sounds. This labourious process would distract the reader inordinately occupied in recognizing each syllable from the meaning and the context. Évelyne Charmeux claims that if reading is giving a meaning 'to' rather than drawing a meaning 'from', reading must be acknowledged as an intelligent, free activity.[2] The search for meaning is the reason for reading, not the consequence of it.

Reading is a complex act that relies on the perception and the cognitive structure of the reader, and requires physiological and intellectual effort.

From eye to reading mechanisms

For a text to be understood, there must be sensory input of a quantity of information. The properties of human vision thus have a considerable influence on the reading process. A complex analysis of the physiological functioning of the eye is not necessary here, but a brief description of it is provided to explain the way in which it interacts with the reader's cognitive structure.

---

1. Philippe Pigallet, *L'Art de lire, principes et méthodes* (Paris: Les éditions ESF – Entreprise moderne d'édition, 1985), p. 26.
2. Isdey Cohen and Annick Mauffrey, *Vers une nouvelle pédagogie de la lecture* (Paris: Armand Colin Éditeur, 1983), p. 69.

Émile Javal was the first to reveal that the eye does not move smoothly along a line, but shifts around in rapid, jerky movements called "saccades". The eye comes to rest at certain points, called "fixation points"; this results in perceptual pauses (fixations), during which words are recognized and information is acquired.

It is during these brief, successive fixations, lasting roughly a quarter of a second, that reading takes place. Overall, these periods represent 94 percent of reading time, the remaining six percent being taken up by eye movements (1/40 second) and saccades during which the reader is functionally blind.

Under normal reading conditions (a distance of 30 to 40 cm, 8- to 12-point characters and suitable lighting), roughly four letters are covered by the yellow spot on the retina, which contains the fovea, the area of the retina where visual acuity is the greatest. However, the eye perceives an additional 15 letters around this point. This ability is called "peripheral vision" and is used to anticipate what will reach the fovea, allowing, despite the imprecision, for the recognition of one to six words, depending on the reader's ability, during a single fixation.

> There is a relationship between the size of letters and the distance needed for good legibility. In an exhibition, the use of large point sizes for a typographic character may have two negative effects on reading efficiency. On the one hand, if readers are too close, their peripheral vision will be impaired and their ability to anticipate words will be diminished. On the other hand, if the text support is placed too far from readers, different elements outside the text will enter their field of vision and disrupt their reading.

The ability to read does not depend on the motion of the eye, but rather on the reader's ability to perceive words and thus units of meaning during each fixation. The average person reads 28 000 words an hour, or roughly 250 words a minute.[3]

---

3. This information is from research conducted by François Richaudeau. See Bibliography for works consulted.

From perception to reading

Unit of perception

The unit of perception in the reading process is not the letter but the word. The eye appears to recognize the contours of an overall form, and seems more sensitive to the outline of each word than to the letters that make it up.[4] The relevance of this premise is reinforced by gestalt psychology which, according to Philippe Pigallet, has confirmed that our sensory field inevitably absorbs a single form (or gestalt) that is not simply a disorganized assemblage but an overall structure.[5]

Our eye discerns global, coherent shapes. When it does not recognize a word, it attempts to break it down. This considerably slows the reading process and hinders spontaneous access to the meaning (later on in this essay, I will examine the importance of reading speed on comprehension and motivation). Ferdinand de Saussure pointed out that while a new or unknown word is spelled out letter by letter, a common, familiar word is taken in at a glance, independently of the letters it contains, and the image of this word acquires an ideographic value for us.[6]

Visual information and the reader's knowledge

Words are the key to meaning. Accordingly, the reader's efforts are not centred on memorizing words, but on deriving meaning from them. In so doing, the reader can come to understand a message and retain it.

The text elements alone assimilated during fixations do not appear sufficient to enable the reader to comprehend the content. Reading requires that the reader acquire a pool of knowledge, i.e. an understanding of the relevant language and the topic dealt with, which he must link to what he perceives in order to grasp the meaning with minimal clues.

---

4. This hypothesis was confirmed by François Richaudeau in his experiments on the reading process. See *Le Langage efficace* (Paris: Denoël-Gonthier, 1973) by Richaudeau.

5. Philippe Pigallet, *op. cit.*, p. 28.

6. *Ibid.*, p. 33.

Frank Smith has observed that reading relies on two types of information: information in front of the eye on the printed page, which he calls "visual information" and information behind the eye, in the brain, which he calls "nonvisual information". He maintains that the more we know "behind the eye", the less visual information we need to identify a letter, a word and the meaning of a text (and conversely).[7]

Thus, a lack of nonvisual information can make any individual "blind"; think of a grammarian reading a scholarly treatise on nuclear physics. The reader's knowledge relies on memory, which remains essential to the act of reading and to many of the mechanisms inherent in our cognitive structure.

Short-term and long-term memory

Memory is a complex process that can be viewed in different ways, depending on the analytical slant adopted. Two kinds of memory are most often referred to: short-term and long-term memory. They are distinguished primarily by their duration of retention and their ability to store information.

Short-term memory is a temporary, "working" memory and is suited to the type of loading and unloading that enables an individual to store information momentarily and subsequently discern its meaning. Its retention capacity is limited to a small amount of information, on average 15 words, so it is important not to overload it, and thereby disable it. Thanks to constant exchanges between the short-term memory and the long-term memory, an individual can not only recognize words, but understand their meaning and the syntactic and semantic links between them.

Short-term memory retains the series of words just read for several seconds. During this brief period of time, various mechanisms, ultimately designed to discern the meaning of the words, are at work. First, the short-term memory asks the long-term memory the meaning of the

---

7. Frank Smith, *Comment les enfants apprennent à lire*, translated and adapted by Michèle Proux (Paris: Éditions France-Amérique, 1981), p. 44.

words. The long-term memory instantly transfers to the short-term memory the portion of the meaning (or mental image) that it finds. The short-term memory then clears and becomes available again.

The signs perceived acquire meaning through a series of mental (conceptual or imaginary) representations: a dictionary definition of a given object does not give the object itself, but assumes that the reader will form an idea of it.[8]

Long-term memory includes the nonvisual information the reader obtains. It presupposes an acquisition phase, after which it organizes the information.[9] The actualization phase makes it possible to use the memory. This phase enables the reader to discover or reconstruct what is evoked by the text.

To this end, the long-term memory works by recognition (it recognizes what the visual information offers) or by recall (in the absence of information in the perceptual field, it searches for acquired knowledge). The reader therefore thinks while reading the text, exploring the range of possibilities, i.e. scanning the pool of information at his disposal.[10]

From reading to construction of meaning

Anticipation and assumption

According to Jean-Paul Sartre, an individual reads by anticipation and assumption, hence the importance of his skill and knowledge.

When reading, an individual anticipates and waits. He anticipates the end of the sentence, the next sentence, the next page. He waits for what he anticipates to be confirmed or denied. Reading relies on a multitude of assumptions, guesses, hopes and disappointments. Readers

---

8. Frank Smith and A. Viala, *Savoir lire* (Paris: Les Éditions Didier, 1982), p. 13.

9. This organization is complex and the different theories on it vary with the researcher. According to Philippe Pigallet, two theses appear to have achieved a consensus, that of the component-based model (semantic approach) and that of the network model (systemic approach centred on nodes or concepts).

10. Philippe Pigallet, *op. cit.*, p. 32.

are always ahead of the sentence they are reading in a probable future that comes into being as the readers progress.[11]

Jean Foucambert defines anticipation as a mechanism that activates an intuitive system based on the probability and the frequency with which words, categories and structures appear.[12] As is the case in any deductive approach, the range of possibilities is vast at the outset and narrows as the reader progresses and reduces his uncertainty by obtaining information. The acquisition of information must be as effective as possible; this means that the parallel process of thinking (retrieval of nonvisual information) must be free of excessive constraints that could distract it from the meaning.

The acquisition of clues

The acquisition of clues is thus essential. This process must remain selective, failing which it will be ineffectual. According to Frank Smith, a text that uses all clues available would slow readers and divert them from the essential objective, which is understanding.[13] The functional acquisition of clues is therefore extremely instrumental in validating or invalidating assumptions.

Readers do not read all visual information. This explains, among other things, why they have difficulty detecting typographic errors or missing words in a text. Instead, they tend to rectify errors or omissions without necessarily discerning them systematically.

The systems of clues used continue to raise numerous questions. While research in this field is inconclusive, three systems of clues, i.e. graphophonic, syntactic and semantic, are used during reading, either together or independently. When one system is given precedence because of various needs or the reading strategy adopted, the other two tend to fade.

---

11. Philippe Pigallet, *op. cit.*, p. 35.
12. Edmond Beaume, *La Lecture, préalable à sa pédagogie* (Paris: Association française pour la lecture, 1985), p. 53.
13. *Op. cit.*, p. 55.

The graphophonic system of clues includes all use of the written word and its phonetic equivalence. It is used most frequently in cases of lexical ambiguity. The syntactic system of clues is based on vocabulary and the order in which words are arranged, i.e. syntax. For example, noun and verb endings and function words such as articles provide a significant amount of information, which helps the reader anticipate. The third and most important system of clues is semantic. Aside from the recognition of words and the links between them, this system looks for key words (subjects, verbs and so on) and their semantic organization. The result may validate or invalidate the reader's initial assumptions. Joël Pynte maintains that the perceptive threshold of a word (the minimum time needed to identify it) is lower when the word is preceded by a semantically congruent sentence.[14] When the word, while syntactically acceptable, is semantically incongruent, the threshold is higher.[15]

Speed of reading and effect on motivation

The speed with which a text is read directly affects the reader's ability to retain the message. The faster a text is read, the better it is stored in memory. Reading speed varies with the number of fixations which, in turn, varies with the difficulty of the words, the syntax, the reader's knowledge, and the originality of the message. Excessive complexity requires rereading and an increase in the fixations per line.

This slows down the reading process, which demands additional effort from the reader, whose motivation may suffer (the same is true of a text in a second language with which the reader is not fully conversant). In any case, it appears that because of this requirement, the understanding and retention of the message are significantly reduced.

The reading process seems to be favourably affected by the "law of least effort".[16] Indeed, the efficacy of a word or a syntactic structure

---

14. Kenneth S. Goodman explains this theory in "Les Universaux psycho-linguistiques et processus de lecture" in *Comment les enfants apprennent à lire*, Frank Smith, editor, translated and adapted by Michèle Proux (Paris: Éditions France-Amérique, 1981).

15. Edmond Beaume, *op. cit.*, p. 58.

16. François Richaudeau uses the expression "law of least effort" in this context.

hinges on the extent to which it is recognized. In other words, the more a word or grammatical construction is common and simple, the faster it is perceived and read, thus facilitating anticipation and the acquisition of clues. Common words and simple constructions offer the advantage of acquired significance because of their high rate of use by the memory.

Conversely, specialized terms and complex sentences require more extensive use of the memory's identification and integration mechanisms. Long sentences, in which the number of words largely exceeds the short-term memory capacity, reduce the potential for retaining the content.

> The foregoing information should influence the writing of exhibition texts. It could serve as a guideline to the development and structuring of messages (see Chapter 4, "Writing"). Readers always evaluate the time and effort required to read a text. They quickly discern the complexity and ambiguities of the text. If the environment in which they are reading is distracting, as is the case in an exhibition, it is essential to facilitate the assimilation of content, and thereby maintain motivation.
>
> The length of texts is an important factor to consider. While there are hard and fast rules in this respect, various studies on reading at exhibitions have shown that the reading time for each word declines as the number of words increases. In other words, the visitor either skims through the text or skips over parts of it. Louise Boucher, referring to the empirical data of Borun and Miller, asserts that short texts are better able to attract the reader and are easier to retain. An evaluation conducted on a 150-word text shows that once the text was divided into three short 50-word texts, the number of readers more than doubled, from 11 percent to 26 percent.[17]

---

17. Information drawn from a report prepared by Louise Boucher for a seminar at the Musée de la civilisation on November 7 and 8, 1991, entitled "La communication dans et par l'exposition." In her report, Louise Boucher refers to an article by M. Borun and M.A. Miller, "What's in a Name? A Study of the Effectiveness of Explanatory Labels in a Science Museum" (Philadelphia: Franklin Institute of Science, 1980).

DIVERSITY OF READING SITUATIONS

Reading goals, motivation and circumstances

Today's readers, accustomed to a steady stream of printed information, have developed reading strategies based on modes of lexical activity that enable them to make choices.

Everyone reads a text for a reason: reading is not a random act but a deliberate one. Reading always serves a purpose or satisfies a need or desire. Readers' behaviour varies depending on their goal and the nature of the printed message. Readers systematically adapt their strategies, without altering the reading process.

Reading is multifaceted and a constant feature of our daily lives. The motivations and circumstances on which it depends call for various strategies. To read in a bus, a café, at breakfast, in the street, on the beach or in a library requires not only that readers adapt to the environment, but that they choose the texts they read. The novel, newspaper, cereal box, tourist guide, popular magazine and philosophical treatise are not read for the same reasons, in the same places or in the same positions. A reader stretched out in a hammock or on a beach does not read the same thing or in the same manner as when visiting an exhibition.

No matter why people read – relaxation, instruction, utility, enjoyment, the quest for prestige – their motivations for doing so lead to different types of reading: utilitarian or functional reading (the search for a telephone number in the directory); cognitive reading (the reading of a theoretical work to broaden one's knowledge); reading for pleasure (the reading of novels or magazines for relaxation, entertainment or escape), and so on. These different types of reading can be grouped into two main categories: studious reading, which is unaccompanied by another activity, and leisure reading, which is always accompanied by another activity, such as a visit to an exhibition.[18]

---

18. Categories defined by Georges Perec and discussed by Philippe Pigallet, *op. cit.*, p. 22.

A single text can serve different purposes and be read in different ways. This indicates the extreme flexibility of the reader, who must constantly adapt his strategies.

Modes of reading

Two modes of reading have been selected for the purpose of this essay, full reading and selective reading.

Full reading

This mode consists in reading a work from start to finish, with or without sustained interest. This strategy is less frequently employed today, but is still used for the novel or other literary genres, such as the essay and biography. Most readers scrupulously respect the semantic and physical organization of a story or specific piece of knowledge. Some readers feel guilty when they abandon a book that has failed to satisfy their needs and which they began with the intention of reading it completely.

Selective reading

The proliferation of texts has led the reader to make choices, not only in terms of the diversity of reading material but with respect to the individual text. He does not read everything. He seeks only the information he wants or needs. He proceeds by way of evaluation and selection. This method of reading is characterized by constant searching.

The evaluation strategy is used to assess the content of documents in order to determine the main topics and the overall organization of the text. The reader must have a clear idea of what he is looking for and the time at his disposal. On the basis of these different factors, he will decide whether or not to engage in a more thorough reading of the sections he has chosen. The reader usually obtains an overview of certain parts of a book, such as the cover page, the table of contents, the summary, the introduction, certain chapters, the conclusion and so on.

Selection strategies that rely on scanning or skimming are designed to locate the desired information quickly. Scanning consists in glancing over the pages of a text, without paying attention to the content, until the desired item is located. This strategy is used when we are looking up a word in a dictionary, for example, or a name in an alphabetical list. In this case, the reader acts as a detector.

Skimming focuses on the main information in a text. It enables the reader to overlook redundancies and ambiguous sentences, and zero in on the main ideas by scanning for key words. Skimming tends to respect the structure of a text. It relies on typographic signs and the hierarchical organization of the content, as indicated by headings, subheadings, sidebars, text boxes and so on. One of the best examples of efficient scanning is reading the daily newspaper. The eye glances over a page on which material is presented according to different levels of reading: headings, subheadings, legends, photographs, introductions, articles, and so on. The page layout and the very nature of the writing, which is concise and informative, are specifically designed to simplify the recognition and assimilation of the messages.

All these selection strategies can be used systematically or individually during the reading process. They depend on the reference points offered by the hierarchical organization of the content, and on the typographic code.

> The exhibition is similar to a newspaper in the way it presents messages. The layout of text (see "Typographic Legibility" in Chapter 5) must enable visitors to identify, at a glance, the textual structure of the exhibition. In this way, they can make efficient use of their reading strategies and thus select what interests them.

*

Regardless of the situation and the reader, the act of reading remains a cognitive and physiological activity that offers an individual access to information and sensibilities that he acquires as he sees fit, according to his interests and knowledge.

The reader we are interested in is mobile and does not necessarily make reading the focal point of his experience. Specifically, he is an exhibition visitor. In this communication situation, the visitor is constantly attracted by various objects, of which texts are only one component. As a result of this complex environment and the nature of the textual support, reading conditions are more difficult, indeed abnormal.

In an exhibition, the visitor adapts his behaviour as a consumer concerned with quickly obtaining the desired information. With the aid of effective scriptovisual documents, he can establish his own reading techniques. Applied research has been conducted in order to describe the behaviour of the typical visitor-reader. An analysis of this behaviour paves the way to a better understanding of the reading mechanisms visitors employ and what motivates them to read.

*

Bibliography

Beaume, Edmond. *La Lecture, préalable à sa pédagogie*. Paris: Association française pour la lecture, 1985.

Cohen, Isdey; Mauffrey, Annick. *Vers une nouvelle pédagogie de la lecture*. Paris: Armand Colin Éditeur, 1983.

Douel, Jacques. *Le journal tel qu'il est lu*. Paris: Centre de formation et de perfectionnement des journalistes, 1981.

Eco, Umberto. *Lector in Fabula, le rôle du lecteur*. Paris: Grasset, 1985.

Goodman, Kenneth S. "Universaux psycho-linguistiques et processus de lecture" in Frank Smith, editor, *Comment les enfants apprennent à lire*, translated and adapted by Michèle Proux. Paris: Éditions France-Amérique, 1981.

Javal, Émile. *Psychologie de la lecture et de l'écriture*. Paris: (Alcan, 1905) Retz, 1978.

McManus, P. "Oh Yes, They Do! How Museum Visitors Read Labels and Interact with Exhibit Texts", *Museum Curator*, Vol. 32, No. 3, 1989, pp.174-189.

Pigallet, Philippe. *L'art de lire, Principes et méthodes* (seminar). Paris: Les Éditions ESF—Entreprise moderne d'édition, 1985.

Richaudeau, François. *Manuel de typographie et de mise en page*. Paris: Retz, 1989.

_____. *La lisibilité*. Paris: Retz, CEPL, 1976.

_____. "Le processus de lecture", *La Chose imprimée*. John Dreyfus and François Richaudeau, editors. Paris: CEPL, 1977.

_____. *Le Langage efficace*. Paris: Denoël-Gonthier, 1973.

Rossi, Jean-Pierre. *Les Mécanismes de la lecture*. Paris: Publications de la Sorbonne, 1985.

Samson, Denis. "L'évaluation formative et la genèse du texte", *Publics & Musées*, Presses universitaires de Lyon, No. 1, May 1992.

Screven, Chandler. "Comment motiver les visiteurs à la lecture des étiquettes", *Publics & Musées*, Presses universitaires de Lyon, No. 1, May 1992.

Serrell, Beverly. *Making Exhibit Labels. A Step-by-Step Guide*. Nashville: American Association for State and Local History, 1983.

Smith, Frank. *Devenir lecteur*. Paris: Armand Collin Éditeur, 1986.

Smith, Frank, editor. *Comment les enfants apprennent à lire*, translated and adapted by Michèle Proux. Paris: Éditions France-Amérique, 1981.

Smith, Frank; Viala, A. *Savoir lire*. Paris: Les Éditions Didier, 1982.

Spencer, Herbert. *The Visible Word, Visual Communication Books*. New York: Hasting House, 1968.

Summary Chandler G. Screven

This paper examines some functions of interpretive labels/graphics and relates these functions to the informal, voluntary conditions in which labels must perform. It examines the often poor results seen when label design does not match the needs and expectations of voluntary, unguided audiences in informal settings. Some common reasons that contribute to the inability to create effective labels are discussed. Methods for improving the quality of attention to labels and some steps for label preparation are summarized.

Motivating Visitors to Read Labels

Chandler G. Screven

Department of Psychology
University of Wisconsin-
Milwaukee

Most visitors read some labels occasionally. Some read nothing at all. But many visitors will read labels if the conditions are right (Borun and Miller, 1980; McManus, 1987, 1990). What are these conditions? Some of the factors that affect whether casual visitors will or will not read labels will be considered here.

First, let's be clear how the term "label" will be used. Normally, the term has referred to the familiar name-date-identification label. As used here, "label" refers to all types of media – print, audio, and grafics and their presentation formats – used to help visitors interpret and relate to exhibit content, have an emotive impact, or motivate attention and effort. Interpretive labels have at least four components that affect their impact on visitors:

- *Content:* text and message components (conceptual level, cause/effect, comparisons, questions, instructions, headings, emotional components).

- *Structures:* legibility, organization, size, typeface, density of information, colors.

- *Presentation Format:* interactivity, sound, graphics, video, computers.

- *Context:* The physical and environmental context in which labels are placed: noise, lighting, sight-lines, competing exhibits, relation of text to exhibit content, entrances/exits.

Most impressions about label effectiveness are based on watching people in museums, zoos, and botanical gardens in which the design and content of the labels mostly reflect the values and needs of their preparers – not the values and needs of users. Those responsible for labels usually are concerned with label aesthetics, maintenance, accuracy of content, and their appeal to expert viewers. Too little attention is given to the reactions (or lack of reactions) of ordinary visitors. Effective labels deal directly with what visitors are looking at in the exhibit because exhibit objects are starting points for many visitors. Also, the information provided by labels should contain information visitors want to know. The common practice of asking script writers to prepare labels before specific objects and other content have been established makes this difficult if not impossible.

FUNCTIONS OF LABELS

As noted by Loomis (1983), the need for interpretive materials to help the general visitor understand exhibit objects – "bridging the knowledge gap" between visitors and objects – is very important. Indeed, surveys by Klein (1978) and others have indicated that a major reason given by visitors for not visiting museums is the difficulty they encounter in finding out why specific objects are there, why they are important, or their connections to the visitor's world. To attract new visitors and encourage repeat visits, museum managers need to become "visitor literate." They should get into the habit of pretesting label effectiveness in the early stages of development. Ineffective label designs, language, and placement usually reflect incorrect assumptions by exhibit managers, label writers and curators about the backgrounds and interests of those to whom they are trying to communicate.

What is an effective label?

It's probably a waste of time planning a label or worrying about which format (print, slides, interactives, etc.) is best for delivering label information before considering the *function* a given label serves. Any label should have a clearly defined function, or it may not be necessary in the first place. Functions for labels include: to attract attention, provide choices, connect unfamiliar objects or topics to familiar experiences, provide a framework for an exhibition theme, provide examples, focus attention to objects, elicit curiosity, answer questions, or communicate messages.

The "message" that labels deliver can include a wide range of functions. For example:

- Facts and definitions: *Not all dinosaurs are meat eaters,*
- Analogies: *Palaeontology is like detective work,*
- Motivational impact: *A rain forest is an interesting topic; Biology is easier to understand than expected,*
- Self-esteem role: *Maybe I'm smart enough to learn things like this after all.*

Topography, layout, interactivity, or other formats serve some purposes better than others: for example, attracting, and holding attention. The particular *content* of a label (e. g., its vocabulary, Socratic questions, graphics) serves other purposes; for examples, helping a visitor to compare things or interrelate elements. Some purposes depend on both the medium and the message.

Without a clear purpose, there is little basis for choosing among alternative formats. Different features serve different purposes. Animation illustrates how an ear works better than a printed diagram or text because the dynamics of the hearing process are lost by the flatness of diagrams and of written language. A large printed sign may work as well or better than an expensive electronic sign to identify a theme area. Arguments over how many words should be allotted, size of type, terminology, colors, or aesthetics often reflect inadequate attention to what a print label is supposed to do and for whom.

Thus, labels serve different functions (for visitors as well as exhibitors) for different circumstances. Some important functions of labels include the following (adapted from Screven, 1986):

1. Provide *information* on the visual content of exhibits – names, dates, uses, relationships, why an object is there, what it does.

2. *Instruct* visitors on what to *do* look for.

3. *Personalize* topics – connect the new and unfamiliar to familiar experiences and questions.

4. *Interpret* the content of the exhibit – its sensory impressions, its meanings, its causes and effects.

5. *Orient* visitors on what to expect, how things are organized, and how they might relate to exhibit content.

In her efforts to help museum professionals improve labels at Monterey Bay Aquarium and other places, Rand (1990) also has emphasized the importance of identifying the objectives (functions) that labels have and how objectives guide decisions about language and presentation. Her examples of objectives include: focusing attention, correcting misconceptions, connecting the unfamiliar with the familiar, challenging visitors to answer a question or solve a problem, expressing the unknown, and drawing analogies.

Additional examples of label headings or text applicable for different label objectives and conditions are listed in Table 1.

CONDITIONS IN WHICH MUSEUM LABELS FUNCTION

The characteristics of museums as teaching-learning environments form the context in which effective interpretive labels must function. The chances a label will be approached, read, and understood is affected not only by a visitor's interest in an exhibit's topic and the quality of its organization, but by design details that affect the visitor's expectations of the amount of effort, time, and value of its content, their control over the type and amount of available information and its sensory modes, and the possibilities for action and problem solving. Over the years, the author has described these characteristics in various articles (Screven, 1969, 1974, 1986, 1990a) and these have been reiterated by Bitgood (1987); Loomis (1987); Shettel (1973), and others. Only a summary is needed here:

1. The majority of museum visitors are unguided people who are exploring museums and zoos on a *voluntary* basis on their own

time and on their own terms. What they do or pay attention to, how carefully they attend, and how they interpret what they see, hear and read are based on *their* needs, expectations, preconceptions – not those of the museum. This means that learning in museums is a byproduct of "fun" oriented activities that are self-directed, self-paced, nonlinear, exploratory, and often social/family motivated.

2. Approaching and attending to exhibits depends on having *positive* experiences when doing so – not, as happens in schools, where maintaining attention often depends on avoiding the consequences of *not* attending (e.g., poor grades). Therefore, the content, structure and presentation modes of museum labels must (a) provide *positive* reasons for visitors to approach and attend to them (require minimum time, are sharable, easy to see, personal, provide challenge, concrete goals, action) and (b) minimize the *negative* reasons for not attending to them (crowded text, too much information, abstract, impersonal, difficult to see, hear or read).

3. When visitors *do* approach an interpretive label, the "quality" of visitor effort and attention can range from relatively passive ("mindless") involvement not directed to relevant content, to *active* involvement, also termed "mindfulness" by Langer (1989a) and Moscardo (1992), in which visitors compare things, ask or answer questions, make choices, notice relationships, make personal connections, and alter existing cognitive structures (Moscardo, 1992), all essential prerequisites for learning. Evidence suggests that much complex daily behavior, including social behavior, occurs with only minimal information processing; i.e., in a "mindless" manner (Grünig, 1979; Langer, 1989a; Moscardo, 1986, 1992). Mindfulness, or high involvement, is more likely in unfamiliar, diverse, unexpected situations, with varied/multisensory media, questions and attention directing devices, visitor control over the type and amount of information, and personally relevant, emotionally charged materials. Active involvement has been associated with better judgement, learning, higher self-esteem, and higher satisfaction (Langer, 1989b).

TABLE 1

Text Examples Serving Different Goals for Using Labels

(Examples marked "•" are from Rand, 1990)

GOALS	1. Attract visitors toward labels or to exhibit content.	2. Focus attention to particular ideas or features of exhibit content.	3. Correct misconceptions.	4. Connect explanations to familiar experiences, phrases, or terms.	5. Encourage active attention to exhibit content.
EXAMPLES	• Squids have orgies, but octopuses have close encounters. • Why Do Otters Scratch So Much? Otters aren't scratching because they itch! They're grooming. This keeps their fur clean and waterproof.	Why are there so many different kinds of living things? • Do you think this thing is a plant? Look more carefully! • They may look empty, but mudflats crawl with life! • Can you find the animal that looks like a stone? This map shows the continents as they are today. Where were they 200 million years ago? Choose one. Which beaks would crush a hazelnut? Why Do These Rocks Look Alive?	• This plantlike creature is actually an animal! What good is a rain forest if it prevents economic development? Hate this painting? Who said you had to like it? Which of these paintings of a green faun do you like best? Is yours the same as Picasso's? How do we know the glacier was here? (Heading over entrance to glacier exhibition.)	Why is a hyena's laugh music to a lion's ears? • *Reach Out and Taste Someone!* An octopus explores with its tentacles. The suckers can taste the difference between sweet, sour and bitter, and can tell if something's rough or smooth. • These dune plants fight for a foothold in shifting sands. • Like vultures, scavenging hagfish keep order on the floor! • Why are there so many kinds of living things?	• Odds are you wont find this cleverly camouflaged fish. Try looking for a blade of kelp that has two round eyes! • Watch the small silvery fish pass in a school and you'll catch some yawning! • That's the hornmouth, one of our more ornamental snails. • They may look empty, but mudflats crawl with life!

TABLE 1 (Continued)

Text Examples Serving Different Goals for Using Labels (Continued)

(Examples marked "•" are from Rand, 1990)

GOALS	6. Make ideas more familiar.	7. Encourage visitors to draw analogies.	8. Articulate questions visitors commonly have about exhibit content.	9. Encourage visitors to fantasize or project themselves into an exhibit situation. Sensitize them to another viewpoint.	10. Challenge visitors to attack a specific problem (not too easy, not too hard).
EXAMPLES	• Flatfishes are quick-change artists! • Like vultures, scavenging hagfish keep order on the floor! A Story Told By Bones. (For exhibit on anatomy)	• Sea Stars Use Suction to Pry Open Their Prey! Pulling on a shell for hours with its small hydraulic tubefeet, a sea star will exhaust even the most clammed-up clams! Think of the generator in a coal-electric plant that turns by steam like your bicycle generator that is turned by your leg muscles.	What's the lady doing among all those men? (From Rembrandt's "Night Watch") What is this painting worth? (From Rembrandt's "Night Watch") Is this bone *real?* Is the diamond in this elephant real? Why do some of these figures have blue skin? (From Egyptian Temple diorama)	If you were here, what would YOU do? (How would YOU feel?) Which of these four versions of the Green Faun do you like best? Is yours the same as Picasso's?	Think of a coal electric plant as a bicycle that turns a generator by coal-fired steam instead of by you. Which beaks could eat from this passion flower? • Can you find the animal that looks like a stone? • What's out there under all that water? • Odds are you won't find this cleverly camouflaged fish. Try looking for a blade of kelp that has two round eyes!

4. Interpretive text and graphics usually are essential if visitors are to understand the larger context of exhibitions. But, in traditional exhibits, many self-directed visitors do not read print labels. One reason is that the *visual, sensory, action, emotional,* and *social* aspects of exhibits (colors, shapes, movements, buttons, touch, smell, texture) usually are intrinsically more interesting than text. While direct sensory-motor-affective experiences sometime can communicate exhibit's messages, usually some kind of text is necessary. If so, this text must be approachable, readable, enjoyable, informative, involving, and pertinent to exhibit content.

5. In most museums, visitor time is limited by fatigue, hunger, appointments, parking, and other practical problems. For many visitors, time is a commodity that is invested at various points between entry and the point when the visit is terminated by fatigue, hunger, etc. Thus, attending to an exhibit and/or reading a label depends on the visitor's perception of the time and effort (cost) required and its expected "value" (Salomon & Globerson, 1987). From a visitor's standpoint, the question is: How much time will the label require compared with alternatives and will this time be worth it? Reading an interpretive label has a "value-added" factor as well as a "cost." This $^{Value}/_{Cost}$ Ratio affects how likely a label will be read. "Value" is the likelihood that the label will make an exhibit more fun, personal, or understandable and "Cost" is the time and effort required to process its content. If the V/C-Ratio>1.0, the label is read. Estimates of "value" may reflect prior experiences, a challenging headline, photo, question, a goal to achieve. (Simple, short paragraphs, familiar language; good illustrations will be perceived to require less time.) "Cost" not only depends on time estimates, but effort factors such as poor lighting, bad placement, too much information, unfamiliar language, and poor organization.

MOTIVATING LABEL USAGE

Given the open, voluntary, time-sensitive, and social conditions of museums, visitor perceptions about time, effort, and value of given actions probably are important influences on their use of text/graphic structures and delivery modes. Learning that takes place under such conditions is not unlike learning a sport or a musical instrument. These require effort and active involvement over time and are motivated by various intrinsic rewards along the way such as personal control over the process, discovery, sharing, surprise, competition, emotional excitement, and progress toward a goal.

In museums, effort and active involvement with exhibits and labels are similarly motivated. As described earlier, creating effective labels is not just a matter of generating lots of attention and effort, but depends on making mindful attention more fun than random or casual manipulations. The "fun" from interacting with exhibits must not be available *whether or not* focused attention is given to the exhibit's intended content or message.

At all educational levels, visitors are more likely to approach exhibit objects, visuals, headlines or text that are personally meaningful (Alt and Shaw, 1984; Samuels, 1988). Personalized writing styles, provocative headlines, leading questions, humor, and challenge increase involvement and focused attention (*What's wrong with this picture? How do we know the glacier was here? Find the animal that looks like a stone. Which of these 4 versions of Picasso's "Green Faun" do you like best? Is yours the same as Picasso's?*) Open ended interviews and focus groups centering around prospective exhibit objects and topics offer rich sources of ideas for potential wording and questions that can be used to create these attributes in labels.

Before discussing more specific formats that encourage label usage, some words about motivation itself may be helpful.

Rewarding mindful reading and attention

Most "rewards" or incentives that can serve as a basis for attracting and sustaining mindful attention and effort are *intrinsic* incentives that are a part of natural explorations of museum environments. Sometimes, however, *external* (physical) rewards may be necessary to obtain the extra time and effort from visitors that more complex tasks or concepts may require.

Intrinsic motivators

"Intrinsic motivators" are ˝rewarding˝ experiences that are natural outcomes from interaction or exploration of environments. Examples would include the excitement of progressing toward or achieving a goal, exploring exhibits with a friend, completing a task, acquiring a skill, solving a problem, or controlling or predicting events. Intrinsic motivators are responsible for many familiar human behaviors that persist without apparent external consequences. Common behaviors that are motivated by intrinsic incentives include playing chess, climbing a mountain, or learning to play a musical instrument (Csikszentmihalyi, 1988, 1990; Screven, 1986, pp. 113-115). Common intrinsic motivators that are operative in museums include curiosity (e.g., pursuing questions), engaging in a challenging goal directed task, uncertainty, novel experiences, and fantasizing Reading labels also can· be intrinsically rewarding if this leads to better understanding of exhibit objects or to new, sharable knowledge. Table 1 and Figure 2 show examples of wording and formats directed to such ends. Intrinsic motivators like discovery and problem-solving probably are contributors to the sustained interest and involvement in label reading seen with interactive (flip) label formats (see below).

External motivators

"External motivators" are things like money, privileges, or symbols given in recognition of an achievement that are under the control of someone or some thing (e.g., computer) that are contingent on some action, achievement, etc. While intrinsic motivators generate much of the attention and learning activities seen in museums, some exhibit goals require more time and effort than can be expected with intrinsic motivators alone. Examples would include exhibits which attempt to teach about food chains, plate-tectonics, biological interdependence, or other complex concepts that visitors know little about.

What if you wanted to create the excitement of discovery or increase the self-confidence associated with succeeding at a challenging task? The difficulty here is that such goals assume that visitors will persist long enough to succeed. But, given their limited time and perhaps uncertainty about their ability to succeed, many visitors will not invest the time needed to find out. Teaching goals of this kind often require more powerful external motivators to entice visitors to try – for example, by providing the opportunity to earn a lapel pin or other take-home prize.

> *To entice visitors to carefully attend to nearby energy exhibits, the author (Screven, 1990b, pp. 120-121) provided take-home prizes to visitors who could answer criterion questions at self-test computers. The questions could be answered by most visitors, but only if key exhibit topics had been carefully attended to and understood. Visitors first had to find out that the questions could not be answered without careful attention to the exhibits. The method produced striking increases in time, effort and mindful involvement, compared with the attention given to the exhibits without self-test computers and take-home prizes.*

Exhibit planners often resist external incentives because they believe that the activities they generate will become dependent on the external rewards. Indeed, this may be correct unless care is taken in controlling exactly how the external incentives are applied. External incentives, indeed, can be counterproductive; for example, when visitors focus on the reward at the expense of reading a label or studying exhibit content. But external incentives need not have negative effects if care is taken to design the "reward system" so visitors cannot earn the reward unless they mindfully use (and learn from) the target exhibits and its labels (Screven, 1986).

Because it is so easy to produce negative side effects, it is important to pretest (formatively evaluate) the impact of extrinsic reward systems and make adjustments that avoid the mindless, reward-driven behavior that, otherwise, may accompany the use of external incentives. Formative testing assures that the "end result" (i.e., involvement, learning, interest, self-esteem) justifies the "means" (use of an external reward). In the application described above, the self-test system was adjusted several times before results were acceptable.

The structure of text

The structure of text includes such things as:

- *Legibility*: typeface, point size, line length; word length, white space, print density, background contrast;
- *Style*: distance between pronouns and their antecedents; specific *versus* general nouns ("*A robin would...*" "*A bird would...*");
- *Reader consideration*: signal words to alert important follow-up information or to anticipate expected information, anticipate causes;
- *Syntactic complexity*: sentence length, number of sentences starting with phrases in which no new information is being added ("*In other words...*", "*In summary...*");
- *Semantic complexity*: number and level of propositions, causal structures, vague, abstract language, concept density (ratio of concrete to abstract concepts).

Such variables can directly affect the readability of text, as well as a reader's perception, effort, memory, and comprehension (Rayner & Pollatsek, 1989; Rothkopf, 1970; Samuels, 1988; Kintsch & VanDijk, 1978; Kintsch & Vipond, 1979). If so, then they also can influence the visitor's motivation to read (or not to read) by affecting the $^{Value}/_{Cost}$ Ratio, or their perception of the effort that reading the text is likely to have, and the likelihood they will "understand" a point, perceive a connection, answer a question, take an action, and so on. Examples of some research results:

- The distance between pronouns and their antecedents should not exceed more than a few sentences.

- Concepts should be kept **specific** whenever possible. *A robin would sometimes wander around the house* is easier to read than *a bird would sometimes wander around the house.* General concepts need to be repeated more than specific concepts.

- More attention usually is given to segments of text that give reader something to do (look for, apply, carry out).

- Cues need to be provided in text to signal a change in topic (paragraphs, italics, indexing, listing, and phrases, such as *The third conclusion about radiation impact is ...*).

- Many readers expect that each sentence will add something new. When a sentence rephrases the same information, reading effort is decreased by devices such as *"In summary..."*

- Average word length and the frequency of words in the general language are good predictors of readability.

- Higher level propositions are remembered better than lower level propositions.

- Chunking text (grouping like information together in nested paragraphs) expands the amount of information persons can "remember" in short-term memory.

Formats and context

Presentation formats include the delivery medium a label uses (print, film, audio, computers), type styles and sizes, text layout, and attributes such as animation, language style, and interactivity. Presentation formats affect readability, visibility, attraction, holding power, the ability to focus attention, and how visitors are likely to *use* or *misuse* labels. As with label content, the purpose or function of a label's presentation format should also be carefully defined before selecting among alternative formats.

The first and easiest step to encourage the reading of print labels is to reduce the "Cost" in the $^{Value}/_{Cost}$ Ratio by avoiding features that *discourage* reading.

The following suggestions should avoid the most common problems (adapted from Screven, 1986).

1. Locate print labels near the objects they are about – preferably *on* them, but at least near them and visually "connected" to them (Bitgood, 1987; Screven, 1986; Serrell, 1983);

2. Select typography that is easy to read. Generally, serif type is easier to read than *sans serif*. Avoid type that is too small, colors that reduce contrast, and poor lighting (Bitgood, 1991; Layton, 1991; Samuels, 1988; Serrell, 1983). There also is the possibility of connotative effects of typefaces on feelings about the message.

3. Distribution and use of white space makes text appear easier to read and more interesting. In general, the more white space the better.

4. As visitors approach text, the text should require only a little time to find the wanted information or to sample short portions of the text. For example, long text can be divided into smaller paragraphs, called *chunking*, so visitors can decide *what* to read and *how-much* as they go along. Different sizes and weights for primary and secondary text is another possibility.

5. Headlines and thematic signs should be short and use large type with simple, eye catching designs and familiar, descriptive language because, from a distance, visitors use headings and thematic signs to help them make a decision.

6. Label language should focus on **specific** descriptive attributes of exhibit object – colors, smells, movements, functions (Bitgood, 1987; Layton, 1991; Rayner & Pollatsek, 1989; Screven, 1986). Tap *existing* visitor interests, naive questions, and personal experiences that can be used in headlines, subheads, cartoons, and other text. Begin where the visitor is (*How much is the painting worth?*) and proceed to where you want the visitor to be (*Money is not useful for evaluating paintings*). Avoid abstract language in headings and lead paragraphs (*Life's Meaning in the Sands*).

7. Use personal language in active voice (we, you, folks) and avoid jargon (Bitgood, 1987; Layton, 1991; Rand, 1990; Screven, 1986).

Some educational and psychologically oriented publications provide research and theoretical models on readability, memory, and comprehension of text applicable to writing and formatting interpretive labels in museums. These include Frase (1968); Hartley (1982); Kintsch & VanDijk (1978); Kintsch & Vipond (1979); Rayner & Pollatsek, 1989; Rothkopf (1970).

Encouraging and sustaining focused reading (Mindfulness)

In addition to avoiding formats that discourage reading, some formats take a more direct approach. For example,

- Using *visual* cues (diagrams, photos) that visitors can use to find desired information in the clutter of other text (Hartley, 1982);
- Inviting visitors to *act* by asking them to touch, smell, compare, sort, predict what will happen if... (Rothkopf, 1970);
- Challenging visitors to solve a problem or pursue a goal (*What's Missing in This Picture?*). (Csikszentmihalyi, 1990).

Visitors must perceive challenges posed by an exhibition to be within their interpretive skills – e.g., the "meaning" of an art work should appear within their reach. Csikszentmihalyi (1988) suggests it is the balance between this challenge and the visitor's view of their interpretive skills that determine the likelihood they will approach an exhibit (or text) and become involved.

Questions

Questions in headings and labels can focus attention and provide a context as well as intrinsic incentives for reading. Questions have been a recommended educational technique for years (Rothkopf, 1970). Some exhibit experiences (and objects) stimulate visitor questions about them (*Is that real? Why do bats hang upside down?*). However, visitors often need help in articulating such questions. One technique for encouraging greater involvement with exhibit content and its text is to incorporate the questions visitors have about exhibit objects into headlines, subheads, and interactive formats. These can be obtained from open-end, informal interviews and focus group sessions during the front-end evaluation stage. Objects, photos, reprints of art, etc. often serve as effective catalysts that can bring out such questions from visitors (Hood, 1986; Screven, 1990a; Shettel, 1989).

The questions visitors have about exhibit content are more predictable than one might expect. A few of the common questions visitors "ask" are the following: (Items marked "*" are from Rand, 1990.)

How much is this painting worth?	How did they paint inside that bottle?
Is this real?	Why are the skins of some figures blue?
Where is that from?	Are all of those things mushrooms?
Can that toxic plant be distinguished from nontoxic varieties?	*Why do otters scratch so much?
	Could I grow that?
Why does the leaf have such a funny shape?	Which berries are poisonous?
*What's out there under all that water?	That painting is ugly. Why is it here?

If questions are introduced into headings and text, immediate and concrete answers need to be provided. Thus,

"Rembrandt got the equivalent of $35 for Nightwatch";

* "Otter's aren't scratching because they itch! they're grooming. This keeps their fur clean and waterproof"

As described earlier, prominently displayed lead questions reduce random observation by encouraging visitors to explore, compare, notice, look for relationships and other "mindful" behavior (see p. 173).

Four presentation formats

The following four presentation formats, which vary in complexity, are examples of some more direct ways to attract and/or sustain quality attention to labels and to exhibit content. The first three formats generally depend on *intrinsic* motivators. While computer formats also depend on intrinsic motivators, computers can adapt label content and delivery modes to much wider differences in visitor interests, background and learning style than other presentation modes.

1. *INFORMATION MAPS* are print labels that are visually coded to identify different categories of information and their logical structure. Finding information in expository text may require considerable time and effort. Visually coding categories of text makes it easier to find particular kinds of information in crowded text. Information maps assume that, as the time needed to access desired label information is reduced, visitors are more likely to use the labels. Figure 1 illustrates one approach to the text you are now reading about information maps. To identify categories of text visually, information maps may *italicize* definitions, **boldface** overviews, <u>underline</u> tasks and practice questions, CAPITALIZE topic headings, indent examples, box technical terms that are defined in margin, and use color, flow charts, or other visual devices (Hartley, 1978, 1980, Horn, 1974, 1976). There are many possibilities for breaking down text content, as well as ways to visually code text.

Table 2a lists additional examples of text categories. Table 2b shows ways of visually cueing text. To use information maps, visitors must be informed about the infomap system – for example, a lapel card or other device illustrating text codes and their meanings.

Text categories should be aimed at serving a broad range of visitor backgrounds, interests, and knowledge on any given topic. Interviewing visitors will help identify categories that meet varied needs. like other interpretive components, information maps benefit from formative evaluation.

FIGURE 1

Information Map

INFORMATION MAPS:

Text which has been visually coded to identify different categories of information and its logical structure.

Finding information in text can require considerable time and effort. Information maps visually code categories of text information to make them easy to find in crowded text. Infomaps assume that, as the time needed to access desired information is reduced, visitors are more likely to use the text.

VISUAL CODING METHODS

To visually identify categories of text, information mapping may:

> Indent and list examples.
> Box technical terms within text that are defined and boxed in margin.
> *Italicize* definitions.
> **Boldface** introductory overviews and concepts summaries.
> Place references, definitions, topic headings, questions, and question feedback in margin.
> Underline practice tasks and leading question in margin.
> Place rules, instructions in parentheses in margin.
> CAPITALIZE topic headings in margin.
> Put feedback to questions in a distinctive "Answer Box" in a consistent place in each exhibit (or in electronic box).
> Use flow charts to depict sequential events, time, etc.

What would you capitalize in an infomap?

For additional coding methods for text and text categories, see Table 2

Some method must be used to alert visitor to the visual codes used to represent information categories.

Infomap

Shorthand term for information map.

What is another possibility for helping visitors use a museum's visual codes?

Visitors might receive a lapel card that illustrates text codes and their meaning to use when encountering a museum's infomap.

Visual coding

Using visual attributes of text to define particular categories of information.

CATEGORIES

Categories depend on the messages to be conveyed and the needs and interests of visitor groups. Museum visitors vary widely in backgrounds, interests and knowledge on any topic so categories should aim at a broad range of visitors. Interviewing visitors will help identify appropriate categories for different visitors.

Flow chart

Depicting sequential actions and time-actions are in boxes, yes-no decisions in diamond shapes, arrows depict time.

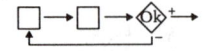

CONCLUSIONS

This infomap illustrates only one approach to mapping the original text. There are many possibilities for visually coding text. Like other interpretive components of exhibits, infomaps benefit from formative evaluation.

See: Hartley, 1978, 1980, 1982;
Horn, 1974, 1976.

TABLE 2A	TABLE 2B
Examples of Text Categories for Information Mapping	**Some Visual Ways to Identify Text Categories**
Overviews, introductory summaries, abstracts, reviews Definitions Examples, quotations Principles Specific applications Technical terms within text (referenced in "definition" area) Passage of time (Processes) Supporting evidence Interrelationships (Connections) Questions (for practice or hints) or tasks to be carried out Feedback to questions or tasks Rules Identification label Property (Distinguishing features) References	**Bold Face** <u>Underline</u> *Italics* Font size Boxed text Chunked text • Bulleted listing Indentation (Parentheses) Flow diagrams (time actions, feedback loops) Margins (definitions, references, questions, feedback). In exhibits, these categories also might be identified in "Answer Boxes" or under flippers. Color or background shading Symbols (→ ☎ ☆ ✚ * @, etc.)

2. *LEADING QUESTIONS*: Table 1 includes examples of leading questions. Leading questions can *lead* visitors to notice or become sensitized to important features in an exhibition. They can focus attention to the shape of a leaf, the hoofs of a tundra animal, or to brush strokes (Hirshi and Screven, 1988). Incorporated into headlines, subheads, text, or placed among objects, they also can alert visitors to underlying issues in thematic exhibits (*How do we know glaciers were here?*). The information visitors need to "answer" leading questions may or may not be immediately obvious in the exhibit, but the "answers" should become apparent when the visitor examines the exhibit, or carries out a suggested "action" (examine a leaf, read a label, make a comparison). Leading questions are intended to motivate and direct the attention of visitors – they usually are *not* intended to measure what visitors have "learned" from an exhibit.

3. *FLIPPER LABELS*: Flippers present text in overlapping layers. The term "flip labels" or "flippers" refers to hiding text and

graphics under one or more layers in some way (Screven, 1986). The visitor lifts up a hinged panel, slides a door, or pulls out a paddle to gain access to "hidden" information under or behind the top layer. Because most visitors can use these either to apply or to obtain information, flippers are a form of a "low-tech" interactive device. Two types of flippers can be distinguished:

Layered Labels consist of two to four hinged overlapping layers that contain questions, statements, or elaborations. The top layer contains a brief statement, *Three Types of Ferns* or a leading question *Are These Berries Edible?* or *Why Do Some of These Figures Have Blue Skin?* Each layer (Figure 2) takes visitors through a linear sequence of points, actions questions, answers, or graphics.

FIGURE 2

Three-layer Label

Figure 2 illustrates an enlarged version of a three-layer label installed on an information rail at an Egyptian Temple Diorama. Layered labels allow visitors to explore a topic, one layer at a time. As they learn one thing, visitors are more likely to seek a little more information (in next layer). Layered labels can be used to do a number of things: direct attention to key features of objects, or encourage visitors to *do* something, notice something, confront a misconception, or in other ways, to encourage them to become actively involved with objects.

Multiple-Choice Flippers (MC-flips) consist of a lead question (*What Material can be Mixed with Coal to Reduce Acid Rain?*) attached to two or more hinged panels with alternative choices, as seen in Figure 3. When lifted, each panel provides feedback. MC-flip-questions provide more precise control than layered labels over exactly how visitors *use* exhibit content to answer questions. MC-flips are particularly useful for concept learning because they can focus attention to differences or similarities among visual elements and teach discriminations between conceptual elements. Better learning (retention) seems to occur when the visitor examines exhibit content *before* choosing an answer, rather than simply guessing. Surprisingly, experience has indicated that visitors over 10 years old usually do *not* guess if the needed exhibit information is easy to locate and does not appear time-consuming. If so, visitors tend to look for answers in the exhibit *before* choosing. Information found under a flip after a random guess appears to have less retention than when the information is obtained before making a choice. MC-flips were first tested in the '70s at a visitor center (Screven, 1986) to provide an interactive print format.

While MC-Flips are now found in many exhibitions, they are often ineffective. Reasons vary. Sometimes the information needed to respond to the choices is not in the exhibit or in nearby labels, or it is not easily found. Note that using questions on MC-flips does *not* guarantee good results. In fact, some questions can be counterproductive. For example, abstracts or trivial questions on MC-flips may *discourage* visitor use or encourage guessing.

FIGURE 3

Multiple-Choice Flip Question

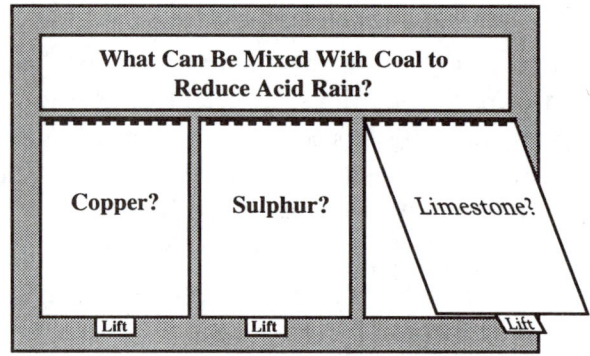

To be successful, layered labels and MC-flips, like conventional labels, not only must connect to familiar experience, but also direct attention to appropriate exhibit content, some of which may be unfamiliar. In spite of their simplicity, layered labels and MC-flips can often dramatically reduce random looking and increase focused, active attention (mindfulness).

Some persons argue that the learning that occurs with layered and MC-flips is due to their manipulability, not to the layered or MC formats. While this hypothesis needs to be experimentally tested, the author's experience indicates that these formats are simply a framework for setting up the *conditions* for learning – i.e., behaviors such as searching, comparing, relating, and applying label and exhibit information. The format might be seen simply as a way to manage the steps involved:

Question → Examine exhibit → Find information → Choose answer → Confirm

On the other hand, what specifically is learned depends on the information given, not the manipulable or interactive format itself.

4. *COMPUTER LABELS*: Label information is presented on computer screens *via* laser disks or other electronic technology. Computer screens become "pages in a book" through which visitors explore alternative pathways of information according to their needs, learning styles and time available (Screven, 1986, 1991; Whitney, 1990; Worts, 1990). Viewers decide what information to pursue and when to pursue it. Computers serve purposes similar to flippers, but have the potential for almost infinite branching and adaptability. They also are useful for managing external motivators, animation, and sound when these are needed. However, those interested in using computers as educational aids in museums should beware! By themselves, computers do not necessarily produce quality attention, reading, or learning (Screven, 1991). Like labels and other interpretive materials, the effective use of computers depends on front-end audience analysis, text analysis, well-defined linkages to exhibit content, and the formative evaluation of the teaching and motivational effectiveness of programs during their development.

Levels of interactive labels

What has been said should not be interpreted to mean that labels need to involve interactive formats like flippers or computers. Even "passive" text can successfully generate active and mindful involvement under some conditions if writers use formative evaluation to make relatively simple adjustments during the label's development.

It may be helpful to distinguish between levels of label "interactivity."[1] Unless there are strong reasons to employ higher levels, this author recommends starting with conventional formats, rather than interactive text. If formative testing indicates that these do not work, one proceeds first to "covert" interactive versions (level 2), then to "secondary" interaction formats (level 3), then on to "direct" formats

---

1. The levels of interaction used here are different than levels of interaction employed in the audiovisual field, which defines four levels: (1) straight linear, (2) branching, (3) computer control, and (4) on disk.

(level 4) and finally to adaptive interaction that usually require friendly computers and video disks (level 5).

Level 1: *Conventional labels* are two-dimensional text panels. These can produce considerable involvement when the "Value" part of the $^{Value}/_{Cost}$ Ratio (see p. 76) is high – which may be the case, for example, with famous artworks, exotic animals, or fantasies generated by gory historical scenes. Even hard-to-read text placed next to the Mona Lisa, a famous Picasso, a mummy, or a Panda, are likely to be read. Visitors seek information about high-interest objects from whatever resources are available. But, even for high-interest objects, it is important that the labels include information that refers *directly* to them. With less exotic exhibit content, conventional text often can be made effective by careful placement, chunking, provocative headings, and readable typefaces.

Level 2: *Covert interaction* involves conventional text formats, but uses questions, challenges, instructions, and/or information maps that encourage covert interaction with the exhibit. They may do this by encouraging visitors to search the exhibit for clues, for "answers" to questions, etc. But again, the specific learning that results depends on the questions, the challenge, and the exhibit's content, not simply on the interactive activity.

Level 3: *Secondary interaction* involves conventional labels that contain information needed to carry out a second, more motivating task – e.g., when information provided in a conventional label can be used to answer an MC-flip question or pursue a problem task. While the conventional label has no push buttons or manipulatives, the motivation to read it is visitor's interest in pursuing the second task. Pre-recorded audio scripts (*via* handheld players, head phones, speakers) also can serve as secondary interactive devices if they ask leading questions about exhibit objects/relationships, describe what to notice, do, or where to go. Audio scripts allow visitors to look at the exhibit and listen to the audio information *at the same time* (see Screven, 1975). Visitors can look *and* listen instead of read *then* look. Applications have shown that voice instructions on what to do or notice is easier for most visitors (i.e., involves lower "cost") than bouncing between reading about objects and then looking at them. However, there are limits. Abstract voice scripts that go beyond immediate exhibit content may be difficult to follow for visitors who do not have good listening skills. When more abstract elaborations are needed, the author has found it better to direct visitor attention to printed text and graphics for these elaborations (Screven, 1975); for example: *You know why that happens? Read text in green frame, then I've got a question for you!*

Level 4: *Direct interaction* is exemplified by layered labels (Figure 2) and MC-flip question labels (Figure 3) that provide more precision in focusing visitor attention and establishing discriminations than do lower levels of label interactivity.

Level 5: *Adaptive interaction* involves electronic labels that, with the help of computers, are able to adapt their responses to different individual interests and needs. This is the highest level of interactive label, best suited when there is a need to adjust the kinds and modes of information available to visitors over a wide range of interests, abilities and learning styles, e.g., in wayfinding, providing overviews, making choices at museum entrances, and adjusting the branching, sequencing, modes, feedback, and depth of information to individual needs. The vast storage and interactive capabilities of computers make it possible for visitors to choose what they wish to see, schedule their time, browse, set goals, ask questions and have 2-way conversations that would be impossible with less powerful devices. For discussions about such computer applications, see Screven, 1986, 1991.

PREPARING LABELS

The role of formative evaluation

Those who believe they can prepare labels that will attract, involve and communicate to unguided visitors should beware! The variables that contribute to label effectiveness vary with different individuals and situations and, therefore, almost always require adjustments of one kind or another.

Formative evaluation (FE) is a process which allows early pretesting of mockups of labels, graphics, formats, and their placement. Formative testing of prospective labels spots deficiencies in their ability to attract, hold attention, generate involvement, and communicate before it is too expensive to make adjustments. Low-cost, quickly made versions of label copy, diagrams, photos, and instructions, are tested with small samples of 5 to 20 target visitors. Because mockups can be quickly modified and retested, it is possible to identify problems, make adjustments, and retest them at low cost. FE also provides writers, curators and exhibit staff with more direct knowledge about visitors that will improve their planning decisions and correct or confirm preconceptions about what visitors will do and not do with labels. After initial training, observations and testing usually can be carried out by label writers in conjunction with curators and staff (Screven, 1990a). Hands-on staff training workshops on FE methods are strongly recommended to assure that staff will be able to efficiently conduct FE procedures by themselves. After one to four weeks of training, only periodic help from a specialist is needed. However, other evaluation activities (front-end, summative, and interview questionnaire planning) often require regular input from experts.

Readers interested in details about formative evaluation procedures should refer to the author's indepth paper on evaluation (Screven, 1990a) as well as other important resources by Griggs (1981), Griggs & Manning (1983), Loomis (1987, pp. 206-248), Miles *et al.* (1988), Shettel (1973, 1989) and Taylor and Serrell (1991).

Stages of label evaluation

The features and formats of labels must be adapted to the characteristics of target audiences, the label's message, and to the functions (Table 1) or impact they are supposed to perform. Integrating the planning and writing of labels with overall exhibit planning is of great practical importance if real progress is to be made. Currently, there is much discussion about how to organize and manage the planning, design, and production stages of exhibitions efficiently and harmoniously. The different approaches to managing the planning and development of visitor-oriented exhibitions over the years, including label preparation, have been compared in a recent paper by Roger Miles (1993) in which he outlines a promising framework currently in use at the Natural History Museum in London.

A host of "management solutions" currently are circulating and being tried by visitor oriented museums. In the hope of contributing to this dialog the following five steps for label preparation focus on label planning within the larger context of exhibit planning.

STEP 1: *Front-end Evaluation* (Before exhibit content has been specified).

The design team (writer, curator, educator, designer, and perhaps director) discuss exhibit ideas and messages over a series of meetings: Who is the audience? What are the two or three most important things to say about the topic? About the objects? What guidelines can be used to organize and deliver the exhibit's messages (e.g., layered, interactive, electronic)? (See Shettel, 1992, *ILVS Review*, pp. 279-284).

STEP 2: *Preparing Preliminary Labels for Team Review*

The person(s) responsible for labels and other interpretive components prepares preliminary statements that describe his/her understanding of the main ideas and supporting materials previously agreed upon by the design team. Rough mockup versions that might be used for testing labels' effectiveness may also be presented.

STEP 3: *Coordination with Exhibit Team*

Results from stage 2 are shared with the design team over several sessions until agreement is reached at least on basic ideas and how the labels and exhibit content will be coordinated. At Stage 3, agreement is limited mainly to key ideas, concepts, potential linkages to exhibit content, and identifying some of the specific functions that given labels are needed to serve.

STEP 4: *Formative Evaluation of Teaching Effectiveness*

The writer tests quickly made "soft" mockups of prospective labels/graphics with "cued" visitors for their teaching effectiveness. ("Cued" visitors know beforehand that they will be questioned or observed.) These are tested with visitors using the objects, pictures or their renditions that are planned for the exhibit, (important because labels must refer to these). Actual testing may be conducted with the help of one or two other persons on the exhibit team. The writer(s) prepare(s) and tests 5 to 20 cued visitors for readability, comprehension, recall or other learning outcomes (for details, see Screven, 1990a; McNamara, 1990). Usually, only one or two panels are tested at a time. Communication problems are corrected as needed and results reported to the exhibit team with recommendations. For scheduling purposes and budget control, time-limits need to be established for mockup testing, based on the number and complexity of label messages and the budget. Only the most important labels (and messages) are tested.

Budgeting and scheduling does not allow formative testing of labels/graphics to be "tested to perfection." Testing must be limited to identifying and correcting only potentially serious problems with readability, layout, illustrations, sequencing, and organization of content. Also, stage 4 normally tests the teaching *efficiency* of labels, *not* their motivational impact (Screven, 1990a).

STEP 5: *Testing Motivating Impact*

Observations are made of *noncued* visitors (who are unaware of being observed) to see if prospective labels or their components attract attention, generate involvement, and produce proper usage of label systems. Photographs, objects, reproductions and other prospective display elements should be present during observation. Observations may include proportion of stops at the target label(s), time spent, holding time, active/passive involvement, social interaction, label or exhibit usage (Do they "play" with it? Guess? Follow instruction?). Noncued observations usually are made on the open floor of the museum (Screven, 1990a, pp. 50-51, 57-59).

There are early and late stages of testing for motivational impact. During early stages, the behavior of passing visitors to mockups is observed; in later stages, visitor responses are observed at more advanced mockups that simulate the final installation (prototypes). As in stage 4, time limits need to be established.

INSTITUTIONAL OBSTACLES TO EFFECTIVE LABELS

Along with label design and content, there are built-in institutional procedures and staff attitudes that often prevent label writers from applying even modest versions of the design guidelines described above. How is it possible that so many competent and dedicated museum staff around the world consistently produce labels that do not work? One likely explanation is that the accepted routines found in many medium- to large-size museums more or less guarantee that most visitors will not use their interpretive text and graphics, or if they do, will not understand them.

Chief among these counterproductive routines and attitudes are the following:

a) **Label preparation does not require planners to define and assign priority to the *purposes* (functions) of given text, graphics, headlines, or signage.** Only cursory attention is given to specific functions of exhibit labels, usually in terms that are too general to be useful (e.g., *"Explains a food chain"*). Instead of checking labels and formats with real visitors, editing labels mainly consists of copy editing for grammar, spelling, accuracy, length, and other such details.

b) **Many planners are biased toward *formal* teaching-learning methods that underestimate the voluntary and *informal* nature of museum settings.** Museums and exhibits are viewed as dramatic, three-dimensional classrooms. But, unlike schools, museums cannot use grades or "top-down" controls to capture attention. Thus, planners tend to overlook or underestimate the role of associating *positive* (rewarding) outcomes to visitors who give time and effort *voluntarily*.

c) **Label preparation routines are not coordinated with other exhibit elements.** Label content must include direct connections to the exhibit objects on display because proper interpretation of objects often depends on information provided in labels. The label formats that encourage (or discourage) attention to and comprehension of these messages varies with the individual needs and learning styles of target audiences. Many museum professionals already recognize this. Yet, in many institutions, label planning and preparation seldom are properly integrated with other exhibit planning. Examples abound, including the practice of preparing exhibits and then turning them over to a third party to prepare interpretive text, or requiring label writers to prepare labels before other exhibit content and organization have been decided.

The educational-motivational-informational aspects of exhibits operate as a *total system*. Creating an effective whole is impossible unless scientists-scholars, designers-fabricators, and labels-graphics specialists work together at every stage of planning. Clearly, better management strategies to facilitate the work of "exhibit teams" seems crucial.

d) **Label and exhibition planners have serious misconceptions and inadequate knowledge about the visitors they serve** (Miles, 1986). Misconceptions about visitors distort decisions about label content and format because they lead to invalid expectations about what visitors will or will not do, need, feel, think, or learn. Inadequate information about the public held by exhibit planners is understandable, partly because their work does not normally bring them into contact with real audiences. Also, normal exhibit and label preparation procedures provide few opportunities to find out what the abilities and limitations of their visitors are like (Miles, 1986). Audiences are viewed as persons with more knowledge, interest, time, and energy than they have – views that may underlay many of the nonproductive arguments in staff conferences over label language, label length, how to present it, where to place it, and what media to use.

A FINAL WORD

While there is much to learn about the complex process by which labels communicate in open environment, more research on the psychology of reading and language media (e.g., Rayner & Pollatsek, 1989) and in cognitive science (Gardner, 1992; Langer, 1989a; and Moscardo, 1992) are being synthesized and made available. But, one need not wait for more extensive research to "tell you how to do it." As we have seen, there already are lots of possibilities for improving the attention of visitors to different kinds of labels and what they learn from them. Also, current experience indicates that the use of "remedial evaluation" (Screven, 1990a, pp. 53-59) can further improve label functioning and productive (mindful) exhibit usage in the post-occupancy environment. To do this, however, planners (and writers) must be better informed about the agendas and learning styles that influence visitor use or non-use of labels within the context of given exhibitions, as well as ways to improve the routines by which labels are prepared.

The facts are mounting that visitors *do* read labels if they perceive that labels will meaningfully help relate exhibit content to them, or will provide feedback and follow-up to exhibit experiences. It is time to become serious about the needs and interests of unguided visitors for meaningful interpretation. The good news is that new tools (e.g., see Layton, 1991) and exciting new strategies are becoming available for the effective design and delivery of interpretive information in open environment. These await only for museum professionals to explore their educational potentials in museum settings.

Bibliography

Alt, M.B. & Shaw, K.M. (1984). Characteristics of ideal museum exhibits. *British Journal of Psychology*, 25, pp. 25-36.

Bitgood, S. (1991). The ABC's of label design. In S. Bitgood, A. Benefield, & Don Patterson (Eds.), *Visitor studies: theory, research, and practice, volume 3* (pp. 115-129). Jacksonville, AL: Center for Social Design.

Borun, M. & Miller, M.A. (1980). To label or not to label? *Museum News*, 58(4), pp. 64-67.

Csikszentmihalyi, M. (1988). Human behavior and the science center. In P.G. Heltne & L. Marquardt (Eds.), *Science learning in the informal setting*. Chicago, IL: The Chicago Academy of Sciences, pp. 79-88.

Csikszentmihalyi, M. (1990). *Flow: The psychology of optimal experience*. New York, NY: Harper & Row, 303 p.

Frase, L.T. (1968). Effect of question-location, pacing and mode upon retention of prose material. *Journal of Educational Psychology*, 59(4), pp. 244-249.

Gardner, H. (1992). *The unschooled mind: how children learn and how schools should teach*. NY: Basic Books.

Griggs, S. (1981). Formative evaluation of exhibits at the British Museum (Natural History). *Curator*, 24(3), pp. 189-202.

Griggs, S. & Manning, J. (1983). The predictive ability of formative evaluation of exhibits. *Museum Studies Journal*, 1(2), pp. 31-41.

Grünig, J.E. (1979). Time budgets, level of involvement and the use of mass media. *Journalism Quarterly*, 56, pp. 248-261.

Hartley, J. (1978). *Designing instructional text*. London: Kogan Page/New York: Nichols.

Hartley, J. (1980). *The psychology of written communication: selected readings*. London: Kogan Page/New York: Nichols.

Hirshi, K.D. & Screven, C.G. (1988). Effects of questions on visitor reading behavior. *ILVS Review: A Journal of Visitor Behavior*, 1(1), pp. 50-61.

Horn, R.E. (1974). Information mapping. *Training in Business and Industry*, 11 (March), pp. 27-32.

Horn, R.E. (1976). *How to write information mapping*. Lexington, MA.: Information Resources, Inc.

Hood, M.G. (1986). Getting started in audience research. *Museum News*, 64(3), pp. 24-31.

Kintsch, W. & VanDijk, T.A. (1978). Toward a model of text comprehension and production. *Psychological Review*, 85, pp. 363-394.

Kintsch, W. & Vipond, D. (1979). Reading comprehension and readability in educational practice and psychological theory. In L.G. Nilsson (Ed.), *Perspectives on memory research*. Hillsdale, NJ: Erlbaum.

Klein, H.J. (1978). Barrieren des eugans eu affentlichen einrichtungen. Unpublished paper. Karlsruhe, Germany; Departement of Sociology, University of Karlsruhe.

Langer, E.J. (1989a). *Mindfulness*. Reading, MA: Addison-Wesley Publishing.

Langer E.J. (1989b). Minding matters: The consequences of mindlessness-mindfulness. *Advances in Experimental Social Psychology*, 22, pp. 137-143.

Layton, J.K. (1991). *Writing for novice visitors: The Minneapolis Institute of Arts handbook of style*. Minneapolis, MN: Education Division of Minneapolis Institute of the Arts.

Loomis, R. (1987). *Museum visitor evaluation: New tool for museum management* (p. 206-248). Nashville, TN: American Association of State and Local History.

Loomis, R. (1983). *Four evaluation suggestions to improve the effectiveness of museum labels*. Austin, TX: Texas Historical Commission.

McNamara, P. (1990). Trying it out. From ASTC series "What research says about learning in science museums." Reprinted in *ILVS Review, A Journal of Visitor Behavior*, 1(2), pp. 98-100.

McManus, P. (1987). Communicating with and between visitors to a science museum. Unpublished PhD Thesis. London: University of London.

McManus, P. (1990). Watch your language! People do read labels. *ILVS Review: A Journal of Visitor Behavior*, 1(2), pp. 125-127.

Miles, R.S. (1986). Museum audiences. *International Journal of Museum Management and Curatorship*, 5, pp. 73-80.

Miles, R.S. (1993). Too many cooks boil the broth – exhibits, teams, evaluation. In S. Bitgood, A. Benefield & D. Patterson (Eds.), *Visitor studies: theory, research, and practice*. (Volume 5). Jacksonville, AL: Center for Social Design.

Miles, R.S., Alt, M.B., Gosling, D.C., Lewis, B.N., & Tout, A.F. (1988). *The design of educational exhibits* (2nd Edition). London: Allen & Unwin.

Moscardo, G.M. (1986). Visitor centers and environmental interpretations: an exploration of the relationships among visitor enjoyment, understanding, and mindfulness. *Journal of Environmental Psychology*, 6, pp. 89-108.

Moscardo, G.M. (1992). *A mindfulness/mindlessness model of the museum visitor experience*. Unpublished doctoral thesis, Townsville, Australia: Dept. of Psychology, James Cook University of North Queensland.

Rand, Judy (1990). *Fish stories that hook readers: Interpretive graphics at the Montery Bay Aquarium*. Technical Report 90-30 Jacksonville, AL: Center for Social Design. (Reprinted from presentation at *AAZPA 1985 Annual Conference Proceedings*.)

Rayner, K. & Pollatsek, A. (1989). Understanding text and representation of discourse, in *The Psychology of Reading*. (Chapters 7 and 8). Englewood Cliff, NJ: Prentice-Hall Inc., pp. 236-321.

Rothkopf, E.Z. (1970). The concept of mathemagenic activities. *Review of Educational Research*, 40, pp. 325-336.

Saloman, G. & Gloverson, T. (1987). Skill may not be enough: The role of mindfulness in learning and transfer. *International Journal of Educational Research*, 11, pp. 623-627.

Samuels, S.J. (1988). *Psychological factors in writing and reading museum labels*. Unpublished paper. Minneapolis, MN: The Minneapolis Institute of Arts.

Screven, C.G. (1969). The museum as a responsive learning environment. *Museum News*, 47(10), pp. 7-10.

Screven, C.G. (1974). *The measurement and facilitation of learning in the museum environment*. Washington, D.C: The Smithsonian Press.

Screven, C.G. (1975). The effectiveness of guidance devices on visitor learning. *Curator*, 18(3), pp. 219-243.

Screven, C.G. (1976). Exhibit evaluation: A goal referenced approach. *Curator*, 19(4), pp. 271-290.

Screven, C.G. (1986). Exhibitions and information centers: Some principles and applications. *Curator*, 29(2), pp. 109-137.

Screven, C.G. (1990a). Uses of evaluation before, during, and after exhibit design. *ILVS Review: A Journal of Visitor Behavior*, 1(2), pp. 33-66.

Screven, C.G. (1990b). A self-test computer system for motivating voluntary learning from exhibitions. *ILVS Review: A Journal of Visitor Behavior*, 1(2), pp. 120-121.

Screven, C.G. (1991). Computers in museum settings. In S.A. Benefield & D. Patterson (Eds.), *Visitor Studies: Theory, Research, and Practice* (Volume 3, pp. 130-138). Jacksonville, AL: Center for Social Design. Reprinted in *Spectra*, 19, 1992.

Serrell, B. (1983). Making exhibit labels: A step by step guide. Nashville, TN: American Association of State and Local History.

Shettel, H. (1993). Exhibits: Art form or educational medium? *Museum News*, 52, pp. 32-41.

Shettel, H. (1989, 1992). Front-end evaluation. *Proceedings*, AAZPA 1989 Annual Conference. Pittsburgh, PA: American Association of Zoological Parks and Aquariums, pp. 434-439; also, reprinted in the *ILVS Review: A Journal of Visitor Behavior*, 2(2), pp. 279-284.

Taylor, S. & Serrell, B. (Eds.). (1991). *Try it! Improving exhibits through formative evaluation*. Washington, DC: Association for Science-Technology Centers.

Whitney, P. (1990). The electronic muse: Matching information and media to audiences. *ILVS Review: A Journal of Visitor Behavior*, 1(2), pp. 68-77.

Worts, D. (1990). The computer as a catalyst: Experiences at the Art Gallery of Ontario. *ILVS Review: A Journal of Visitor Behavior*, 1(2), pp. 92-108.

Summary   Denis Samson

Reading Strategies Used by Exhibition Visitors

The historic development of the thematic exhibition, the highlights of which are reviewed in the first part of this essay, bears witness to the increasingly important role of text in museum practice. The fact that text pervades exhibitions has prompted visitors to develop new reading strategies that experts have endeavoured to analyze from various standpoints. Some studies differentiate several types of readers and specify the factors that determine their choices: length of the texts, location, legibility and so on. How do visitors read exhibition texts? To answer this question, we must first take a look at the distinctive characteristics of the museum environment. Because visitors are free to circulate, they determine their own reading itinerary, deciding when they stop and draw on the information that interests them. As a result, they can reorganize the overall content of panels according to the itinerary they choose and, in so doing, derive meaning from them. That being the case, it is extremely important to anticipate visitors' reading strategies to ensure that they receive the target message. The formative evaluation is a highly useful tool in this respect, as the author shows using as an example the On a marché sur la Terre *exhibition, mounted by the Muséum national d'histoire naturelle in Paris. Elements of this exhibition were tested on visitors prior to and following their visit. This evaluation made it possible to measure the importance of the reading itinerary on visitors' understanding of concepts, a factor that must be considered when an exhibition is designed. In the next chapter, Anne Decrosse and Jean-Paul Natali go on to show how the written document can be used in a special way through a spoken text.*

Reading Strategies Used by Exhibition Visitors

Denis Samson

Museum Consultant and
Lecturer in Curatorial Studies,
Université du Québec à Montréal
(UQAM)

Today, the exhibition text plays a pivotal role in the way in which a museum communicates with visitors, although this has not always been the case. The exhibition had to gain recognition as a communications medium before text could play a preponderant role in the dissemination of messages. This vital contribution from American museology has profoundly altered the relationship between the exhibition text and visitor. Because of the pervasiveness of text in exhibitions, visitors have been prompted to develop new reading strategies that affect the efficacy of communication. The purpose of this essay is to explore these reading strategies in the museum environment.

In order to define the reading strategies adopted by visitors, it is important to understand the historic development of the thematic exhibition on which text and its most widely used form, the exhibition panel, depend. The evaluation of texts as they affect visitors began with impact studies of the message during the 1940s and 1950s, followed by educational evaluations in the 1960s and 1970s, then reception studies during the 1980s and 1990s. The reading strategies presented in this essay focus on the latter current, i.e. on reception.

THEMATIC EXHIBITIONS

Since exhibitions have been required to tell a story (Cummings, 1940), the text has undergone spectacular development in museum practice. The idea of telling a story, attributable mainly to the Americans, was strikingly apparent at the Chicago (1933) and New York (1939) world's fairs. The Hall of Science (1933) and Medical and Public Health Building (1939) drew the attention of numerous American museologists. The works of Cummings are evidence of this. Cummings, director of the Buffalo Museum of Science, along with several museologists from American museums, studied the impact of the 1939 World's Fair on visitors to find out what museums could learn from the experience (Cummings, 1940). In the United States, world's fairs have provided an opportunity for museological experimentation and many museologists have participated in the development of the events.

The 1933 and 1939 world's fairs were innovative in several areas: the narrative framework, lighting, colour, sound, demonstrations, interactivity and visitor circulation. One radical innovation was the presentation of works in relation to a story line, i.e. the objects illustrated a narrative. The idea of telling a story had already crossed peoples' minds. The earliest mention of a story line was made by Dana (1921), who deemed it a noteworthy precedent. The 1933 and 1939 world's fairs featured thematic pavilions on science and health and were the first to present a predefined message on a large scale[1] (Alwood, 1977). These advances in the realm of thematic exhibitions mark the growing importance of the text in museum practice.

The panel was the main support for the message underlying this new form of exhibition. In 1933 and 1939, the popularity of the multimedia panel seemed to be on the rise. The example of the "Structure and Location of Digestive Organs" panel (see illustration), presented in the Medical and Public Health Building (1939), already displayed the essential features of the exhibition panel: a relationship between text and image, the presence of textual identifiers (titles, headings and labels), and the use of information mapping.

---

1. After World War II, the thematic exhibition diversified and underwent spectacular development, primarily in the form of travelling and temporary exhibitions (Robinson, 1960).

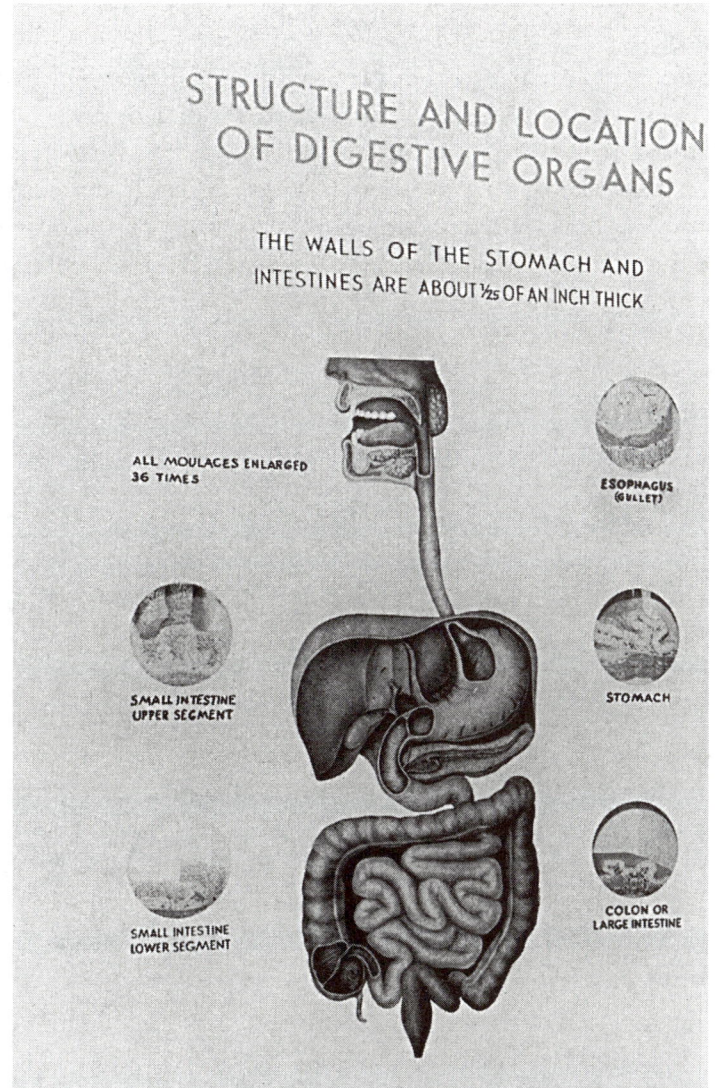

Excerpted from C.E. Cummings, "East is East and West is West. Some
Observations on the World's Fairs of 1939, by One Whose Main Interest
is in Museums" (Buffalo: *Bulletin of the Buffalo Society of Natural Sciences*,
Vol. XX, 1940), p. 239.

"Structure and Location of Digestive Organs"

*Panel displayed in 1939 at the New York World's Fair in the Medical
and Public Health Building.*

Starting in the 1930s in the United States, the exhibition was considered a communications medium, which made people think about the planning of the message. Various authors distinguished different types of thematic exhibition[2] and institutionalized the process of designing an exhibition in different stages, i.e. first, defining overall intention and, second, constructing the story line or narrative framework.[3] The importance that the text assumed had a bearing on the structuring of an exhibition (Calver, 1939; Lane and Tolleris, 1948; Gebhard, 1948). The text became indispensable not only in presenting a thematic exhibition, but in designing it. Thus text became an integral part of museum "practice".

FROM AN EVALUATION OF THE MESSAGE TO AN EVALUATION OF READING

At the outset, the exhibition evaluation was dominated by the measurement of behaviour. The first generation of American evaluators focused on the concepts of drawing power and ease of retention (Robinson, 1928; Melton, 1935). Shortly thereafter, the development of the thematic exhibition and the influence of a growing communications science encouraged professional evaluators to examine the efficacy of the message. During the 1940s and 1950s, evaluators raised two questions. Who visits an exhibition? Does the audience grasp the message? (Derryberry, 1941). The impact studies conducted during the post-war period focused on evaluating the message. The text was not evaluated directly, but gradually received more and more attention as an important part of the message.

During the 1960s, Shettel and Screven introduced the concept of evaluation by objectives (Shettel, 1968; Screven, 1969). This period marked the systematization of the exhibition design process and the first evaluations of reading in the museum environment. The key contribution

---

2. Lane and Tolleris (1948) distinguish two types of exhibitions, those designed to change behaviour and those designed to exhibit something.

3. Intention and story recounted have become concept and scenario in current North American exhibition design practice.

138

of the learning-oriented evaluation school was to clarify the problem of the specificity of the museum environment. Screven and other museologists after him defined the museum as an informal learning environment. This definition, while only partially true, did initiate discussion on the specific characteristics of museums that affect visitors' reading.

The first scholars to evaluate reading data were Shettel, Borun and Wolf. The first question of concern to them was whether or not visitors read text panels. In 1968, in a lengthy investigation of *The Vision of Man* exhibition, Shettel studied visitors' reading of various texts. He showed that visitors spent, on average, 20 seconds in each section of the exhibition, although the necessary reading time was two or three times as long. He concluded that visitors did not read the text panels or devoted very little time to reading them (Shettel *et al.*, 1968: 124-128).

At the Franklin Institute in Philadelphia, Borun also focused on the question of reading. She challenged Shettel's conclusions and the average reading times he established. On the basis of a study, she showed that visitors read, on average, 18 percent of the texts in an exhibition overall, but that they read 68 percent of the specific texts they stopped to read (Borun, Miller, 1980: 9-10). This broad range of behaviour pointed up the need to take several factors into account.

At the Smithsonian Institution, Wolf delved further into the significance of reading data. In his evaluation of the *Our Changing Land* exhibition, he distinguished different types of readers: those who read from one to five texts (51 percent), those who read from six to 15 texts (23 percent), and those who read 15 or more texts (26 percent). He also listed the factors that determine their choices: first, the length of a text and its location, then lighting, the type font, and legibility[4] (Wolf, Tymitz, 1979: 42-46).

These quantitative approaches to reading indicate not only that exhibition texts are read, but that they are read by a large number of

---

4. Screven recently conducted a study on the impact of the form of texts on visitors (Hirschi, Screven, 1988). Studies have also been carried out on the reading of texts in art museums (Wolf, Tymitz, 1980; Gottesdiener, 1992).

visitors. So how do visitors read exhibition texts? To answer this question, it is essential to consider the characteristics of the museum environment that affect reading.

READING IN THE MUSEUM ENVIRONMENT

Information selection

Reading conditions in a museum setting are inextricably linked to the very definition of the exhibition medium. Visitors move around in an exhibition in order to take it in. Freedom of movement, even within defined itineraries, is a constant feature of the visit. An itinerary is established by selecting among all the information provided by the exhibition as a whole. Even within the sections where visitors decide to stop, the selection of information is how they determine the choice of texts to read, how much attention they pay to artifacts, the length of time they stop, and so on.

In order to understand this more fully, we must consider the concepts of drawing power and ease of retention defined by Robinson (1928) and Melton (1935). We know that texts have little drawing power over visitors. It is the artifacts or specimens rather than the texts that attract visitors and, in a sense, communicate with them. The location of texts in relation to the artifacts or specimens is thus decisive in encouraging visitors to read.

Visitors also select the information they read on text panels. At the Natural History Museum in London, McManus (1989) showed that visitors approached the texts in a manner resembling a dialogue, asking themselves two questions. What is it? What are they talking about? They selected information on the basis of these two questions. The length of the communication depended on the answers that the visitors found.

Another factor affecting the selection of information is the social context of the museum visit. Three-quarters of the visitors studied by McManus were in groups and attached a great deal of importance to maintaining group cohesion. One of the members of the group read for the others. In studying visitors' conversations, McManus found text echoes[5] in 85 percent of cases (McManus, 1989: 182-186). Thus, information selection and transmission often go hand in hand.

Conceptual orientation

Visitors do not read everything and usually do not read in the prescribed order. Not only is there a problem of general orientation in museums, but there is also a specific orientation problem in terms of reading. For several years now, a distinction has been drawn between topographic orientation and conceptual orientation. To find one's way in an exhibition and to understand the organization of its content are two distinct problems (Griggs, 1983; Loomis, 1987; Bitgood, 1988). Wolf took this distinction even further, maintaining that visitors establish a "conceptual itinerary" in attempting to link the elements of the exhibition to discern their meaning (Wolf, Tymitz, 1981; Wolf, 1986).

The foregoing distinctions apply to exhibition panels as well. Visitors do not necessarily follow the prescribed itinerary, but reorganize the exhibition content by developing their own reading itinerary. It is important to trace this itinerary if we are to understand how visitors reorganize content. The reading itinerary sheds light on visitors' reading strategies in the museum environment.

Integration of messages

When Wolf conducted his evaluations at the Smithsonian Institution, he stressed the strategic importance of the location of texts in relation to the objects displayed. Separating texts from the objects appreciably hinders transmission of the message. In fact, it is not simply a problem of positioning text, but of integrating the content (Wolf, Tymitz, 1981: 20).

The proximity of texts and the items displayed on a panel or in an exhibit case does not guarantee the assimilation of their content. To understand the approach of visitors, Loomis suggested applying the concept of bodies of knowledge to describe the grouping of information

---

5. Text echoes are segments of exhibition texts quoted to members of a subgroup and used as a basis for discussion and interpretation (McManus, 1989: 175-179).

around a given topic (Loomis, 1987: 241). Visitors integrate messages by redividing contents into information blocks that appear to carry meaning for the readers. The theory of the reading schema takes visitors' redivision of the contents into account. This theory, formulated by Bartlett in 1932, claims that understanding is guided by pre-existing schemas. The theory was revived 15 years ago and is now applied to reading. Meaning is not dictated by the text, but is determined by the reader, who relies on preconceived conceptual scenarios.[6] The text provides readers with ways to construct the meaning on the basis of their previously acquired knowledge. The text must also sustain and orient the reader-text interaction. As a result, visitors restructure the content.

ANTICIPATING READING STRATEGIES

Formative evaluation is a very useful tool for anticipating visitors' reading strategies. Before designers decide on the final version of an exhibition panel or exhibit case, they may ask to test different types of organization of the content on visitors. This exercise is designed to anticipate visitors' reading itineraries and the repercussions on their reconstruction of the meaning. This experimental situation introduced by the formative evaluation makes it possible to understand the major problems visitors are likely to encounter in their attempts to give meaning to a particular content.

During the preparation of the *On a marché sur la Terre* exhibition at the Muséum national d'histoire naturelle in Paris, an extensive formative evaluation program was implemented.[7] All told, seven panels and exhibit cases prepared in collaboration with the scientific team were tested on visitors, using two-dimensional models. The problems encountered in certain projects resulted in the redesigning of the models and the rewriting of texts. An evaluation of the panels and exhibit cases once the exhibition opened made it possible to ascertain whether the exhibition objectives had been attained during actual visits. In all

---

6. This theory has been called "preconceived scenario" (Schank, Abelson, 1977), "advance organizers" (Ausebel, 1963) and, above all, "schema-theoretic" (Adams, Collins, 1985).

7. This program was carried out jointly by the Cellule de préfiguration (Muséum), the CNRS-URA 887 (Paris) and the CREST/UQAM (Montréal).

instances studied, the reading itinerary proved to be a decisive factor in visitors' reconstruction of the meaning.

"VIVRE HORS DE L'EAU, C'EST SE SOUTENIR" ("LIVING OUT OF WATER MEANS SUPPORTING YOUR OWN WEIGHT")

In an experimental situation

One of the exhibit cases pretested for the *On a marché sur la Terre* exhibition[8] was entitled"Vivre hors de l'eau, c'est se soutenir".[9] Simple two-dimensional models, accompanied by little text, were designed to help visitors understand the relationship between the emergence of animals or plants from water and the strengthening of support structures. The explanations supplied tended to show that gravity caused these changes and that the oxygen content of air made them possible. The interrelationship between the concepts is essential to an understanding of the overall idea suggested by the title.

Model A compares the differences between the fish and the tetrapod with respect to energy required to move around, oxygen, and the effect of gravity on support structures. It includes a title, an editorial, two headings with explanatory texts, four illustrations and labels accompanied by arrows. Model B compares the similarities between the on-land support structures of the tree and the human being. It includes an editorial and five illustrations, accompanied by three labels. Visitors were asked to read models A and B one after the other, then to answer the questions in front of the models.[10] The information derived from these qualitative evaluations was analyzed according to the text echoes visitors used.

---

8. The *On a marché sur la Terre* exhibition recounts part of the story of evolution, with particular emphasis on the emergence of plants and animals from the water. The exhibition is part of a sweeping 6 000-m² project on the theme of evolution to be housed in the former *Galerie de zoologie*, renamed *Galerie de l'évolution*. The new natural science museum opened in 1993 at the *Jardin des plantes* in Paris.

9. D. Samson, J. Eidelman and B. Schiele, *Vivre hors de l'eau, c'est se soutenir* (evaluation report). (Paris, Montréal, Muséum national d'histoire naturelle, URA 887-CNRS/Paris V, CREST/UQAM, 1991), 16 pp.

10. The recorded interviews lasted from 10 to 15 minutes. In the case of the presentation of models A and B, a sampling of 10 visitors was sufficient to reveal the reading problems.

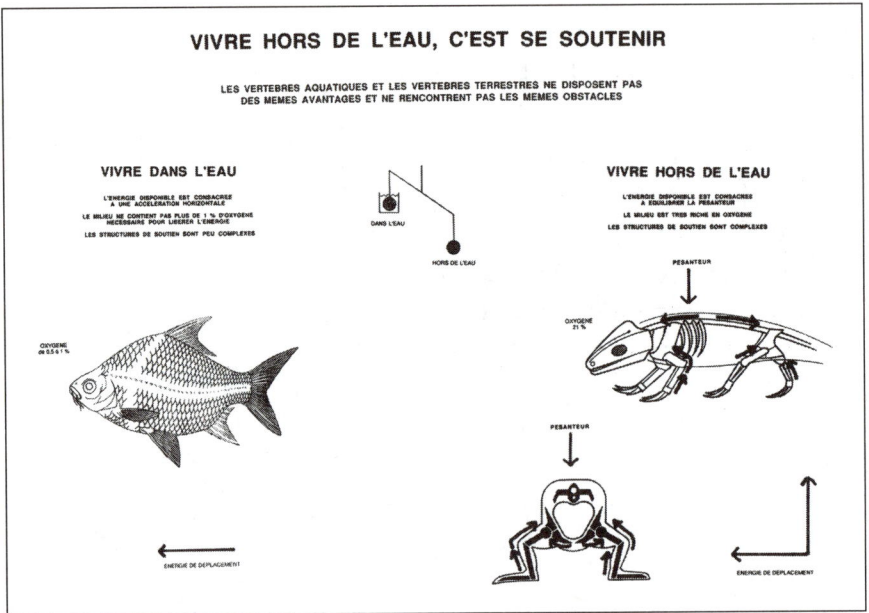

Formative evaluation model A

This model represents part one of the "Vivre hors de l'eau, c'est se soutenir" study.

It was readily apparent that visitors recognized the theme through a reading order that focused first on the illustrations, then on the labels, the title, the headings, the texts and then the illustrations again.

The reading order does not follow the same logic as the design of the models, which provides the text first, then the illustrations. Visitors rarely read from top to bottom, starting with the title. Instead, they establish their own order when reading the panel. Surveys of visitors have revealed that the reading is usually a two-stage process that involves reading for identification then reading for interpretation. In the first stage, visitors seek to discern the general theme on the basis of the images and the title. In the second stage, they interpret the theme by identifying and putting together blocks of information deemed significant.

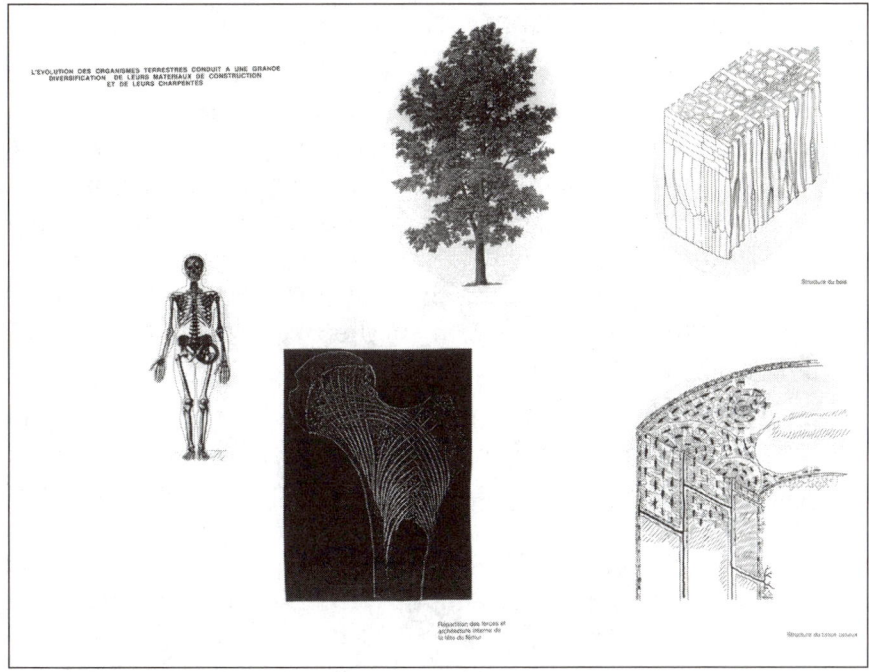

Formative evaluation model B

This model represents part two of the "Vivre hors de l'eau, c'est se soutenir" study.

During the surveys, the numerous text echoes in visitors' remarks indicated a structured understanding of model A: the frequent use of the terms "energy", "oxygen" and "gravity" in conjunction with the distinction between "in water" and "out of water" confirmed that visitors read model A by pinpointing the key concepts and grouping the blocks of information[11] in the way the model suggested.

Model B, however, proved incomprehensible to the visitors.[12] The lack of headings and the inadequacy of the labels prevented visitors from

---

11. In this instance, there are two blocks of information: "Vivre dans l'eau" (living in water) and "Vivre hors de l'eau" (living out of water). Both blocks include a heading, an explanatory text, one or two drawings, labels and pictograms. An isolated element, the drawing of the scale, serves as a bridge between the two blocks. These blocks are read in a vertical manner.

12. The blocks of information in model B are horizontal (the tree at the top and the bone at the bottom), which most of the visitors failed to see.

understanding the additional information this model provided in relation to model A. The introduction of a new element, the tree, exacerbated the problem. The reading order of model A remained self-contained and failed to link the content of the two models. Moreover, the main problem with model B was that most visitors established a circular reading order.[13] Their difficulty in organizing the elements into meaningful blocks of information is shown by circular reading that isolates each element. The arrangement in two horizontal blocks conveyed no meaning to the visitors. They tended to contrast the tree and the human being, rather than seeing similarities between them.

In order to overcome the harmful effect of circular reading and to prevent any difficulty in comparing the wood and the bone, the designers, scientists and evaluators designed model C, intended to replace model B. The illustrations and texts were assembled into two separate blocks presenting the skeleton and the structure of bony tissue (linked to the tetrapod in model A) on the left and, the tree and the structure of wood on the right. A title and headings were added. Model C was then tested[14] in conjunction with model A. Most of the visitors correctly read model C, i.e. not in a circular fashion, and were able to compare wood and bone.

This evaluation reveals the importance of reading order on the understanding of concepts. It also made it possible to pinpoint a major problem experienced by visitors, i.e. linking the comparison of plants and animals to the theme of the support structure. While model C solved this problem, the difficulty of linking the comparison reveals a hidden social idea, which could be formulated as follows: evolution occurs along parallel, independent lines in the plant or animal kingdoms. According to this logic, the fish/tetrapod comparison is understandable, but the wood/bone comparison is not.[15]

---

13. Circular reading overlooks blocks of information and moves clockwise from one element to the next. It reflects a complete misunderstanding of the way the information is organized.

14. A sample of 15 visitors was selected for the study on models A and C.

15. The vast majority of visitors thought that plants and animals did not leave the water at the same time. Therein lies a sort of consensus on the gradual conquest of the Earth (Eidelman, Schiele, Samson *et al.*, 1992: 16-17).

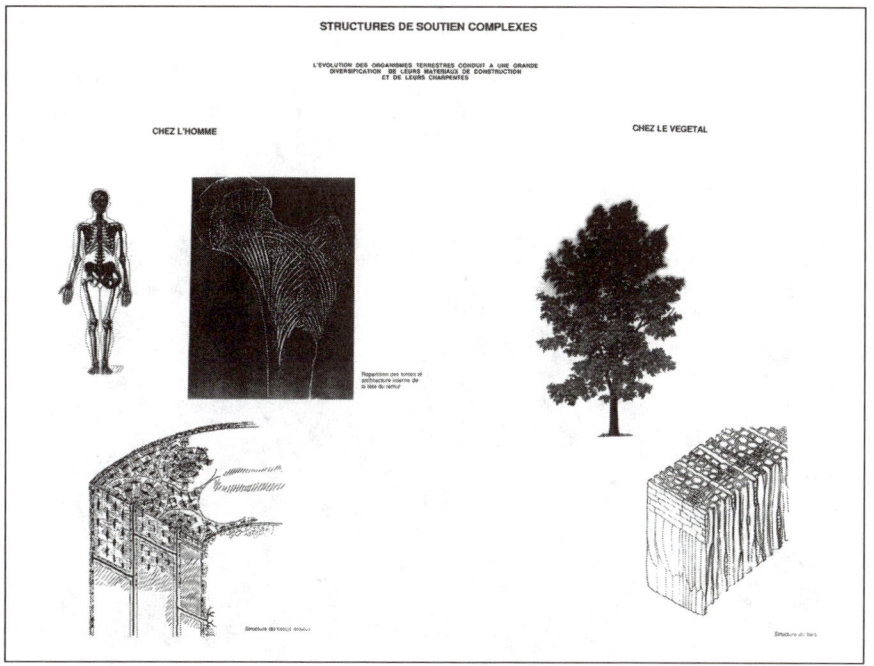

Formative evaluation model C

This model represents part two of the "Vivre hors de l'eau, c'est se soutenir" study, second version.

AT AN EXHIBITION

When the formative evaluation was carried out, exhibition designers had not decided whether the "Vivre hors de l'eau, c'est se soutenir" exhibit would be presented in the form of a panel or an exhibit case. This is not an obstacle to the formative evaluation. It is possible to use two-dimensional models to pretest an exhibit that will be three-dimensional. The evaluation team at the Natural History Museum in London became interested in this transposition. Through a series of visitor surveys, they showed that the predictive validity of formative evaluation is not affected by the fact that the eventual form the exhibit took was three-dimensional (Griggs, 1981; Griggs, Manning, 1983).

A similar situation occurred with respect to the "Vivre hors de l'eau, c'est se soutenir" exhibit case. When the designers built the exhibit case, they used specimens to encourage visitors to compare the bone structure of the fish and that of land-based vertebrates. The visitors surveyed[16] correctly answered questions on the content: they understood the comparison between the fish and the salamander in relation to the effect of gravity, and the comparison between the salamander and the deer in relation to the development of support structures.

On a marché sur la Terre exhibition, Muséum national d'histoire naturelle, Paris.
"Vivre hors de l'eau, c'est se soutenir" exhibit case

However, visitors found the comparison between bone and wood enigmatic and incomprehensible. Most of them had read the texts at the bottom of the exhibit case, but were unable to answer the last survey question: What do wood and bone have in common? They did not understand what the piece of wood was meant to illustrate. The same problem arose among these visitors as in the case of the formative evaluation: the evolution of the bone structure of fish and land-based vertebrates was logical and comprehensible, but the evolution of marine plants and trees met with stubborn resistance.[17]

This situation was rectified only in the travelling version of the exhibition. "Vivre hors de l'eau, c'est se soutenir" was presented on an

---

16. Semistructured interviews with 11 visitors who stopped in front of the exhibit case.

17. Here is an example: "The appearance of wood is what gives the tree structure, what holds it up. I can understand that animals changed, but it is hard to understand that plants did. If trees existed, they were always like that."

exhibition panel, and its designers established the similarity between a bone and a piece of wood. In this instance, the objective was achieved more rapidly. Focusing the panel contents on this difficult theme enabled visitors to make the desired comparison between the wood and the bone.

*

To conclude, the reading strategies of exhibition visitors open up an entirely new field of research. Through such strategies, it is possible to discern the conditions under which reading takes place in the museum environment: selection of information, conceptual orientation and assimilation of messages. More importantly, reading strategies shed light on the specificity of the processes at work.

Applying the idea of a reading itinerary to a panel or exhibit case satisfies a need for conceptual orientation. This reading order is structured by the search for meaning. Key elements play a vital role. Illustrations often precede the text. Labels, which are marginal elements, are brought to the forefront with the title or headings to indicate the content. Explanatory or interpretative texts come at the very end of the reading order, after quick looks for identification purposes. Reading does not follow the order of presentation from top to bottom and from left to right. Successive readings appear to be a major trait of the processes at work.

The reconfiguration of the panel or the exhibit case into blocks of information results from the need to integrate the messages. When the groupings go against what the exhibit proposes, the concepts cannot be successfully integrated. Nothing is more disastrous than dividing information in a manner that visitors find disorganized. This applies to many types of intellectual activity. It was apparent in the panels and exhibit cases that were intended to compare elements, follow narrative frameworks or analyse graphs.

Visitors' understanding of the concepts of a thematic exhibition hinges on reading conditions and processes. To take account of them when an exhibition is designed and anticipate reading strategies is to help ensure the assimilation of information and the reception of messages.

*

Bibliography

Adams, M.J.; Collins, A. (1985). "A Schema-Theoretic View of Reading" in Singer, H.; Ruddell, R.B. (editors). *Theoretical Models and Process of Reading*, third edition. Newark: International Reading Association, pp. 404-425.

Allwood, A. *The Great Exhibitions*. London: Studio Vista, 1977.

Bitgood, S. "Problems in Visitor Orientation and Circulation" in Bitgood, S.; Roper, J.T.; Benfield, A. (editors). *Visitor Studies 1988, Theory, Research and Practice*. Jacksonville: The Center for Social Design, Jacksonville State University, 1988, pp. 155-170.

Borun, M.; Miller, M. *What's in a Name? A Study of the Effectiveness of Explanatory Labels in a Science Museum*. Philadelphia: Franklin Institute and Science Museum, 1980, 70 p.

Calver, H.N. "The Exhibit Medium", *American Journal of Public Health*, 1939, No. 29, pp. 341-346.

Cummings, C.E. "East is East and West is West: Some Observations on the World's Fairs of 1939, by One Whose Main Interest is in Museums", Buffalo, *Bulletin of the Buffalo Society of Natural Sciences*, Vol. XX, 1940, 382 p.

Dana, J.C. "The Story", *Museum Work*, 1921, No. 3, pp. 185-186.

Derryberry, M. "Exhibits", *American Journal of Public Health*, 1941, Vol. 31, No. 3, pp. 257-263.

Eidelman, J.; Schiele, B.; Samson, D. *et al. Suivi évaluatif de l'exposition de préfiguration, rapport final, 1re partie.* Paris: Cellule de préfiguration MNHN, URA 887 (CNRS Paris V), CREST (UQAM), 1992, 59 p.

Gebhard, B. "Exhibit Planning and Analysis", *Journal of the American Dietetic Association*, 1948, Vol. 24, No. 5, pp. 394-398.

Gottesdiener, H. "La lecture de textes dans les musées d'art", *Publics & Musées*, 1992, No. 1, pp. 75-88.

Griggs, S.A. "Formative Evaluation of Exhibits at the British Museum (Natural History)", *Curator*, 1981, Vol. 24, No. 3, pp. 189-202.

_____. "Orienting Visitors within a Thematic Display", *International Journal of Museum Management and Curatorship*, 1983, No. 2, pp. 119-134.

Griggs, S.A.; Manning, J. "The Predictive Validity of Formative Evaluations of Exhibits", *Museum Studies Journal*, 1983, Vol. 1, No. 2, pp. 31-41.

Hirschi, K.D.; Screven, C.G. "Effects of Questions on Visitor Reading Behavior", *ILVS Review, A Journal of Visitor Behavior*, 1988, Vol. 1, No. 1, pp. 50-61.

Lane, J.; Tolleris, B. *Planning Your Exhibit.* New York: National Publicity Council for Health and Welfare, 1948, 28 p.

Loomis, R.J. *Museum Visitor Evaluation: New Tool for Museum Management.* Nashville: American Association for State and Local History, 1987, 306 p.

McManus, P. "Oh Yes, They Do: How Museum Visitors Read Labels and Interact with Exhibit Texts", *Curator*, 1989, Vol. 32, No. 3, pp. 174-189.

Melton, A.W. *Problems of Installation in Museums of Art.* Washington, DC: American Association of Museums Monograph, New Series No. 14, 1935, 269 p.

Robinson, E.S. *The Behavior of the Museum Visitor.* Washington, DC: American Association of Museums Monograph, New Series No. 5, 1928, 72 p.

Robinson, P.V. *An Experimental Study of Exhibit Arrangement and Viewing Method to Determine Their Effect upon Learning of Factual Material.* Los Angeles: University of Southern California, Ph.D. thesis, 1960, 415 p.

Samson, D.; Eidelman, J.; Schiele, B. *"Vivre hors de l'eau, c'est se soutenir", Rapport d'évaluation.* Paris, Montréal, Muséum national d'histoire naturelle, URA 887-CNRS/Paris V, CREST/UQAM, 1991, 16 p.

Screven, C.G. "The Museum as a Responsive Learning Environment", *Museum News*, 1969, Vol. 47, No. 10, pp. 7-10.

Shettel, H. "An Evaluation of Existing Criteria for Judging the Quality of Science Exhibits", *Curator*, 1968, Vol. 11, No. 2, pp. 137-153.

Shettel, H.; Butcher, M.; Cotton, T.S.; Northrop, J.; Slough, D.S. *Strategies for Determining Exhibit Effectiveness.* Pittsburgh: American Institutes for Research, 1968, 230 p.

Wolf, R.L. "The Missing Link: A Look at the Role of Orientation in Enriching the Museum Experience", *Journal of Museum Education: Round Table Reports*, 1986, Vol. 11, No. 1, pp. 17-21.

Wolf, R.L.; Tymitz, B.L. *"East Side, West Side, Straight Down the Middle": A Study of Visitor Perception of "Our Changing Land", the Bicentennial Exhibit.* Washington, DC: Smithsonian Institution, National Museum of Natural History, 1979, 54 p.

_____. *"When Will the Fourth Floor be Open?" A Study of Visitor Perceptions of the Hirshhorn Museum and Sculpture Garden.* Washington, DC: Smithsonian Institution, 1980, 55 p.

_____. *"Hey Mom, that Exhibit's Alive". A Study of Visitor Perceptions of the Coral Reef Exhibit.* Washington, DC: Smithsonian Institution, National Museum of Natural History, 1981, 29 p.

CHAPTER 3

HEARING

Summary   Anne Decrosse
                                          Jean-Paul Natali

The Oral Text as a Singular Form of the Written Text in an Exhibition

While an exhibition is, intrinsically, a very special space, there is a tendency to reproduce in it language practices modelled on a standard system of written text. The science exhibition La Douleur *(Pain), presented recently at the Cité des sciences et de l'industrie in Paris, is used here as a starting point for a discussion of what an innovative written text could be. The text in its traditional forms, e.g. panels and documents, gave way to the oral text and visitors proceeded through the exhibition with headsets. This original approach fostered an intimate, emotional relationship between the scientific discourse and each visitor's internal universe, notably by means of the narrative text, which reflects the discursive tradition of the theatre, and by means of the information transmitted, mid-way between specialized knowledge and common opinion. The authors analyze at length the writing and the linguistic processes used and establish a parallel with those that are usually adopted in science exhibitions. They reveal that this form of the oral text, which relies on the visitors' understanding, reasoning and imagination, facilitates the overall apprehension of scientific concepts. In the opinion of the visitors themselves, the narrative approach, primarily because of the key role the voice plays, creates a place that elicits receptiveness in a way that reading alone can rarely create. The essay by Hélène Lamarche, which marks the transition between the theoretical and practical portions of this book, shows how the oral text serves other communication objectives.*

The Oral Text as a Singular Form of the Written Text in an Exhibition

Anne Decrosse

Professor, École des hautes
études en sciences sociales
et en muséologie des sciences et
techniques, Paris, and Associate
Professor, Stanford University

Jean-Paul Natali

Research Project Manager, Cité
des sciences et de l'industrie
de La Villette, Paris, scientific
designer and author of the texts
for the exhibition *La Douleur*

A SPECIAL MUSEOLOGICAL APPROACH TO TEXTS

Over the past decade or so, the proliferation of science exhibitions has become a notable feature of our society. The scope of this socio-cultural phenomenon, which involves governments, granting agencies, scientific institutions, educators and ordinary members of the public, those much-discussed visitors, has established a radically new language practice: writing the exhibition!

The exhibition text or, as people may prefer to say, text in the exhibition medium, thus indicating the distance between the exhibition space and language, has scarcely been subject to analysis, in contrast to the analyses devoted to communication or information. It is to be noted in this regard that the study of text in the exhibition medium is, in relation to the broad field of linguistics, a poor relation, overshadowed by the written word in general, literature, different types of discourse, and so on. In the case of science exhibitions, the question of the text is, however, fundamental. Indeed, the exhibition text is a restructuring[1] of the specialized language and the hypothesis-deduction discourse of the sciences.[2] Consequently, text in the exhibition medium represents a discursive educational experience that differs radically from a book. While the space of a book constitutes a relationship to language in which the body is silent, the exhibition itinerary implies the visitors' physical presence in a global environment and in a movement. The itinerary interweaves various systems of verbal and non-verbal signs. Understanding relies as much on processes involving perception and sensation as on reasoning. The visitors' relationship to the science exhibition calls into play the multiplicity of relationships that the individual maintains with others, and the implementation of a logic of knowledge.

While researchers have examined, on the one hand, general ways of "presenting" textual materials in the exhibition in order to understand how they are appraised and received according to their height, the typography used, the layout of surfaces, and so on, and on the other hand, the relationships between text and image, the general question of the exhibition text as a genre has never been dealt with.

Problems of a semiotic nature, rather than problems pertaining to the theory of communication or information, such as the difference between scholastic texts and exhibition texts, or the difference between scientific texts and "panels", are issues that must be unravelled. A science exhibition cannot be reduced to a series of objects, documents that include the text, and experiments.

---

1. See J.-P. Natali, *La transtructuration des savoirs par l'exposition*, thesis in progress at the Université de Paris 7, concerning the concept of restructuring by the exhibition.

2. We are referring here to the scientific method that consists of posing a working hypothesis, elaborating an experimental protocol that isolates the phenomenon to be studied, and collecting a series of measurements that enable a reexamination of the initial hypothesis and that may involve the modification or the confirmation of the theoretical model that made it possible to formulate the hypothesis.

The exhibition is formally specific, a semiosis as linguists and semioticians would have it, i.e. a complex ordering of signs. Reformulation[3] and transcoding[4] are complex operations inherent in the formal specificity of the exhibition. The text and, consequently, the act of writing, have a very special consistency in this visual and sensitive atmosphere.

However, the chief criticism levelled at science exhibitions is that they are "panel-exhibitions", i.e. exhibitions in which the text takes up too much space as a text, irritates, bores and fails to mediate between meaning and ideas. The design and study of the exhibition text undoubtedly has a bright future in both a creative and a hermeneutic sense.[5] We are obviously only at the stage of the premise of a readable exhibition text, given that we are still bound in the strait jacket[6] of the standardized scholastic text that the 19th century has bequeathed to us. It is the project for a standardized language and school textbooks ensuring such standardization, notably with respect to the system of the sentence, that underlies this scholastic text, which is markedly different from the literary text. This type of representation of the the written word has contaminated our environment and overall perception of learned discourse. The exhibition, like newspapers, although the media are radically different from this prime example of learned discourse, reproduce the latter's formal practices in a space that cannot, as we have already pointed out, be subsumed under the space occupied by the book.

What we are proposing in this essay, based on the case of an exhibition that attempted to present the text in another guise, is a reflection on what an innovative exhibition text might be, with the implicit hope of advancing the study of the specific characteristics of

---

3. Reformulation occurs when a message is disseminated over a communication medium that differs from the original one. See, in this regard, the work of Professor J. Peytard and D. Jacobi.

4. Transcoding occurs when the process of transforming basic scientific discourse modifies the concepts themselves by dramatizing them. See, in this respect, the work of A. Decrosse and J. Davallon.

5. The study of the question of meaning.

6. Its constraints are prescriptive and at the same time contribute to standardization.

such an exhibition text, particularly in its relationships with other semiotic systems, and with the main sociocultural narratives in which and through we think.

La Douleur (Pain): **Problems concerning one type of text in an exhibition and the ambiguous distinction between written and oral materials**

The characteristics and particular bias of this exhibition context have made for an original museological approach. The exhibition entitled *La Douleur*, presented in 1992 and 1993 at the Cité des sciences et de l'industrie (CSI)[7] in conjunction with the thematic year devoted to health, was also intended to be a travelling exhibition. Entirely bilingual (French/American English) and covering an area of roughly 1 000 m², the exhibition was designed according to a series of biases emphasizing an intimate, sophisticated relationship between scientific discourse and its reception by visitors. Text, in its traditional forms associated with exhibitions, i.e. panels, display cards and documents, occupied very little space, but in the form of an oral text, underpinned the entire itinerary the visitor followed, wearing a headset. The oral text evoked a genre that is literary and, occasionally, dramatic, while communicating highly complex scientific information. At the same time, the text avoided neither the specialized vocabulary nor the sociocultural effects of pain, which, over the centuries, have interwoven the history of the body and care of the body with scientific discoveries.

The exhibition focuses on major themes, each of which is organized around a broad landscape.[8] This complex organization of various systems of signs, including language, makes coherent various scientific objects (diagrams, models, interactive experiments), æsthetic presentations (objects crafted by artists, historical engravings, dioramas, and audiovisual,

---

7. The exhibition ran from October 15, 1992 to August 28, 1993, then toured North America.
8. See J.-P. Natali and J.-L. Martinand, "Une exposition scientifique thématique... Est-ce bien concevable?", *Éducation permanente*, No. 90, October 1987; M. Marie, "Paysage, tourisme" in *L'objet expose le lieu*, Cahiers Expo-Média No. 2, 1986; and J.-P. Natali, "Le plaisir de comprendre sa douleur", *Bulletin Sciences-Muséo*, No. 3, Cité des sciences et de l'industrie, July 1993.

graphic and multimedia displays), along with art works (paintings and sculptures by contemporary artists) and texts to be listened to or read.

The scientific content, rendered difficult because of the complexity of the concepts and systems underlying it, e.g. neurophysiology, behaviour, medicine and the neuropharmacology of nociperception, demanded a significant transformation of the formulation of the basic scientific concepts inherent in the subject. Through a narrative text heard on individual headsets, each field was subject to a single, broad explanation in three or four episodes, involving only those concepts that the visitors needed in order to understand the overall message.

La Douleur, exhibition at the Cité des sciences et de l'industrie de La Villette, Paris

The oral text

The audiotape was produced by professional broadcasters. Each space was "covered" by an element of the audiotape: soundscape, music and texts spoken by actors. Visitors to the exhibition wore headsets using an infrared transmission system that enabled them to hear 30 sound sequences. The series of sequences, consisting of loops lasting three minutes, on average, represented roughly 90 minutes of texts commenting on and explaining the explicitly visual structures of the exhibition. Consequently, the scriptovisual portion was reduced to a strict minimum: titles of presentations, names designating the components of interactive diagrams, and a few indications concerning interaction with the diagrams.

Formatting of the audiotape for visitors

Actors read all of the exhibition texts. The way the texts were written reflected theatre tradition and helped to partially overcome the neutrality and authoritative tone of scientific discourse. The visitor heard someone saying in simple language that once pain has been felt, we remember it and we remember the state in which it put us, we talk about it and it becomes a fact of life.

La Douleur, exhibition at the Cité des sciences et de l'industrie de La Villette, Paris

The puppet, a narrator-character personifying pain

Among these voices, a dramatic character, the puppet, personified pain. He appeared throughout the exhibition in various poses. He mentioned the relativity of the knowledge presented, summarized its history or indicated its field of application. He pointed out the difficulty that scientists or patients encounter in understanding and modelling the entire range of knowledge acquired on the subject, in the case of the former, and what they are experiencing and suffering, in the case of the latter. For example, he remarked that, while scientists were at one point enamoured of gate control theory, pain turned out to be much more complicated than that, and in any event, it is when a signal reaches the brain that you really feel a sensation of pain.

The puppet, an emblematic character who expressed his reactions frequently to underscore the contradictions and gaps inherent in this field of knowledge, was surrounded by major sociocultural and historico-scientific reconstitutions of pain. These frescoes reconstructed the everyday experience of pain familiar to all, but also the world of the laboratory or medical care.

The visitors were thus thrust into a discourse which, without being entirely theatrical, was nonetheless transmitted by human voices, each with its own personality. As a result, the distinction between the oral (speech) and the written (scientific knowledge in the form of text) was blurred for visitors, caught between their inner world and the world of medical knowledge. The pedagogical or didactic discourse, personalizing the speaker and his relationship with the person listening to him, the physician, moved to the background so that the information could be transmitted through a particular cognitive activity: the emotional aftershock of scientific knowledge.

Exhibition texts, knowledge and opinion

The exhibition text, a text that the visitors listened to and did not read, interwoven with some basic formulas and a few words that referred to the items exhibited, created suspense and thus revealed the uncertainties of a science that presents itself more as a human activity in its processes and achievements than as a purely intellectual abstract construction.

Thus, the distance between scholarly knowledge and common opinions was to a large extent reduced in this place specially created by the scientific designer to elicit a state of receptiveness.[9] Visitors could compare their own knowledge with the knowledge transmitted in a framework that was as emotional as it was rational. This method of all-embracing communication-information tends to foster the restructuring of the visitors' knowledge more than it contributes new, specific information.

STUDY OF THE CONTIGUITY AND NON-CONTINUITY OF SCHOLASTIC LANGUAGE AND MUSEUM-RELATED LANGUAGE

Starting in the school system, contrasting factors arise between the spoken and written word in the reasoning process. Specifically, we are referring to the relationship between the lesson (oral), the textbook (read but also commented upon) and written homework. In the exhibition entitled *La Douleur*, the use of an oral text meant that speech was instituted between the person and the world. The museum-oriented writing selected differed from the scholastic turn of phrase that is usually adopted in the scientific texts in science exhibitions. This decision has numerous implications with regard to reasoning processes and the understanding of language itself.

The text, a changing historical concept

Generally speaking, the text in a science museum can be perceived as both related to and transcoding the discourse of knowledge that precedes it. Similarly, it constitutes a special discursive genre because of the reformulation implicit in the shift from the page to the panel.

While the museum-related text thus imposes a modified expression of a common prescriptive language phenomenon, its various mani-festations in the display of a science exhibition lead more often than not

---

9. This differs from the design of *Explora*, a permanent CSI exhibition in which visitors must play the role of Robinson Crusoe discovering his island. See A. Decrosse, J. Landry, J.-P. Natali in *Museum* 155, 1987, UNESCO, "Les expositions permanentes de la Cité des sciences et de l'industrie: Explora".

to the implementation of a recurring argumentation process, i.e. reference to the formula, the law, the phenomenon on which a decision has been handed down.

Very few studies have checked the consistency of this argumentation process in the museum, a process that refers to the very basis of the scientific text. We might still wonder whether this process is genuinely effective in enabling the different types of visitors to absorb the knowledge being disseminated.

The form usually taken by this type of text is a reproduction[10] of the modern distinction between the spoken and written word, which was unknown, for example, to the 16th-century humanists who paid such close attention to oral rhetoric, or the scholarly texts of the classical era, in which the sentence, constructed by stressing the indications of the reasoning process, makes little distinction between the written and spoken word.

Neither is the current museum-related text closely related to the procedure typical of the encyclopedia, in which words and objects are organized in a general text that provides labels for the world around us.[11] The modern era, with its compulsory school attendance, has tended to reject the use of spoken language because of the disruptive effect it has on the content and articulation of the knowledge alluded to earlier. Text in science exhibitions has found a place in this larger discursive educational experience, probably through a failure to understand the distinctive traits of the scientific community, in which text rendered orally (exchange of ideas via oral communications, conferences, seminars) and purely oral discussions occupy a fundamental position alongside written language (reasoning and findings set down on paper and published).

---

10. With respect to the concept of reproduction, see the work of Professor Pierre Bourdieu, Chair of Sociology, Collège de France.
11. A. Decrosse, *Histoire de la langue française, tome 1: Généalogie des systèmes de signes*, research conducted in collaboration with the Centre national des lettres (Paris: Hermann) (to be published).

From the ordinary language practices of visitors to the places that elicit receptiveness in the exhibition

La Douleur is a specific example of an exhibition that highlights the heterogeneous nature of text. There were fragments taken from scientific texts, such as diagrams, but also examples of such texts to which visitors did not have access, i.e. a stack of scientific reports in a glass case. There were "dictionary" words, a scientific vocabulary whose paradigm for the general public is the written rather than the spoken word, even if such words are spoken in the scientific (biology) and medical communities. Such words were few in number in the exhibition. They transmitted a great deal of information and were essentially all spoken by the puppet or in the interactive audiovisual displays. There were also everyday words, like the commemorative plaques, or the words designating objects, which became virtual objects in themselves. There were other words: the oral text accompanying the exhibition itinerary, which spoke of science and of life, of ordinary experience and of the scientific classification of pain.

This writing is a baroque text in which opposites meet and which, exactly like baroque culture, focuses on life and death. It finally accords a fundamental place to language in the exhibition: not overtly, but as an integral part of the general system of the exhibition, the writing is discernable without being presented for the visitors to read.

In the wake of our initial evaluations of the exhibition and the format of the text, it appeared that visitors experienced the text, first and foremost, as the organization of a whole, a sort of all-embracing, coherent thematic landscape. The type of textuality that visitors confronted was perceived as a factor that facilitated reasoning.

The complex, heterogeneous text in the exhibition enabled visitors to institute cognitive activities by constructing places that stimulated receptiveness which were based on comprehension, reasoning and imagination. This type of text, tied to the enactment of large sequences of ordinary life, refers to the daily semioses of perception and comprehension of the surrounding environment. At the same time, the text contains an otherness, i.e. scientific knowledge, which is always held in check by the suspension of the surrounding environment but also by its own form, the puppet's speech.

An approach centred on linguistic processes that favour information in the exhibition: rendering the text orally

From the standpoint of the exhibition designer, the oral text has been conceived as a written text that is "spoken" with a view to providing special elements of rhetoric adapted to the immediate dissemination of scientific discourse in a broad context.

From a linguistic standpoint, it is also true that the spoken word, for the speaker, always seems closer to his usual ways of communicating and generally understanding the surrounding universe. As linguists are aware, text is actually a negative factor with respect to understanding in the exhibition. The text is often little read and its appeal and intelligibility are limited, while iconicity and schematization have significance without requiring the semanticization of the content.[12] Only rarely does the text to be read on the scriptovisual structures of the science exhibition lead to retention or comprehension. Museums know this: like the Palais de la découverte and the CSI, other museums have often given priority to the facilitator, who explains scientific experience in the first instance and scientific content in the second.[13] In general terms, text, while it reassures educators and generally accompanies images, is only rarely functional, intelligible and user-friendly in the contemporary science exhibition for those who are not much accustomed to it. The prestige of the experiments in the exhibition ranks first, along with interactivity, among practices that visitors prefer. In experiments, text is often subject to the logical principles by which computers operate, and acts as a complement to the image.

In *La Douleur*, the oral rendering of the texts constitutes, according to what we know about the text in the exhibition medium, a

---

12. A. Decrosse and J.-P. Natali, editors, *Sciences et medias, penser, imaginer, connaître*, afterword by G. Delacôte (Paris: Didier Érudition, 1989).

13. A. Decrosse and J.-P. Natali, editors, *Muséologie des sciences* (Paris: Hermann), published with the support of the Ministère de la Recherche (to be published).

transgression. Textuality serves totally as an organizing factor in the form of text rendered orally, and style transcends formulas and reasoning. Indeed, style is truly presented here as a factor that facilitates the overall assimilation of scientific concepts.

Text, which for a long time had been relegated to an adversarial text-image, text-object and text-sensation role and which had lost a great deal of its ability to effectively transmit meaning within the exhibition, occupies a new place and is regaining a genuine role in the sociocognitive activity that is represented by a science exhibition. The oral rendering of the text makes it possible to introduce linguistic processes that can help prevent the loss of meaning. Areas of enunciation are marked in the exhibition and pointed out by the speaker.[14] Indeed, the scientific text is transmitted by characters, including the puppet, who speak to the visitors and talk about them. The puppet, which is strongly rendered as a type and contrasts with the human of which he is the distanced image but also the radical other, the instructor in pain, introduces a meaningful voice into the exhibition that prevails over the neutral utterances of science. The fragments of scientific or everyday texts that punctuate the exhibition thus take the form of fragments of the great ordinary text that any speaker encounters in the contemporary world.

STUDY OF THE FIGURES OF TEXT RENDERED ORALLY WITHIN THE FRAMEWORK OF THE EXHIBITION: THE NARRATIVE APPROACH

A danger may persist in this type of general exhibition writing. This form of expression can structure information around a dramatic connotation and introduce simplistic effects that may impoverish the scientific discourse. Obviously, such writing, which may seem adapted to a subject in which the visitors are keenly interested, as is the case with respect to pain, could not be chosen as is for a subject such as mathematics. Not all scientific domains are equivalent as for their immediate interest. The

---

14. "Linguists oppose this enunciative structure (discourse and deixis with the opposition I/YOU) to that constituted by history (third person and, depending on the languages, the presentative: "it is", "there is", "one"...)." Benveniste, "L'appareil formel de l'énonciation", p. 79, in *Problèmes de linguistique générale* (Paris: Gallimard, 1976).

scientific quality denoted by the hypothesis-deduction model of knowledge[15] applies to subjects of study that involve the interest and need for knowledge of each one of us to varying degrees. While biological and medical topics are amply explored by the mass media, this does not mean that the knowledge underlying these questions has actually been assimilated.

However, it remains to be seen how the type of expression chosen here can constitute a discursive type, i.e. a method to design discourse for the exhibition and, in particular, how it is possible to prevent simplistic effects from impoverishing scientific discourse.

A method of argumentation in a continuous loop

A thorough analysis of the process of writing the texts rendered orally in the exhibition allows us to better understand the nature of the linguistic operations applied to the discourse constructed in this demonstration space and to derive a typology from it.

From the outset, we note that these texts, midway between commentary and narration, have been written in order to function in a loop, i.e. the visitors "enter" the acoustic space at any point as it progresses. The circularity of the discourse has made it necessary to simplify the development of the argumentation. Only one concept is brought to the fore, accompanied by examples or elements that contribute to understanding. However, through the loop structure, a conceptual meaning can be reached without adopting a demonstrative turn of phrase, which the visitors often find obscure.

---

15. See footnote 2.

EXAMPLE OF TEXT IN A CONTINUOUS LOOP

(The puppet's voice is in italics.)

.../...

...In this way, you'll see how all this coded information spreads and becomes, in your brain and so in your consciousness, a subjective sensation of pain.

Oh, my, it's a lot more complicated than that! Here, you are only seeing a simplification of my systems. In any event, while scientists have learned a great deal to date about pain perception, they don't know everything about it. Good luck.

✳

I am pain. I am singular and multiple. People know me as the expression of ills that affect the body. In fact, I am the perception of what hurts. I exist only when there is a subject who is suffering.

As for scientists, they study the objectifiable portion of pain. They call it nociperception, that is, the entire range of stimulations and processes which, once they reach the brain, are experienced as pain.

For example, when your finger gets caught in a door, you experience a sensation of pain that is intended to let you know what is wrong.

They could say thank you! I am, after all, a useful signal: I warn you when danger is present, which often enables you to avoid something worse. I care about you and I don't want to lose you...

In this space, you'll see around you objects and representations that show you the structures of the nociceptive system. When signals from this system reach your brain, you interpret them, that is, you feel them as a painful and sometimes even unbearable sensation. That is what pain is.

Here, they're showing you everything they know about my circuits, neurons and molecules. They are telling you how I function and how I spring forth in your consciousness.

They've looked through their microscopes, recorded nerve impulses, built models, even invented equipment to look inside the body and the brain in an attempt to translate me into images.

You're going to become familiar with the biological components of this system, that is, the nerve cells or neurons. Neurons generate the nociceptive signal in the form of a nerve impulse, which moves from the affected area to the brain. Next, you'll see how particular molecules can regulate this impulse.

Then, you can follow, step by step, the origin, transmission and modulation of the nociceptive signals along the networks of nerve fibres. In this way, you'll see how all of this coded information spreads and becomes, in your brain and thus in your conscious mind, a subjective sensation of pain.

Oh, my, it's a lot more complicated than that! Here, you're only seeing a simplification of my systems. In any event, while scientists have learned a great deal to date about pain perception, they don't know everything about it. Good luck.

I am pain. I am singular and multiple. People know me as the expression of ills that affect the body. In fact, I am the perception of what hurts. I exist only when there is a subject who is suffering.

As for scientists, they study the objectifiable portion of pain…

…/…

From a second standpoint, the scientific vocabulary has been considerably reduced to avoid interfering with an understanding of the message. The construction of the meaning is based on legible text in conjunction with simplified objects: the nerve cell, the contact point between neurons, the nervous system, and functional zones. Aside from several anatomical terms that have become very commonplace, such as "brain", "neurons" and "synapses", only two very precise terms have been used and figure in the oral rendering of the text, i.e. "nociperception" and "endorphins". When the exhibition was designed, a third term was contemplated, "placebo effect". However, the difficulty in describing it and, in particular, the possible confusion with "placebo" as a substance, led to its being abandoned.[16] At the lexical level, it was replaced by the phrase "quality of the patient/physician relationship".

16. By definition, a placebo is biochemically or molecularly inactive. It is used in complex protocols to test the medicinal effect of active substances by enabling any effects caused by the psychophysiological contingencies of their administration to be eliminated

Third, it was possible to study, especially from the standpoint of reception, how basic is the rhetorical procedure using repetition, redundancy and a multiplicity of viewpoints. These rhetorical processes became increasingly numerous as the visit progressed. They tired the visitors, rekindled attention, stressed the quasi-supra-segmental nature of the information itself (melodic effect, rhythmic division of the spoken sequences, tone of the voice and so on), but still did not resort to any metalinguistic procedure.[17]

The text rendered orally, between unconscious knowledge and the sciences

Because each theme began with a sequence that referred to the entire zone in question, a two-tiered reference was created. Once the visitors had listened to the three-minute general introduction, they could skip the next two or three texts, which dwelt in greater detail on scientific concepts, by leaving the area or removing their headsets. They could also find, in subsequent texts, the ideas already presented in the preliminary sequence and enter into a more emotional or mood-related relationship with the environment. The emotion will organize itself contextually with the scientific information, but also with recollection and memory, and make possible advanced development of cognitive processes. Moreover, these processes will not be internal to the code of the scientific discourse, but poietic,[18] in that they connect self, world and knowledge.

---

from the analysis. In contrast, the placebo effect is a pscychophysiological effect sought by the therapist. It facilitates the success of the treatment. The introduction of the term "placebo effect" would also have implied the introduction of "nocebo effect", equally difficult to understand in scientific terms. Nocebo effect refers to negative psychophysiological effects that disturb or, indeed, inhibit the efficacy of the treatment. The absence of clear meanings in scientific terms and the resemblance to interpretations of a magical nature would have considerably interfered with the intention of presenting medical research as a full-fledged scientific activity.

17. There is no attempt to explain the terms themselves, which is what a metalinguistic operation such as a definition in a scientific dictionary entails. See, in this regard, the article by Josette Rey-Debove, "Le Petit Robert et les Sciences" in *Sciences et médias* (*op. cit.*).

18. From the Greek *poiein* (to produce), signifying the emergence (the production by a system) of an organization or a structure, here stylistic in nature.

Moreover, the puppet representing pain prefers to express a viewpoint diametrically opposed to the objective or neutral viewpoint of the scientists. He is pain itself, expressing itself and emphasizing what is not strictly the subject of science. To the extent that the relationship between this monologue and the space close at hand is emphasized, even without its being explicitly indicated, the intertext[19] occupies a fundamental operational place.

Here, it is intertextual globality that functions as a dictionary of concepts rather than the objects displayed, which are only rarely pointed to by the discourse. In this intertextual relationship, the visitors have considerable latitude to engage in association, analogy and comprehension. However, in the scientific fields considered, the text rendered orally that pertains to basic cognitive concepts of science carries referential meanings. In order to construct the understanding of these scientific meanings, the text rendered orally bears linguistic marks, such as the explanatory verb or the presentation of various stages that follow one another logically in order to draw the visitors' attention to the development of reasoning. However, the exhibition restructures these concepts by paraphrasing them, i.e. they are no longer in the form of metaphors but in the form of derivations.[20] Thus, reception does not purely and simply imply access to the normative codes of the sciences. Meaning, which eludes the designer as much as it does scientists, is created by the reasoning of the visitor, on the spot.

A study of visitors: the voice of the text

A study[21] was conducted from the beginning of the exhibition, in collaboration with the Groupe de recherche sociosémiotique de la Maison

---

19. The intertext is the series of relationships that link the text to all texts at a given time in a given society. The concept underscores the fact that a text has no closure: it is open to all texts and, as a result, understanding of the text is not rigid.

20. Paraphrase is, in fact, a process of discursive derivation on an initial word. It is not the fabula, i.e. the narrative perspective that leads us beyond the universe of the initial reference.

21. The panel consisted of roughly 100 visitors of different age groups, belonging to various socioprofessional classes and reflecting the makeup of the general public that attended the exhibition. The investigation was sociolinguistic in nature, notably in order to

des sciences de l'homme, on the behaviour and receptiveness of visitors. Observations over a period of several months and the initial findings of our analysis allow us to offer a broad picture of the receptive behaviour of visitors who were drawn into the exhibition's content by their relationship with the oral text.

The role of the voice was regarded as paramount, both the puppet's voice and the voices heard in the interactive audiovisual displays. The voices heard were those of actors, and they contrasted sharply with the neutral, lofty tone usually associated with learned discourse. The voices engaged in monologues and dialogues, addressed the listener, and delivered asides. They surrounded the visitors and dwindled to whispers and silence. Thus, visitors were listening to the "voice" of the world, which for one instant was virtually embodied in the presence speaking to them. This "voice" established a "gentle" relationship to language, contrary to the "harsh" relationship characteristic of institutions. Here, it was not the "machine" of society or the "system" of the scientific community that was speaking. It was a personalized voice, welcoming and friendly, which, in a confiding way, produced echos of the "voice" of the world that enables us at once to be ourselves and a part of society.

Individual listening was thus strongly elicited. Special and prolonged attention – some visitors spent a lot more time in the exhibition than was necessary to listen to all of the audiotapes – to what was said was constantly aroused by the supra-segmental and melodic story line, in contrast to the usual practice of quickly passing through the exhibition. As one of the visitors put it, it was virtually impossible to "zap" between the contents.

Contrary to reading practices, the visitors moved about and submitted to the sudden voluntary or involuntary passage from one text to another, even though they might not have finished listening to what was being said. Most visitors found this hiatus caused problems in understanding the exhibition itinerary itself, although, strangely enough, it did not hinder their understanding of the scientific concepts presented.

---

analyze the levels of reception from a terminological and stylistic standpoint. Special attention was paid to the reception of the narrative program, especially the cognitive processes set in motion by the puppet.

If some visitors found it strange not to be able to use rapid reading techniques, e.g. to randomly select words in a sentence or ignore linking words, this type of narrative program did not hinder their reflection on the content. Other visitors found that adopting the pace of the speaker whom they heard on the headset, entering into his time frame while they occupied a space (an islet), facilitated access to the content.

However, that is not all: the visitors also had to enter into the psychological coloration induced by the particular traits of the voice and the text. The designer wanted the relationship between the text and visitor to be emotional: the relationship with knowledge is achieved through feelings. During their visit, many visitors received an emotional impression of tranquil or gentle comprehension[22] that is not to be found in the "hardness" of reading scientific texts.

Moreover, the isolation of the headset and accompaniment by the character of the puppet, who guided the visit in a special way, elicited attitudes of understanding knowledge that were based on individual contemplation. Schools during the Third Republic put forward the idea that reading and writing were tied to the notion of a state language that made for territorial unity. Today, language and the discourse it conveys are always viewed as implying inclusion in a geopolitical entity. In the science museum, the relationship may still be considered utopian, since science is universal, despite the constraints inherent in national languages. In *La Douleur*, scientific writing encountered the voice of the world, which speaks out of its diversity, specific characteristics and universality. The visitor, by becoming an integral part of the production, through individualized listening, became one of the characters in this great collective text.

What was most striking in the exhibition was to see all the attentive faces absorbed in listening and private reflection: the headset compelled visitors to interiorize the act of receiving information, demanded their attention and caused their momentary withdrawal from the human environment, i.e. family, friends, teachers. Some visitors

---

22. See the advertising slogan used to describe the Cité des sciences et de l'industrie, "Le plaisir de comprendre" ("The pleasure of understanding").

spontaneously divided their time between individual listening and discussions (with the headset removed) with those accompanying them. In this respect, this type of scientific exhibition may constitute a new use of the relationship between writing and reading. It could be dubbed popular writing-reading.

*

Barthes spoke of writing as a mechanism that "engages" the individual. The study conducted among visitors to the exhibition reveals a similar phenomenon. The exhibition seems to be experienced not as a medium for viewing or action, but instead, as a structure that attracts and captivates the visitor, although, paradoxically, there were only a few interactive elements (seven) in the entire space.

One of the strengths of this kind of input is attributable to the oral form of the text and the investigation it induces. According to our survey among visitors, they appeared (with the exception of those who cannot abide headsets) to visit the exhibition in a state of constant shuttling back and forth between their own experience and the messages they heard. The visibility of the object and the legibility of the text were not of paramount concern. Indeed, the visitors' "interior" language came to the fore, their own interior voice, with which mingled the voices of the world and of science as personified by the actors. The oral rendering of the texts and the resulting attitude of the visitors appeared to make it easier to realize that text in the exhibition medium cannot, ultimately, be anything more than intertext.

An examination now under way of the numerous comments in the visitors' book tends to confirm visitors' interest not only in the content of the exhibition but in its very particular textuality. The vast majority of comments reveal a mixture of emotion and understanding. While there is occasional criticism of the technical limitations of the process of disseminating the texts, partly because of improper use of the headset or difficulty in recognizing the boundaries between the different audio zones, visitors frequently alluded to the quality of the audio messages, the content and the textuality, all perceived as part of the pleasure of listening.

*

Bibliography

Benveniste, E. *Problèmes de linguistique générale*. Paris: Gallimard, 1976.

Bourdieu, P.; Passeron, J.C. *La reproduction, éléments pour une théorie du système d'enseignement*. Paris: Minuit, 1970.

Chalmers, A.F. *Qu'est-ce que la science? Récents développements en philosophie des sciences : Popper, Kuhn, Lakatos, Feyerabend*. Paris: La Découverte, 1987.

Davallon, J.; Decrosse, A. *Transformation des discours scientifiques en discours d'exposition*, fact-finding report on the museum's vocation. Paris: EPPV, La Villette, 1986.

Decrosse, A., editor. *Sociosémiotique*, Langage et Société, 28, two parts, CNRS. Paris: MSH, 1984.

_____. *Les manuels scolaires, histoire et linguistique*, Actes de la Table Ronde, Langage et Société, École normale supérieure. Paris: MSH, 1984.

_____. "En quoi les musées diffèrent de la bibliothèque?", *Protée*, Vol. 16, No. 3, Québec City, 1988.

Decrosse, A.; Natali, J.-P., editors. *Sciences & médias, penser, imaginer, connaître,* "Discours et Sociétés" collection, No. 5. Paris: Didier Érudition, 1988.

Decrosse, A.; Landry, J.; Natali, J.-P. "Explora, les expositions permanentes de la CSI de la Villette", *Museum,* No. 155. Paris: UNESCO, 1986.

Desportes, E.; Natali, J.-P.; Raffin, A. (editors). "Muséologie et Information", *Brises,* No. 10. Paris: CDSH/CNRS, 1987.

Feyerabend, P.K. *Contre la méthode. Esquisse d'une théorie anarchiste de la connaissance.* Paris: Le Seuil, 1979.

Fuchs, C. *La paraphrase.* Paris: PUF, 1982.

Holton, G. *L'imagination scientifique.* Paris: PUF, 1988.

Jacobi, D.; Schiele, B., editors. *Vulgariser la science. Le procès de l'ignorance.* Seyssel: Champvallon, 1988.

Jacobi, D.; Jacobi, E. *Analyse sémiotique des panneaux dans l'exposition scientifique,* fact-finding report. Paris: EPPV, La Villette, 1984.

Kuhn, T.S. *La structure des révolutions scientifiques.* Paris: Flammarion, 1970 (University of Chicago Press, 1962).

Maldidier, P.; Boltanski, L. *La vulgarisation scientifique et ses agents,* report on inquiry, Centre de sociologie européenne. Paris: EHESS, 1969.

Natali, J.-P. "La conception des expositions scientifiques et la restructuration des savoirs" in *Actes du colloque Culture technique et formation,* 1988.

Natali, J.-P.; Martinand, J.-L. "Une exposition scientifique thématique... Est-ce bien concevable?", *Éducation permanente,* 90, Paris, 1987.

Natali, J.-P. "Les classes-Villette: l'exploitation pédagogique d'un lieu muséologique", *Bulletin de la Société française de physique,* No. 67, 1988, pp. 21-23.

Peytard, J.; Jacobi, D.; Petroff, A. "Français technique et scientifique: reformulation, enseignement", *Langue française*, No. 64, 1984, pp. 1-125.

Rivière, G.-H. *Muséologie selon Georges-Henri RIVIÈRE*. Paris: Dunod, 1989.

Serres, M. (editor). *Éléments d'histoire des sciences*. Paris: Bordas, 1989.

Veron, E.; Levasseur, M. *Ethnographie de l'exposition; l'espace, le corps et le sens*. Paris: BPI, Centre Georges-Pompidou, 1987.

Veron, E. *La semiosis sociale: fragments d'une théorie de la discurvité*, "Sciences du langage" collection. Saint-Denis: Presses universitaires de Vincennes, 1987.

Summary   Hélène Lamarche

The Audioguide as an Aid to Understanding an Exhibition

The exhibition text can take several forms, including a sequential narration that visitors listen to using an audioguide, which is an excellent teaching medium, particularly in art museums, where it often replaces scriptovisual displays. However, because the text is intended to be listened to, its design requires a special approach that is discussed in this section. As the author of this essay explains, the method usually employed consists of constructing the audioguide scenario by adapting a given content to visitors' comments about the exhibition. Moreover, it is necessary to define, within the general exhibition itinerary, a secondary itinerary that will determine which works are to be commented on. In addition to the usual information, the writer must include instructions concerning the itinerary and the location of the works, without making the text cumbersome. As for the writing itself, the problem that arises is the same one encountered in any attempt at popularization, i.e. to transmit specialized information in simple, clear language. The euphony of sentences, the voice of the reader and the quality of the reading are also very important. The author describes the main types of equipment used, recording methods and new transmission and listening systems. To conclude, she notes that the text intended for an audioguide cannot be designed like a text for a catalogue or a panel: it has its own style of writing, which is more sound-related than visual.

The Audioguide as an Aid to Understanding an Exhibition

Hélène Lamarche

Head, Educational and Cultural
Service, The Montreal Museum
of Fine Arts

The audioguide is one of the key teaching media that museums make available to their visitors. It is an individual listening device that offers a pre-recorded tour of a site or an exhibition. Its most common form, which will be the main focus of this essay, is a sequential narration, which visitors listen to by means of a headset and a cassette player slung over the shoulder. Random access transmission systems have also appeared in recent years.

Introduced in the late 1950s as part of the audiovisual revolution, the audioguide has ridden the crest of the high-technology wave to become an adjunct to major exhibitions.

NUMEROUS CHOICES

Modern museums are defined as much by the objects they preserve as by the themes that link them and give them meaning. They are open and accessible to everyone: they welcome both scholars and casual visitors, along with more regular visitors, families, school groups, tourists, organized tours and so on. In order to build bridges between the museum and its public, it is essential to adopt clear communications objectives aimed at reconciling the demands of specialized knowledge with the numerous ways in which such knowledge is disseminated.

What seems obvious to exhibition designers is not necessarily evident to everyone. A choice of interpretive activities and written, visual or electronic media, such as the audioguide, make it possible to organize visits tailored to individuals and groups, whose diversity in terms of their origins, education and expectations is the only common denominator.

Unlike guided tours offered at set times and group visits that must be reserved in advance, a museum visit with an audioguide, which is available at all times, is suited to individuals who, by reason of circumstance or choice, are not interested in group activities. Moreover, the presence of the audioguide in no way impinges upon the exhibition space. While teaching media are often perceived as a necessary evil in art museums, where the need persists for visitors to be alone to contemplate the works on display, the audioguide, which encourages individual contemplation, is an acceptable solution.

THE APPROACH

The audioguide specifies the context of the exhibition by indicating angles of approach or aspects that the presentation emphasizes. These angles must be established even before the text is written.

The method frequently used at The Montreal Museum of Fine Arts consists in developing the synopsis of the audioguide by taking visitors' questions or comments noted during visits or animation activities and adapting them to a given content. The social and historical context and artistic movements will be mentioned. Elements of the artists' lives that facilitate an understanding of the artistic process will be described. A discussion of objects or art works will provide information on their use and origin, or technical details on their production.

COLLAGE OR DÉCOUPAGE

Like any other teaching medium, the audioguide directly reflects the exhibition text, whether it summarizes or emphasizes certain aspects of it. While the audioguide often has its source in a catalogue, it has its own particular requirements regarding visual references and spatial division. Unlike published texts that contain the necessary illustrations, the audioguide, which is designed to be heard, cannot accommodate visual references other than those that are immediately visible to the visitor. An assemblage of catalogue excerpts supported by illustrations that are not included in the exhibition would not constitute an acceptable audioguide text.

Moreover, because visitors move about in a given space while listening to the audioguide, the content must take into account the arrangement of the exhibition space and include, without making the text more cumbersome, the necessary instructions to move from one spot to the next. Using a cassette tape involves the assumption that the information is gradually distributed throughout the itinerary in a rational manner. However, in the case of random access systems, where there is no predetermined order, each block of information must be complete and independent.

Regardless of the electronic technique used, the audioguide must be adapted to the itinerary logically and coherently, through meticulous scripting. Before the text is written, it is important to mark off a secondary itinerary within the general exhibition itinerary, which will determine the works or groups of works on which comments will be made. All available information must be assembled, i.e. catalogues and background texts, photographs and colour slides of the works, and the complete, final hanging plan.

"...ON YOUR LEFT"

Instructions about the itinerary and the location of art works must be kept to a minimum. Some instructions, such as "on your right" or "on your left" are ambiguous because a visitor's exact position while listening to the audioguide can never be taken for granted. It is better to relate spatial indications to fixed visual elements, which should be as visible as possible. The best way to pinpoint the art works described in the commentary is to mark them with symbols or special numbering. Often, more than one person will be standing in front of a given work. It is essential that the markers indicating the works covered by the audioguide be sufficiently large and positioned so that they are clearly visible. Ideally, the numbering should be part of the design of the exhibition.

It must not be forgotten that the choice of works covered in the commentary can facilitate or, to the contrary, impede the movement of visitors. To avoid bottlenecks, too many comments should not be concentrated in a given sector, especially when the art works are small or the items are displayed in an exhibit case. Moreover, it is wise to avoid selecting works that are located close to other sources of information, such as videos or display panels.

LENGTH AND INTERVALS

The length of an audioguide visit is neither proportional to the scope of the exhibition nor limited to the capacity of the tape cassette. On the contrary, it is museum visitors who decide how much time they will devote to listening and adapt it to their own needs. Most playback devices can be stopped and started at will and rewound. Some pauses, needed to enable visitors to move on to the next point, which is denoted by a predetermined visible marker, are indicated by an audible cue. These stops dictated by the itinerary must not be confused with reading pauses, which, like intonation, modulate the text by letting it "breathe".

A TIGHT SCHEDULE

Everyone involved in mounting an exhibition must collaborate on the production of the audioguide, as it is almost impossible to alter the presentation of the exhibition once the text has been recorded, at least as regards the works selected along the itinerary. While specialized firms can execute all of the steps in the production of an audioguide, it is usually much simpler to ask museum staff to design, write and record the script. Collaboration among curators, educators and exhibition designers is advisable. Museum staff are familiar with internal work methods, and it is easier for them to establish a realistic, flexible timetable. Although the planning of an audioguide is important, it must not be subject to a standardized procedure. Too many unknowns come into play, especially when an exhibition is mounted in collaboration with foreign museums.

"FINDING THE RIGHT WORDS..."

Even though the audioguide is used above all by lay persons, it is not necessary to trivialize the language used. It is better to briefly explain a technical term or elaborate on information already presented. The golden rule of education, which consists of moving from the known to the unknown, from the concrete to the abstract, from the simple to the complex, also applies to the writing of an audioguide script. Because the text is heard and not read, it is preferable to use short sentences and avoid departures from normal word order and nested subordinate clauses.

POLISHING THE TEXT IS A MUST

The text is intended to be heard, not read, and it must be clear and also euphonious. It should be properly revised, translated if need be, and annotated with indications on the pronunciation of foreign names or terms. Experience shows that professional actors are often very good judges of the quality of the texts they are asked to read. Their recommendations and questions may lead to last-minute alterations.

A professional reader should be used, bearing in mind the close sensory contact established through the ear. Male or female? Beware of stereotypes: a man's voice is not necessarily authoritarian, or a woman's voice more seductive. The qualities of a good reading – intelligence, humour or solemnity, depending on the subject – are first and foremost a question of experience, not the sex of the reader.

TECHNICAL CONSIDERATIONS AND FINANCIAL CONSEQUENCES

Audiotapes can be played on portable cassette tape players of the Walkman® type, or on players designed for prolonged, intensive use. Portable tape players are inexpensive but are prone to break down. Museums looking for the appropriate equipment can take advantage of special services offered by companies under agreements that cover initial costs, revenue-sharing and the exact nature of the services, e.g. installation of display shelves on which the players and cassettes are stored, recharging of batteries and equipment maintenance.

QUIET, TAPING IN PROGRESS!

To obtain the best sound quality, a 45-minute cassette is recommended. Aside from a brief introduction, the text should not run for more than 40 minutes.

In order to ensure a flawless master tape, the recording must be done in a professional studio with the assistance of a sound technician and a studio manager. The recording can be made without editing if it is done in small segments several minutes long, separated by an imperceptible pause in the voice. Once the segment is recorded, it should be verified immediately. The slightest error in reading or the smallest noise, such as the rustling of paper, should be eliminated by rerecording the text, starting at the previous pause.

When the recordings are made abroad, it is advisable to have the work done in a local studio, in the presence of people familiar with both the exhibition and the text.

RANDOM ACCESS SYSTEMS

Other sound systems are available, in particular infrared sound transmission and computer-based transmission in which the sound is transmitted by a central modulator to predetermined transmission zones. Visitors can obtain selective information using different types of receivers and listening devices. Unlike the audiotape, which presents a sequential itinerary, these techniques are called random access systems. Their main advantage is that it is possible to present several programs simultaneously from the same transmitter and alter portions of the content without re-recording the entire text. The need to incorporate the components of the system into the architectural environment, transmission problems, lost signals, background noise and the discomfort to users of some headsets (which require the wearing of hygienic ear pads) are all factors that continue to limit the use of such devices to some extent, although it is only a question of time before they gain widespread favour.

*

To conclude, the preparation of an audioguide, like any other teaching medium, centres on the problem of specialized information as opposed to popularization. It would be a simplistic mistake to limit the audioguide text to a patchwork of catalogue excerpts or texts originally intended to be read. The audioguide, the information handout and the display panel are not interchangeable tools. They are designed for different purposes and, consequently, demand individual treatment. In the case of the audioguide, the writing must be more sound-oriented than visual.

*

Bibliography

Goodes, D. "Qualified Democratization: the Museum Audioguide", *The Journal of Canadian Art History*, Vol. 14, No. 2, 1991, pp. 50-73.

Greenberg, R. "The Acoustic Eye", *Parachute*, 45, March-April 1987, pp. 106-108.

Howze, W. "Audio Tours, Slide Shows, Video and Computers" in Berry, N.; Mayer, S., editors. *Museum Education: History, Theory and Practice*. Reston, VA: National Art Education Association, 1989.

Nadeau, M. "L'Audioguide, un instrument de concertation et d'éducation", *Muse*, Vol. 7, No. 2, 1989, p. 33.

Roth, E. "Audio Tours: Next Best Thing to a Personal Guide", *Museum News*, Vol. 70, November-December 1991, pp. 72-73.

Taylor, P. "A Vox on You", *Manhattan Inc.*, October 1986, p. 195.

PART 2

PRACTICAL
CONSIDERATIONS

CHAPTER 4

WRITING

Andrée Blais

Writing, a Critical Process

This essay marks the end of the theoretical section of this book and the beginning of the practical. It reviews the tasks involved in the writing and displaying of exhibition texts, summarizes the main stages of production and provides a checklist of the essential points. The author presents an overview of the work involved by looking at three basic points: when to start, where to start and who to call on. There are three main steps in drafting the texts: the first consists in preparing an outline of the texts and planning the graphic design. The second involves the actual writing of the texts. Once the form and content of the preliminary version have been checked the final version is prepared, then checked from a technical and linguistic point of view. Publication, the third and final phase, includes the preliminary page layout, proofreading, the preparation of camera-ready material and printing. The subsequent essays examine some of these stages in greater detail, zeroing in on the writing and graphic presentation of texts and highlighting the key factors that ensure their effectiveness.

Writing, a Critical Process

Andrée Blais

Project Manager and Production
Assistant, Exhibition Services,
Musée de la civilisation,
Québec City

The texts we read at an exhibition are the result of many stages of elaborate preparation. An analysis of their production is particularly useful as it can provide guidelines for the writing of exhibition texts.

The overview of the writing process described in this essay is based on interviews with three museum professionals: Marie-Claude Dion, former Director of Museology, Groupe Média Science de Montréal, now Project Manager at Métamorphose, Claude Benoît Inc.; Sylvie Dufresne, Director, Research, Conservation and Outreach, Pointe-à-Callière, Musée d'archéologie et d'histoire de Montréal; and Cécile Ouellet, Project Manager, Exhibition Services, Musée de la civilisation.[1] This consultation and collaboration process provided insight into different methods and made it possible to determine the main points they share, which are described here and presented in the form of a checklist.

PRE-PLANNING PHASE

Text planning is always preceded by research and concept development. The concept can take on different forms, depending on the institution concerned, e.g. orientation, preliminary scenario. It is precisely at the

---

1. Interviews with Marie-Claude Dion and Sylvie Dufresne were conducted with the participation of Louise Boucher, Locus Loisirs et Culture.

concept stage that both the content and the communication strategy are determined. Numerous choices must be made and reflected in functional and conceptual guidelines. These choices include:

- the subject of the exhibition, or unifying thread
- communication objectives
- the theme and sub-themes
- target audiences
- the treatment and means of communication (including the text).

Thus, the development of the exhibition concept already provides guidelines, according to which museum officials will either seek an outside writer or produce the texts themselves. For example, the type of audience targeted – the general public, specialists, a specific age group or visitors from two different language groups – will directly affect the choice of writer and the editorial approach.

PLANNING PHASE

Editorial planning

WHEN TO START: Editorial planning begins once the research has been conducted and the exhibition concept developed. Ideally, a plan should be drawn up which combines, balances and rounds out the theoretical, strategic and technical data.

WHERE TO START: Shaping the editorial plan requires an analysis of the objectives established at the outset and the findings of the research carried out. It is essential to assess the information produced by the research (quantity, gaps and so on), and carefully determine whether a written text or a spoken document is best suited to transmitting the message.

It is at this stage that the typology of the texts, which will enable the public to understand the exhibition program and the physical division of the space, must be established. Because of the unique nature of each exhibition, it is impossible to create a theoretical model applicable to all exhibitions. The typology must be carefully designed for each project in

194

order to reveal its unique character and the hierarchical organization of its content. Once the typology has been developed, it should adequately reflect the exhibition theme. In this respect, the typology acts as a functional system that facilitates the reading and assimilation of messages throughout the exhibition itinerary. For example, the introductory texts in each exhibition area should be written in a uniform style and contain a similar level of information. They should also adopt a similar structure and be placed in similar, strategic locations in the exhibition space. The designer establishes the role and objective of each text in the overall plan.

It is also at this stage that any formative evaluation of the exhibition texts can be planned.

WHO TO CALL ON: It is essential to decide at the outset who will write the exhibition texts, i.e. a member of the in-house team, a specialist from the firm producing the exhibition materials or a professional writer. Outside resources must be sought according to the communication objectives and the tone of the texts. It is advisable to screen applicants by means of a "writing test". Applicants cannot be assessed strictly on the basis of a curriculum vitæ and portfolio. The finished work they present does not necessarily reveal the supervision received from a project manager or the editing carried out by a reviser. Once the writer has been chosen, the exhibition director must provide an editorial plan that will serve as a framework for the writing of all texts.

SAMPLE TYPOLOGY			
TYPE OF TEXT	GENERAL OBJECTIVE	SPECIFIC OBJECTIVE	FORM OF TEXT
General	Make the visitor feel	Reveal the atmosphere: establish the psychological and physical context	General introductory text
		Show what prevailed in the thematic development	Area text
Conceptual	Make the visitor understand	Communicate more abstract or conceptual information	Theme text
		Express the logical links in the argumentation or the story line	
		Create a unifying thread	
Specific	Make the visitor aware	Communicate concrete, specific information (core of content)	Sub-theme text
			Vignettes
Illustrative	Make the visitor see and know	Transmit precise information that links what the visitor sees and reads	Labels (simple or grouped)
		Reduce the polysemy of the object or the image by linking it to the theme	Legends

Planning the graphic work

WHEN TO START: The graphic concept of the exhibition is usually determined before the actual writing of the texts begins, although it can be decided later on. It is preferable to begin planning the graphic concept once the editorial plan has been finalized, so that it is an integral part of the planning process.

WHERE TO START: It is advisable to consider the type of text support adopted, e.g. audio, panels, the manner in which the supports will be arranged along the exhibition itinerary. Consideration should also be given to the placement of the texts on the supports and the printing processes. These considerations must result in the development of a visual system, based on conventions, that structures the text and organizes the space.

A final proposal for the graphic presentation of each type of text must then be agreed upon according to the hierarchical organization of the content (microtypography and page layout). In other words, the typography and the arrangement of the scriptovisual texts must be determined according to reading level, register, language and editorial decisions.

WHO TO CALL ON: The graphic design work should be carried out by a specialist, who may be sought through a call for tenders in the event that the firm producing the exhibition materials does not employ a graphic artist. However, if the scope of the project does not warrant employing specialists, exhibition officials should be able to perform the work and ensure that the finished product is appropriate in light of the typology of the texts.

SUMMARY OF THE PLANNING PHASE

- Editorial planning begins after the exhibition concept has been developed
- Development of the editorial plan: choice of the text support, creation of the typology and definition of the objectives and function of each text
- Choice of the writer
- Planning of graphic work after the editorial plan has been adopted
- Choice of the supports used, the placement of the text on the supports and the arrangement of the supports along the exhibition itinerary (displaying of the text)
- Design of a graphic grid (microtypography and page layout)
- Choice of a graphic designer

WRITING PHASE

Preparing the preliminary texts

When to start: The preliminary writing can begin once the overall content of the exhibition has been established (research has been carried out, artifacts selected, iconography determined, scenario established, audiovisual material selected, and so on), i.e. during the production phase.

WHERE TO START: The content must be rigorously analyzed and organized in relation to other means of communication to avoid unnecessary repetition and carefully link what will be read, seen and heard. Once the content has been established, the appropriate style, tone, syntax and so on can be determined.

There are no hard and fast rules governing the writing of labels. It is, however, important to adopt a procedure and adhere to it. Label writing frequently differs from one exhibition to another, even within a given institution. In the absence of an established procedure, each exhibition director or curator is obliged to create one, thereby leading to an incredible lack of uniformity. Here are some sample labels, taken from the exhibition entitled *So Goes the City*, mounted by the Musée de la civilisation and presented at Marché Bonsecours in Montréal in the summer of 1992. These samples could be used to develop a procedure.

SAMPLE 1: OBJECT LABEL	
Identification of the object	**Globe by Matteus Greuter**
Materials	Papier-mâché, wood
Date	1632
Collection	Collection of the Société historique du Lac Saint-Louis de Montréal
Lender	David M. Stewart Museum
Identification No.	68-8-1

SAMPLE 2: ART WORK LABEL	
Identification of the art work	***Montréal, vue de la montagne***
Artist	F.X.A. Rapin (1868-1901)
Material	Oil on sized canvas
Date	Late 19th century
Lender	Musée du Château de Ramezay
Identification No.	988.20

SAMPLE 3: OBJECT LABEL	
Identification	**Model of the Dorchester locomotive**
Scale	One-half, built by Raoul Fortin
Remark	The first locomotive in Canada, the Dorchester was built in England by Robert Stephenson in 1836. It belonged to the Champlain and Saint Lawrence Railroad, which built the first railroad in Canada.
Date	1979
Lender	Musée régional du Haut-Richelieu

It is not necessary to include all these headings or to use them in this particular order. It is important, however, to bear in mind that they should not appear on the labels. Typographic marks such as italics boldface and the typeface must be chosen according to need, then rigorously applied so as to create a coherent reading system.

WHO TO CALL ON: The preliminary writing can be done either by a member of the in-house team – the person responsible for the project or the research – or by a writer who would assume the entire task from the first draft to the final copy. The initial draft could be prepared in-house then submitted to an outside writer for completion.

In the event that the writing is assigned in whole or in part to a subcontractor, the latter should be given all the information necessary to do the work, namely the editorial plan clearly describing the typology, and the role and function of each text.

WHICH VALIDATION MEASURES TO USE: After the preliminary texts are drafted, it is important to conduct an initial validation to ensure that the content is adequately communicated and coherent. Has the right tone been used? Is the average length of the texts satisfactory? Are the ideas well organized and reading levels clear? Are titles and headings informative and eye-catching? It is essential to examine all these factors, as they affect the readability of the text.

One or more members of the project team can carry out this careful first reading of the texts; an expert on the content, i.e. the research, does not necessarily have to be called in at this point. If need be, a list of instructions or recommendations can be drawn up for the writer.

PREPARING THE FINAL TEXTS

FOLLOW-UP: If the writing of the exhibition text is assigned to someone outside the museum, it is important to check the progress of the work regularly to ensure compliance with the instructions, the desired style and the timetable stipulated.

BALANCE: After corrections are made in light of the initial validation, it is essential to visualize the entire exhibition (floor plan, elevation, model) to check its overall balance and ensure that the communication objectives are being achieved. This stage makes it possible to measure the amount of text needed and to examine the question of its balanced distribution. Different criteria can be used in the analysis: redundancy, clarity, total reading time, space required, and so on. In short, it is essential to ensure the coherence of the messages as they relate to the overall content and the exhibition space.

TECHNICAL VALIDATION: The technical validation of the content is carried out on the revised version of the texts and is performed by the research manager and team.

READER VALIDATION: Ideally, you should find a reader, or a group of readers representing a cross-section of the museum's visitors. An excellent way to check whether the objectives have been achieved is to ask someone who was not involved in writing the texts to read them. A reader examining the texts with a fresh eye can ensure that they are interesting. If the reader fails to comprehend the general intent, a rewrite may be in order.

The translation of the texts, if need be, must be planned at this stage. Moreover, if the writer is not part of the project team, the texts must be submitted to the project manager after reader validation.

LINGUISTIC REVISION: Once the final version of the texts has been completed, it is time for a language specialist to examine them. The reviser's work ranges from the simple correction of spelling mistakes to reformulation and depends on the needs and goals of the exhibition director.

SUMMARY OF THE WRITING PHASE

- Preliminary writing begins once the overall content of the exhibition has been established
- The content is carefully analyzed and organized in relation to other means of communication
- An initial validation of the texts is carried out
- Writing of the final version of the texts begins
- A team member verifies the overall balance of the texts and ensures that communication objectives are being achieved
- Technical validation
- Reader validation
- Translation, if need be
- Linguistic revision

In the event that the texts are translated, in this case into French, the French version should be verified by a French-speaking expert to avoid shifts of meaning or awkward formulations, which could affect the readability and intelligibility of the message.

PUBLISHING PHASE

Prepress activities

WHEN TO START: Once the linguistic revision has been completed, the texts can be submitted to the graphic artist or to the member of the graphic design team.

WHERE TO START: The final layout of the scriptovisual areas (arrangement of headings, texts, illustrations and other graphic elements) can now be determined. Printing instructions can also be formulated.

If the graphic work is performed by an outside firm, the final layout should be submitted to the project manager for approval.

Proofreading

WHEN TO START: Once the final layout has been approved, the graphic artist can print out each page of text, which can then be proofread.

WHERE TO START: First identify mistakes. Locate misprints, check the spelling of place names and proper names, and look for other anomalies.

Do not overlook titles, headings and sources. These text snippets, which are known by heart and read superficially, often contain unfortunate typographical errors. This reading will also make it possible to check the accuracy of the sources cited for the items displayed, iconography and so on.

Once any errors have been noted, the graphic artist makes the necessary corrections, then prepares the camera-ready material.

If the graphic concept calls for panels made up of units of photocopied text, the final texts are now assembled, otherwise the following steps need to be taken.

WHO TO CALL ON: The project manager is responsible for this last check, along with the other members of the team, depending on their areas of responsibility.

Camera-ready material

The person responsible for graphic design prepares camera-ready material. One final check is necessary. Because of the material used for the blueprints, this check is usually carried out in the graphic design studio.

Printing

The person responsible for graphic design then sends the material to the printer. This marks the final phase of the production of exhibition texts.

SUMMARY OF THE PUBLISHING PHASE
• Texts are submitted to the graphic artist once the linguistic revision has been completed
• Final layout is determined
• Directions concerning printing are formulated
• Final graphic design is validated
• Proofreading begins as soon as the texts are printed
• Second-to-last general check
• Graphic designer prepares camera-ready material
• Final proofreading of the blueprints
• Printing

*

The writing and printing processes described above may differ appreciably depending on the needs and experience of the individuals mounting the exhibition. It is important to establish procedures based on the practices of your particular institution.

*

Summary   Hélène Baños

Writing Exhibition Texts

The text is a point of contact between visitors and the exhibition and it must be accessible to most of them. As a result, the exhibition text must be readable and intelligible, two fundamental aspects that the author seeks to define while proposing guidelines for the writer. Concision, precision and clarity are criteria that the writer must always keep in mind. The writer's goal is to communicate the essential information in simple but correct language that is within the grasp of the general public, and able to arouse their interest. The author proposes a number of ways to achieve this goal: simple syntax, appropriate punctuation, common vocabulary, and so on. The use of such straight-forward language helps visitors remember the content and affects reading speed. What is read quickly is better retained. Thus the importance of choosing precise, predictable words and using polysemous words and repetition sparingly. All these factors combined contribute to the text's readability and, as a result, its intelligibility, which depends not only on linguistic standards, but also on the semantic content and the organization of ideas. The key to writing exhibition texts lies in achieving simplicity and clarity. The following essay, by Laurent Marquart, goes on to examine different methods of presenting exhibition texts.

Writing Exhibition Texts

Hélène Baños

Lecturer, Department of
Linguistics and Translation,
Université de Montréal, Writer
and Translator

The principles of text writing examined in this essay are not specific to exhibition texts. They apply to any form of writing intended for a wide audience.

One of the main constraints of exhibition text writing is that the message must be understood by as many people as possible. It is thus essential to use a simple, but not simplistic, writing style in order to reach visitors, regardless of their knowledge.

Readability is imperative as the exhibition text is a point of contact between the visitor and the exhibition. If no contact is made, the message cannot be transmitted. Intelligibility is also essential as it helps the visitor retain the message. The information presented must be complete, concise and coherent in order to be accessible.

If these criteria are satisfied, the exhibition text can potentially arouse or sustain the visitor's interest. However, the visitor's background is a variable that affects interest. This is a fact that the writer must constantly bear in mind.

The extent to which a text is accessible depends by and large on its readability and intelligibility, which in turn depend on the form and content.

READABILITY AND INTELLIGIBILITY OF TEXTS

> Readable: "**1**. Capable of being read, legible. **2**. Capable of being read with pleasure or interest. Usu. Of literary works: Agreeable or attractive in style. Hence **Readability**.[1]
>
> Intelligible: "**2**. Capable of being understood; comprehensible [...]. Hence **Intelligibility** [...].[2]

The effective organization of exhibition texts is governed by three criteria: concision, precision and clarity.

Concision

Because optimal *readability* must be reconciled with space limitations, the exhibition must convey ideas that are complete, but distilled to their essence.

Precision

Exercising care in the choice of vocabulary units can ensure both concision and *clarity*, as the English language has the means to express complex ideas in simple terms.

Clarity

The content must be condensed, yet understood by the greatest possible number of visitors whose interest the museum wishes to capture. The *intelligibility and readability* of a text depend on the clarity of the message. Clarity can make a text easier to understand, thus potentially interesting, and easier to retain.

Level of language

It is necessary to use general language in most cases to facilitate reading and attract the attention of the entire spectrum of visitors. Readability and intelligibility are thus improved. However, it is inappropriate to use

---

1. *The Shorter Oxford English Dictionary on Historical Principles* (Oxford: Oxford University Press, 1978).
2. *Id.*

familiar language. While it may suit some visitors, it could ultimately irritate others. It is preferable to opt for a level of language or register that is neither too familiar nor so elevated that it becomes abstruse. Ideally, the text should use simple vocabulary and syntax and convey optimal information that can be understood by the majority of visitors.

Familiar or colloquial language refers to any structure, form or expression that is commonly used in everyday conversation but not used in written texts, which call for slightly more formal language. We do not express ourselves in writing as we do in ordinary speech, unless we are seeking to create a stylistic effect.

Sentences such as *to have a bone to pick with* ➙ *to have an unpleasant matter to settle with someone; pick up the tab* ➙ *to pay for something, e.g. a meal, an entertainment; pick up* ➙ *to meet casually* are unquestionably expressive, but they belong to spoken language and, in some instances, their use has become limited to a specific region. These expressions, which can be very colourful, should be used with discernment bearing in mind their intended audience.

Usage can create the standard. For example, some people feel that hindclipping, the deletion of one or more syllables at the end of a word is best avoided because it can ultimately create confusion and give rise to familiar language. However, other people maintain that certain words shortened by this process, such as *cinematograph* to mean *cinema*, are so firmly established in the language that they have made the original term (in this instance, *cinematograph*) obsolete. In this case, as in many others, use has created the norm. The trick for the writer is to achieve the appropriate level of language, which is based on linguistic standards, as prescribed in traditional grammars and dictionaries, and on general usage.

READABILITY

Richaudeau's research on readability shows that all readers, whether fast or slow, read a text word by word as opposed to letter by letter, and that words thus take on an ideographical value (see "The Reading Process in Chapter 2). The result is a more efficient reading of the text.

Elements of Richaudeau's theory on the function of the short-term memory in the reading process can be used to propose a method of writing exhibition texts. Moreover, Richaudeau's findings can be used as a reference point with respect to the organization of material. They can be used to make a text easier to decipher. The fact remains, however, that the exhibition text is intended for a group of people whose linguistic and extralinguistic knowledge and thus ability to decipher a text, vary.

READABILITY CRITERIA

Deciphering word by word

Richaudeau's work reveals that an individual reads a text on a word-by-word basis. However, the unit of readability is not a single word, but a series of words that bear sufficient semantic features to convey a message. This unit is simply a *phrase*.

Language structures

Richaudeau makes a distinction between lexical units with a high semantic content, i.e. *vocabulary*, and those with low semantic content, i.e. *function words*. The former are better retained if they are placed at the beginning of a phrase. The latter, which are syntactically necessary, can then be anticipated. The two categories are essential to readability as they are complementary: the second acts as a framework for the first.

As a result, in an overall text, only the words not explicitly dictated by the syntax, i.e. function words, are chosen.

According to Noam Chomsky[3], the acquisition of human language depends on language universals that apply to all languages. They are inherent in the language faculty, which is itself a mental faculty. The brain possesses language structures or mechanisms that are innate. However, vocabulary is not innate, it is acquired and the size of our vocabulary is proportional to our experience: the more educated and cultivated we are, the broader our vocabulary will be.

---

3. Noam Chomsky, *Aspects de la théorie syntaxique* (Paris: Éditions du Seuil, 1971).

Linguistic screen

It is preferable that the structure of phrases be simple and free of any linguistic screen, which could affect legibility. Richaudeau defines "linguistic screen" as a series of words in a phrase that separates two linked units, such as subject and past participle in the following phrase:

> A shard of pottery, <u>extremely high in colour</u>, dated circa 100 BC.

The underlined portion creates a screen between the subject, *pottery*, and the rest of the phrase.

Linguistic screens can often be avoided; in this case, one word, placed before the subject, can be used instead of the screen:

> A <u>colourful</u> shard of pottery dated circa 100 BC.

Number of words

Depending on whether readers are slow or fast, cultured or uncultured, their short-term memory can retain between 8 and 16 words (Richaudeau does not dwell on the notion of "cultured" that he uses in his classification. See the table "Number of words per phrase". It should also be noted that the capacity of the auditory memory is 16 percent greater than that of the visual memory, regardless of the subject's reading speed. In other words, all visitors have a greater short-term memory capacity for what they hear, regardless of how fast they read. This detail is particularly important when the exhibition text is presented on audiotape.

The unit of readability is a phrase, which is defined as a sequence of grammatically linked words that imparts a meaning. The readability of this unit is increased by the following factors:

- The use of punctuation, if appropriate
- The placement of key words at the beginning of the phrase, which makes it easier to retain the message

- A more cultivated reader
- The use of short, common words
- The use of all the syntactically necessary items in the phrase
- The use of affirmative turns of phrase such as "that is why" and "thus", which favour predicative statements
- The absence of a linguistic screen in the sub-sentence
- A predictable choice of words.

These factors contribute to greater legibility, which in turn increases their retention in memory.

Affective, mechanical and mental factors make it possible to retain something in memory. The affective factor refers to the interest that must be aroused. The mechanical factor imprints in the memory what has been repeated several times. The mental factor relies on association, a mnemonic technique that facilitates retention in memory.

FACTORS AFFECTING MEMORY RETENTION		
AFFECTIVE FACTOR	MECHANICAL FACTOR	MENTAL FACTOR
Arouses interest	Facts imprinted in memory	Mental association of facts for the purpose of memory retention
Contact	Assimilation	Integration

The following table shows F. Richaudeau's findings on short-term memory retention.

NUMBER OF WORDS PER PHRASE		
	NUMBER OF WORDS RETAINED 100%	NUMBER OF WORDS RETAINED 85%
Slow reader		
– Moderately cultured	8	9
(*Reader's Digest*)		
Average reader		
– Fairly cultured	13	15
(specialized magazines)		
Very fast reader		
– Cultured	16	19
(scientific works)		

The readability of a word depends on how rapidly it is read, since theoretically, the faster a text is read the better it is retained. Reading speed, in turn, depends on the reader's knowledge. When readers come across words that are unfamiliar to them, their perception is automatically slowed. The length of a word and number of syllables also affect reading speed and retention of the message.

This theory points up the need for a universal formalism that is decipherable by all speakers of different languages. Richaudeau illustrates his remarks with the example of the Chinese, who speak 50 different dialects, while using a single written language made up of ideograms. Ideographic symbolization based on mathematical thinking of the sort used to express scientific concepts would be the ideal solution. However, this kind of abstract formalization is not inherent in the mode of communication we usually use.

In light of the foregoing discussion and the need for concision in exhibition texts, the choice of words is of the utmost importance and must be guided by the various points raised in this essay.

Choice of words

As we have just seen, the overall text may depend on the writer, who has the freedom to choose some of the words that make up the exhibition text. According to Richaudeau, the writer's choice is exercised with respect to *vocabulary*, which refers to all words that designate a concept, as opposed to *function words*, notably determiners such as *the*, which serve to qualify and have a lesser semantic value. However, Richaudeau seems to be forgetting the indirect information communicated by these particles. Indeed, the omission of these so-called formal elements would hinder reading.

Many linguists wonder whether it is possible to dissociate semantics from syntax. To illustrate the semantic content of function words, let us take the following example:

I saw *a* vase in the store window.
(Could be any vase, i.e. indefinite)
I saw *the* vase in the store window.
(One in particular of which both listener and speaker have previous knowledge)

Or take a preposition, for example:

I went *up* the hill.
versus
I went *over/around/down* the hill.

While the leeway accorded writers is limited, they have every reason to be concerned with the choice of words. They enjoy sufficient latitude to guide the reader within the framework chosen. Visitors will benefit from greater readability if the text is designed in such a way that it transmits complete information in the simplest possible manner.

Common words and neologisms

Generally speaking, scientific or technical jargon should be avoided although, in most instances, it is better to employ the appropriate terminology even if it is specialized and initially daunting, provided it is accompanied by a brief definition between dashes. The educational goal of the exhibition will still be attained: visitors will have access to condensed information. They will also have an opportunity to broaden their vocabulary by being exposed to new words and their meaning. The texts will read smoothly, and continue to be stimulating and thus sustain interest.

The writer would be well advised to focus on *common* words, which most people are familiar with. However, new terms are coined as advances take place in certain fields. Telecommunications is a prime example: five years ago, no one spoke of the *information highway* because it did not exist. Today, people are familiar with the term but do not necessarily know what it means.

It is therefore up to the writer to familiarize visitors with the appropriate terminology and the concepts to which it refers. Accordingly, all relatively specialized terms should be followed by a brief explanation so that visitors can fully understand them.

Co-occurring expressions

Aside from the items that make up the framework of the sentence, there are certain lexical items that are typically used together and are thus noteworthy for their predictability. Co-occurring expressions are made up of two or more lexical items, usually from different grammatical categories, which repeatedly appear in combination.

Habit is important in the case of co-occurring expressions. The items, e.g. verb-noun, adjective-noun and so on, have come to form a unit through accepted use.

Idiomatic forms

English, like other languages, uses idiomatic forms, i.e. expressions that are peculiar to the language, for example, mount a play/exhibition.

These are idiomatic forms and obviously set expressions. Every language has its particular idioms and the writer must be familiar with them.

Co-occurring expressions offer a degree of predictability in a text. According to Richaudeau, the more *predictable* words there are in a sentence, the easier it will be to retain.[4]

---

4. François Richaudeau, *Le Langage efficace* (Paris: Les nouvelles éditions Marabout, 1973).

In the following example, predictability is impaired by the use of an inadequate co-occurrent.

> "The gap between rich and poor has intensified
> here in Mexico."[5]

The meaning of this proposition taken on its own is confusing. Usually *gap* would occur with *widened*, if the gap has gotten bigger, or *narrowed*, if it has gotten smaller. The term "intensified" in the example above does not provide information on the situation. The context indicated that the economic situation was widening the gap between the two social groups. The meaning of "intensified" would be clearer and more explicit if it were expressed thus:

> The gap between rich and poor has widened here in Mexico.

This last example is much more intelligible and the reader does not have to stop and mull over the possible interpretations.

Polysemous expressions

Richaudeau points out that polysemous expressions – words with more than one meaning – are a valuable resource and should be used.

---

5. Comments by Carlos Herrera, Mexican economist, on *Le Match de la vie* (May 18, 1993 edition, broadcast on the TVA network).

EXAMPLE OF POLYSEMY

Pin

- A short piece of wire with a sharp point at one end and a round head at the other, used to fasten things together
- A piece of wood, metal, etc. having a similar use, such as a clothespin, hairpin, or hatpin
- An ornament, badge, or jewel fitted with a pin and a clasp
- A cylinder inserted into a hole as a fastener or anchoring device
- In golf, a pole with a small flag which marks the hole on a green
- A bottle-shaped wooden peg, used as a target in bowling.

However, it cannot be overemphasized that the writer should exercise caution and discernment in determining the extent to which the context allows for the use of polysemous terms – when they are heard, they become homonyms, e.g. *discreet* (careful and tactful in speech and action) and *discrete* (separate and distinct) – without creating ambiguity and causing confusion in the reader's or the listener's mind. The same recommendation concerning the writer's discernment applies to the choice of synonyms: true synonymy does not exist and account must be taken of the shades of meaning dictated by the context.

Redundancy

Unnecessary repetition can impair the *readability* and the *intelligibility* of a text. It can also make a text tedious and affect the reader's interest. According to Ducrot, since speaking to someone means demanding his attention, we can only speak legitimately to others about what is supposed to interest them.[6]

---

6. O. Ducrot, *Dire ou ne pas dire. Principes de sémantique linguistique*, "Savoir" collection (Paris: Hermann, 1980).

However, repetition can be necessary and useful, as Richaudeau points out.[7] All or part of a message can be repeated to avoid misunderstanding, especially in the case of didactic works. Repetition is also used in advertising. The same term is often repeated systematically to ensure that it is retained by the audience.

In the case of the exhibition text, the use of a technical or scientific term, followed by a brief definition in order to inform as many visitors as possible, is a useful form of repetition. Repetition of this type serves educational purposes and is not only necessary but indispensable.

Condensing technique

Condensing consists in eliminating unnecessary redundancy or repetition in a text, thus preserving a minimum number of words in order to enhance readability. In this way, the reader is brought directly into contact with the essence of the message. Condensing makes it possible to suppress linguistic screens that impair readability.

> The Carmelite then appeared as a queer fish. His striped coat meant he was rejected by ordinary people, who associated it with the jellaba of the <u>Muslim infidels</u>.[8] (20 words).

In order to maintain a high degree of readability, according to Richaudeau's method (see the table "Number of words per phrase"), the number of words in the last sentence must be condensed in the manner indicated below. The meaning of the sentence remains intact and its structure is simplified.

> Associating his striped coat with the Muslim jellaba, the people rejected him. (12 words)

---

7. François Richaudeau, *La Lisibilité* (Paris: Éditions Retz, 1976).
8. Label text from the *Drôles de zèbres* exhibition, Musée de la civilisation.

Even when the longer version of the sentence is preserved, the example contains a redundancy that must be eliminated, as there is an overlap between *infidels* and *Muslims*. The first term demands that the visitor possess a certain cultural referent. For this reason, it would be logical to eliminate it and keep the second word.

During the condensing process, sentences and phrases are shortened. However, the statement being made is strengthened as it achieves the density needed to sustain interest.

> On the basis of this information, it is possible to apply certain rules that bolster the readability, interest and retention of the message. (23 words)

> Certain rules based on this information can be used to bolster the readability, interest and retention of the message. (19 words)

There are many works that outline rules of writing and ways of reducing verbosity. These works rightly remind us that wordiness can be avoided through proper use of punctuation. The colon, for example, can replace more than one word in many instances. Irène de Buisseret[9] has proposed simple, effective methods of condensing text, which also eliminate linguistic screens. The following list provides a number of examples.

---

9. Irène de Buisseret, *Deux langues, six idiomes* (Ottawa: Carlton-Green Publishing Company Limited, 1975).

EXAMPLES OF CONDENSING	
VERBOSE FORMULATION	**SIMPLIFIED FORMULATION**
The dangers that may arise	Possible dangers
Monday of next week	Next Monday
Such a way of acting	This act
This text reads as follows	This text states
I drew his attention to the fact that	I informed him that
The measures that we are proposing to adopt	The proposed measures
This runs contrary to the law and to the facts	This contradicts the law and the facts

Generally speaking, it is preferable to keep the number of words in exhibition texts to a minimum. This will make them straighter to the point and more readable. It is the writer's responsibility to use all available means, including the devices discussed earlier such as co-occurrence, the use of common words, polysemy, didactic repetition and shortening, to sustain the visitor's attention and interest.

Sentence

An exhibition text is almost always concise. It is constructed using sentences that are linked or juxtaposed, depending on needs.

> **Sentence**: 3: *a grammatically self-contained unit consisting of a word or a syntactically related group of words that expresses an assertion, a question, a command, a wish, or an exclamation, that in writing usually begins with a capital letter and concludes with appropriate end punctuation, and that in speech is phonetically distinguished by various patterns of stress, pitch, and pauses.*[10]

It should be noted that François Richaudeau speaks of phrase, without specifying its grammatical nature, as a linguistic unit that imparts meaning. This unit includes from 8 to 20 words and can be

---

10. *Webster's Third New International Dictionary* (Springfield, MA: Merriam-Webster Inc. Publishers, 1981).

retained by the short-term memory of readers or listeners, depending on their knowledge.

Richaudeau maintains that readability has more to do with structure than length.[11] However, he concedes that the shorter the sentence is, the more likely its structure will be simple and correct.[12]

The latter observation is noteworthy in that a short sentence is usually simple. Two of the objectives sought are thus attained: because the sentence theoretically contains fewer words, its structure is more likely to be correct. Moreover, if the sentence is predicative, it will be even better assimilated by visitors. The predicative sentence, as described here, is intended to make an objective statement.

> The child is eating an apple.

In this sentence, a fact is stated without any other information. In an expressive sentence, unlike a predicative, the subject reveals his state of mind in relation to the fact stated. The objectivity in the predicative sentence is replaced by subjectivity in the expressive.

> I am angry that the child is eating an apple.

Readability depends on the use of well established rules. Such rules ensure the coherence of the message, and the transmittal of the meaning. To write (or speak) requires the systematic use of not only syntactical rules but of semantic and logical rules as well.[13]

Grammarians and linguists agree that the boundary between syntax and semantics is tenuous. If we blindly apply the rules of syntax as they are set forth in traditional grammars, i.e. the subject/verb/complement sequence, logical coherence is not guaranteed, as the following example clearly illustrates.

---

11. F. Richaudeau, *op. cit.*, p. 118.
12. *Id.*
13. F. Richaudeau, *La Lisibilité* (Paris: Éditions Retz, 1969), p. 112.

> The apple is eating the child.

Unless the context is surreal or supernatural, the sentence is meaningless. Everyone will agree that it is agrammatical.

While this example clearly illustrates the point, it does not reveal all of the problems that arise in accurately pinpointing the dividing line between syntax and semantics and the overlapping of the two. The sentence below provides an example that linguists cite frequently to illustrate the multiple interpretations of certain structures.

> The love of God is great.

Not only is this sentence well constructed syntactically, it is also semantically acceptable. The problem is that is can be read in two ways:

> God's love for us is great.
> Our love of God is great.

The reader has a choice of interpretation. The exhibition text can be conceived in such a way that it raises questions. Reading such a text cannot fail to be stimulating. However, it is not advisable to write turns of phrase that encompass two underlying interpretations as the reading is more likely to be slowed and the retention of the message jeopardized.

INTELLIGIBILITY *

To write an intelligible text calls for simplicity with respect to forms, words, and the application of grammatical, syntactical and stylistic rules in order to produce a clear, concise, precise statement. It is important to observe these three criteria scrupulously to achieve a legible, intelligible result.

---

* The term is defined in the section "Readability and intelligibility" at the beginning of this essay.

220

The intelligibility of an exhibition text depends above all on its readability. The easier it is to decipher, the more accessible it will be to visitors and, consequently the fuller the visitors' understanding of the exhibition will be. When the basic structure is simple, it is highly likely that visitors will grasp the exhibition's contents more fully and rapidly. Moreover, the exhibition will capture their interest.

In this respect, intelligibility goes far beyond the sentence level. It is part of the framework of the exhibition: the way in which the exhibition is structured determines the clarity of the text. Furthermore, the intelligibility of the text is attributable to a coherence that is both extrinsic (the text supports the exhibition in relation to the framework chosen) and intrinsic (the discourse is prepared using legible, concise structures that interweave according to a logic designed to ensure rapid comprehension).

The factors that contribute to intrinsic intelligibility fall under the linguistic standards that govern writing in general. While the writer respects the rules of syntax and grammar, some problems attributable to the overlapping relationship between syntax and semantics arise in the course of writing. They modify the scope of the text and, consequently, singularly complicate the reading of it. They impair readability and alter the visitor's interest and ability to retain the message.

Syntactical-semantic relationships

All writing is structured around syntax. However, the semantic value of each syntactical unit produces relationships that linguists define as syntactical-semantic relationships, as it is difficult to ascertain whether they fall under syntax or semantics because they are indissociable.

Some syntactical structures may be rudimentary, but they nonetheless harbour pitfalls for the writer. While they are syntactically correct and, as a result, legible in principle, these structures may impart a meaning that escapes the author's intention and, occasionally, attention.

Ambiguities

Ambiguities also result from overlapping in syntactical-semantic relationships. They, too, affect the semantic impact of the statement.

221

However, the grammatical correctness of the structure is no less valid. For example:

> This remarkable individual devoted his existence to the dissemination of an art that is now recognized the world over. His financial situation allowed him to do so.

The ambiguity in this statement results from the use of the pronominal form in the second sentence. (Allowed him) *to do so* can refer to two segments in the preceding sentence, i.e. *the dissemination of an art* or the recognition implicit in *that is now recognized the world over*. The nuance is not, it might be argued, very broad, as the dissemination of an art or the recognition of it are more or less the same. However, we must be certain that the *financial situation* of the individual in question reflects means that made possible the dissemination of this art the world over.

The last example illustrates a statement that raises questions, which are different from those that would enable visitors to delve deeper into the exhibition's theme, because of an ambiguous formulation. The text's readability is still valid because of the simplicity of the structures used, but its intelligibility has been jeopardized.

To summarize, the fewer pitfalls the visitor encounters in a text, the clearer the text is and, consequently, the more legible it is. The text's intelligibility is thus enhanced. The text arouses visitors' interest, attracts their attention and is more likely to be retained. The writer's objective has been achieved.

Paragraph

A paragraph is recognizable by its typographic presentation and the grouping of sentences that present an idea. However, each part maintains its coherence as it is conceived as an autonomous entity. An acceptable reading time is required to decipher the information in a paragraph. According to Desjardins and Jacobi,[14] as a result of a *fragmenting* process,

---

14. *Op. cit.*

visitors can choose what they want to read and the length of the passage they read.

In light of Richaudeau's criteria concerning readability, the ideal exhibition text should be constructed in paragraphs of three or four sentences, each of which contains not more than 16 words.

Most exhibition texts are presented in paragraph form. This means of organization shapes the text. Jean-Paul Simard[15] distinguishes two types of paragraphs, open and closed. However, both types of paragraph are self-contained and can be read as an autonomous unit or as part of a whole.

Open paragraph

The open paragraph satisfies the utilitarian criteria inherent in texts intended for the general public, rather than logical organization criteria. It appears in fragmented form. New lines are used without any set pattern, simply to enumerate particular points in the main idea. It is a valuable tool for popularizing a theme, transmitting a message, and attracting the attention of readers who are scarcely accustomed to reading. The following example illustrates this type of paragraph in the museum setting.

> "The poor man spends nothing as he has no money. While the rich man has a fortune in land or in livestock, he no longer has any money! The community organizes itself around an exchange of services. There is no waste and no refuse.
> Cow dung serves as a fuel.
> A bone becomes a bolt or a latch.
> Lumber used to build cottages is reused as many as three or four times."[16]

15. Jean-Paul Simard, *Guide du savoir-écrire* (Montréal: Les Éditions de l'homme, 1984).

16. Example of an exhibition text appearing in an article by Julie Desjardins and Daniel Jacobi, "Les étiquettes dans les musées et expositions scientifiques – Revue de la littérature et repérages linguistiques", *Publics & Musées*, No. 1, 1992.

Closed paragraph

The closed paragraph contains demonstration elements specific to the essay, informative text and description. The structure of this type of paragraph satisfies the needs of argumentative texts. It encapsulates the coherence of the logical argumentation of the idea being developed. Such an idea is found in the first sentence and imposes a logical order on subsequent sentences that is readily recognizable from a semantic stand-point as a result of the syntactical elements that ensure its development. The following example, drawn from an exhibition,[17] clearly illustrates this type of paragraph.

"A DUBIOUS UNIFORM"

The scandal of the Carmelites is the first historic evidence of the loathing of people in the Middle Ages for the striped motif. In 1254, Louis IX returned from the Crusades accompanied by some peculiar monks: the friars of Notre-Dame du Mont-Carmel.

Discreet and a member of an order with little power, the Carmelite appeared then as a queer fish. His striped coat meant he was rejected by ordinary people, who associated it with the jellaba of the Muslim infidels.

Insults and blows flew, but the proud monks clung to their stripes. Pope Alexander IV attempted to intervene, but in vain. It was only in 1287, following a bitter polemic, that the "striped friars" opted for a simple white cope.

Their long coat earned the Carmelites the nickname "striped friars".

Aspects of paragraph structuring

Certain syntactical units make possible the structuring of discourse. Inherent in their grammatical function is a semantic trait in that they

---

17. *Drôles de zèbres*, Musée de la civilisation, Québec City.

reflect a special link within the clause. These units include, among other things, conjunctions, conjunctive locutions, adverbs, coordinating and subordinating pronouns, and so on. In the following example, the structuring terms are the possessive adjective *his* and the pronouns that refer to the antecedent *Carmelite*. In this example, syntactical links contribute in several instances to structuring.

> "Discreet and a member of an order with little power, the Carmelite appeared then as a queer fish. His striped coat meant he was rejected by ordinary people, who associated it with the jellaba of the Muslim infidels."

Title

Most of the time, the title consists of a nominal group, i.e. a syntactical unit governed by a noun, e.g. "A dubious uniform", compared with a verb phrase, in which the verb dominates, e.g. "Sell immediately!", and encapsulates in few words the main idea of the text. The title should be:

- forceful, to arouse interest and encourage readers to read the text;
- succinct, i.e. not more than two to six words long as the exhibition text itself is not very long;
- evocative, i.e. the link between the title and the text must be obvious.

Usually, it is the text that suggests the title. Consequently, the title becomes clear once the writing has been completed.

To summarize, readability and intelligibility are the main criteria governing the writing of exhibition texts. They are the cornerstones of the exhibition text, without which the latter's role as an aid in interpretation and a source of information and entertainment may be impaired or even completely impeded. The key to attaining these objectives lies in syntactical-semantic relationships. When these conditions are met, the exhibition's objectives, i.e. to interest and inform visitors, capture their attention so that they retain the message and thus further spur their interest, are achieved.

Bibliography

Chomsky, Noam. *Aspects de la théorie syntaxique*. Paris: Éditions du Seuil, 1971, Presses universitaires de France, Paris.

Cressot, Marcel. *Le Style. Précis d'analyse stylistique*, 1991.

De Buisseret, Irène. *Deux langues, six idiomes*. Ottawa: Carlton-Green Publishing Company Limited, 1975.

Deguée-Bertrand, Chantal. *Exercices de réécriture – Syntaxe du français*, Montréal, author's draft, 1992.

Desjardins, J.; Jacobi, D. "Les étiquettes dans les musées et expositions scientifiques : revue de la littérature et repérages scientifiques", *Publics & Musées*, No. 1, 1992.

Ducrot, Oswald. *Dire et ne pas dire. Principes de sémantique linguistique*, "Savoir" collection. Paris: Hermann, 1980.

Dupré, P. *Encyclopédie du bon français dans l'usage contemporain*. Paris: Éditions de Trévise, 1972.

Grevisse, Maurice. *Le Bon Usage*. Paris-Gembloux: Duculot, Éditions du renouveau pédagogique, 1980.

Guiraud, Pierre. *La Syntaxe du français,* "Que sais-je?" collection. Paris: Presses universitaires de France, 1980.

Phal, André. "De la langue quotidienne à la langue des sciences et des techniques", *Le français dans le monde,* Paris, No. 61, December 1968.

Richaudeau, François. *Le Langage efficace.* Paris: Les nouvelles éditions Marabout, 1973.

_____. *La Lisibilité.* Paris: Éditions Retz, 1976.

_____. *La linguistique pragmatique.* Paris: Éditions Retz, 1981.

Simard, Jean-Paul. *Guide du savoir-écrire.* Montréal: Les Éditions de l'homme, 1984.

Yaguello, Marina. *Alice au pays du langage. Pour comprendre la linguistique.* Paris: Éditions du Seuil, 1981.

Sauvageot, Aurélien. *Français d'hier ou français de demain?,* "Langues en question" collection. Pairs: Éditions Fernand Nathan.

CHAPTER 5

SHOWING

Writing in Space

The optimal format of a text satisfies precise criteria that the author summarizes in two words: legibility and visibility. Before this result is achieved, it is essential, from the outset, to design a visual scenario geared to communication, in order to define the role that scriptovisual messages will play in the exhibition and establish their visual relationship to the objects exhibited and the setting. Not all messages are equally important, and it is essential to adopt from the start a hierarchical ranking of their location, typographic treatment and supports. The author indicates five categories of scriptovisual messages, ranging from macro-scale to micro-scale and including large-, medium- and small-scale messages. He discusses the main criteria that the designer must consider to emphasize the messages, i.e. the spatial positioning in relation to the visitor's eyes, the relationship between the eyes and the message with respect to reading distance, the scale of the message in relation to the spatial reading conditions, the medium of execution and, last but not least, creativity. The essay also looks at the choice of treatment, supports and lighting, all of which depend on the initial concept. The author concludes by stressing the importance of verifying the validity of conceptual choices through practical experimentation. Visitors' successful reception of the scriptovisual message will depend on the appropriateness of these choices, as Rock Anctil's essay on typographic treatment shows.

Writing in Space

Laurent Marquart

President, GSM Design,
Montréal

Talking about scriptovisual messages is like talking about a poor or occasionally embarrassing relation, one we are obliged to put up with.

This essay has the following objectives:

- to situate the treatment of scriptovisual messages at a level comparable to that of other components of museography;
- to establish basic rules for the design and execution of scriptovisual messages;
- to promote a creative attitude and a willingness to call into question the teaching of the past in order to create new ways of seeing and doing things in a more dynamic way that enables more effective transmission of scriptovisual messages.

To the foregoing objectives should be added the need to be as open-minded as possible and to maintain an overview, when designing a project, which allows for enlightened choices and the achievement of the best possible balance among the components of the exhibition.

The ability to examine a project in a broad perspective will enable museographers to completely rethink the relationships between scriptovisual messages and the other components of museography in a different context.

AMBIVALENCE AND CONTRADICTIONS INHERENT IN THE USE OF TEXT

To speak of text in conjunction with museum practice is like talking about vacations. The possibilities are virtually limitless in terms of places, activities, means and personal approach. And of course, to speak of the text in a museum is to admit from the outset that the subject is elusive.

For example, there have been exhibitions in which text was of inordinate importance and which have enjoyed considerable public acclaim, although everyone knows that reading a text in a museum is physically very tiring.

There have been exhibitions in which the lack of text frustrated visitors, who would have liked to know more about the subject. How many examples spring to mind of unimportant messages given pride of place and messages laden with fascinating information that were almost impossible to read?

In fact, the optimal text format satisfies precise criteria.

Broadly speaking, there is one unbreakable rule, in fact, a rule about rules: there is no unique and absolute solution, but there are rules that must be obeyed.

Moreover, the objective can be summed up in one word: legibility. The very mention of legibility immediately calls to mind visibility, without which legibility is unattainable. In principle, there is no magic formula, no limit to the imagination or to invention, but certain criteria must be respected. While compliance with these criteria can create constraints, it paradoxically paves the way for innovation and creativity.

THE ROLE OF SCRIPTOVISUAL MESSAGES IN THE EXHIBITION

The need to design a visual scenario geared to communication

Using your knowledge of the basic rules to know how best to break them

All too often, scriptovisual messages in an exhibition are relegated to the subsidiary role of providing secondary or tertiary information. Before we pass judgment on this situation, it should be noted that it often reflects a consistent, entirely justifiable conceptual approach.

However, it must be acknowledged that, in other instances, this subordinate role results from the compartmentalization of areas of specialization and from the absence of a broad perspective on the concept of the museum. Scriptovisual messages are treated rather like glorified legends and used at far below their real potential, akin to driving a Formula 1 race car at 50 km/h. It is essential to draw up an overall visual scenario geared to communication in order to accord each component of an exhibition its rightful place and ascertain the role it must play at any given time in the exhibition itinerary.

The relative importance of the scriptovisual message

From a practical standpoint, designing an overall visual scenario geared to communication means establishing in advance the relative importance of various scriptovisual messages in relation to the components of the exhibition. The weight accorded these messages and their treatment must be thought out clearly when the initial concept of the exhibition is developed. At this point, a number of conceptual guidelines will be adopted that will affect a whole range of detailed decisions that must be made as the project unfolds. For this reason, it is important to correctly develop the concept by taking into account the remarkable potential of scriptovisual messages to emphasize what needs to be emphasized.

In many ways, the macro-scale approach must be handled in the same way as the use of big billboards along highways. To attract attention and be read, a message must be strong, direct and unambiguous.

The Automobile exhibition, Musée de la civilisation, Québec City
(Photo: Pierre Soulard)

**Relationship and hierarchical ranking of scriptovisual messages
in a scriptovisual framework**

This requirement alone is insufficient. It is essential to decide on the visual relationship between a message and the three-dimensional elements of the decor, the objects, the artifacts and the dynamic or audiovisual components. Will the scriptovisual message be incorporated into a three-dimensional display item? Will it be a freestanding component? Should it contrast with its surroundings or act as a discreet support?

All of these questions and many others that must be broached at the beginning of a project clearly show that the communication of messages by means of typography must not be regarded as a minor element amid the array of communications tools available.

Importance of the text in a scripted itinerary

To show, without being dogmatic, that there is a need to look seriously at the transmission of messages by means of typography, we must ask an almost sacrilegious question: Is text really necessary?

The question can be asked in another way: What could be created to transmit the message without the help of a text?

While the question may seem banal, it must be acknowledged that text often serves as an easy solution, a quick fix that enables museum officials to have a clear conscience and maintain that they have done what is necessary to transmit the message to visitors. However, if visitors fail to read the text, then the content has not been transmitted. From this standpoint, the text is a very poor means of communication, because it is highly likely that some percentage of the visitors will not read it.

To meet the utopian challenge of mounting an exhibition without a text is in fact the most daunting communication criterion that can be undertaken because in that case the medium really does become the message.

Viewed from this perspective, text assumes a relative value and can be exploited to the utmost as a communications tool or, on the contrary, can virtually disappear or become very unobtrusive, given that other means are used to adequately communicate the exhibition's content.

Different levels of communication

The same sort of weighing carried out with other exhibition components must be performed within the specific domain of scriptovisual messages. Objectively speaking, not all messages have the same importance, nor are they necessarily aimed at the same kind of visitor.

Consequently, they must be weighted accordingly, with a view to effectively reaching as many visitors as possible.

Visitors seeking specialized, in-depth information will find such information, provided it is properly presented. Moreover, some members of the general public may suddenly discover a subject that fascinates them, and information must be presented in a way they can comprehend.

Early on in the planning process, it is important to establish a hierarchical ordering of scriptovisual messages corresponding to specific locations along the exhibition itinerary, weak points, varied, colourful typographical treatments and a wide array of supports.

It is all the more important to establish this structuring of the content at the outset because it will affect the writing of the texts. Failure to coordinate this precise, specialized task with the overall concept may mean that the writing is not geared to thematic or museum-related criteria, or that the length of the texts or the importance accorded them does not reflect the type of visitor and, consequently, the type of reading desired.

For the sake of simplicity, scriptovisual messages can be divided into five categories:

- macro-scale texts, which encompass all the exhibition zone titles, catch phrases or slogans that are read by all visitors;

- large-scale texts, which include all headings and subheadings, catch phrases or major slogans that facilitate understanding of the thematic or museum-related content and must be read by all visitors. This category can also include certain texts one or two paragraphs long whose scale will encourage the majority of visitors to read them;

- medium-scale texts, i.e. support texts such as subtitles or continuous text dealing with a broad topic or a specific exhibition item. The average length of texts in this category indicates that such texts can clearly not exceed four or five paragraphs, without becoming impossible to assimilate;

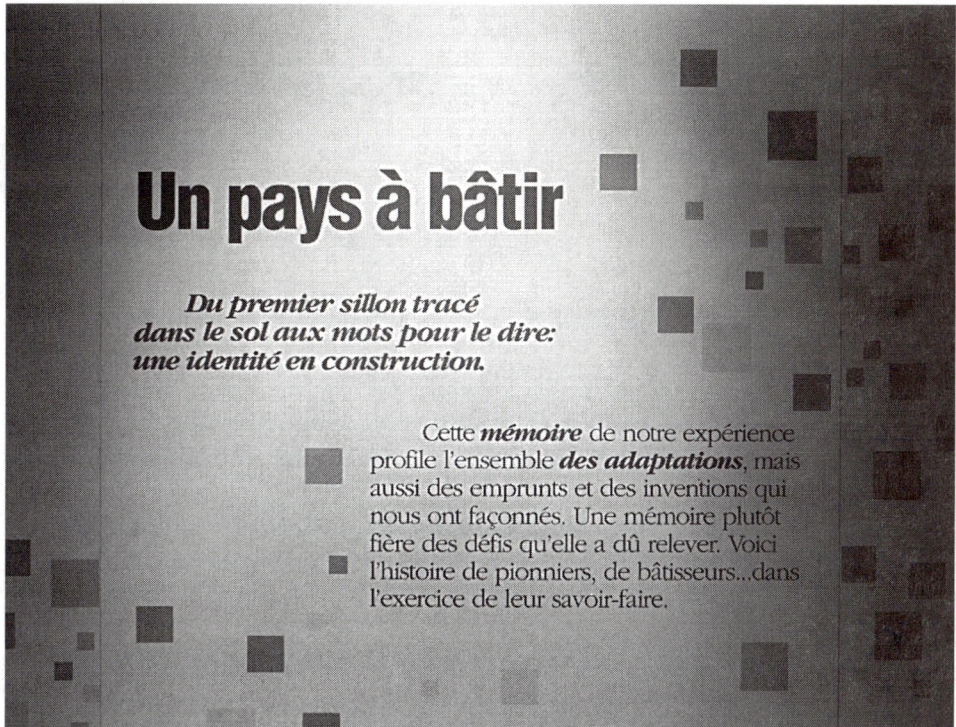

Memories exhibition, Musée de la civilisation, Québec City
(Photo: Pierre Soulard)

Large-scale scriptovisual message

- small-scale texts include titles, headings and texts that develop a topic and provide more specific or in-depth technical, thematic and descriptive information. This category should be approached cautiously: the length of the texts must be limited to make them accessible to as many visitors as possible. If, to the contrary, relatively long texts are presented, it should be done with full awareness that only visitors genuinely interested in the subject will take the time to read them;

- micro-scale texts include all small-scale texts that provide extremely specific information on a theme, subject or object.

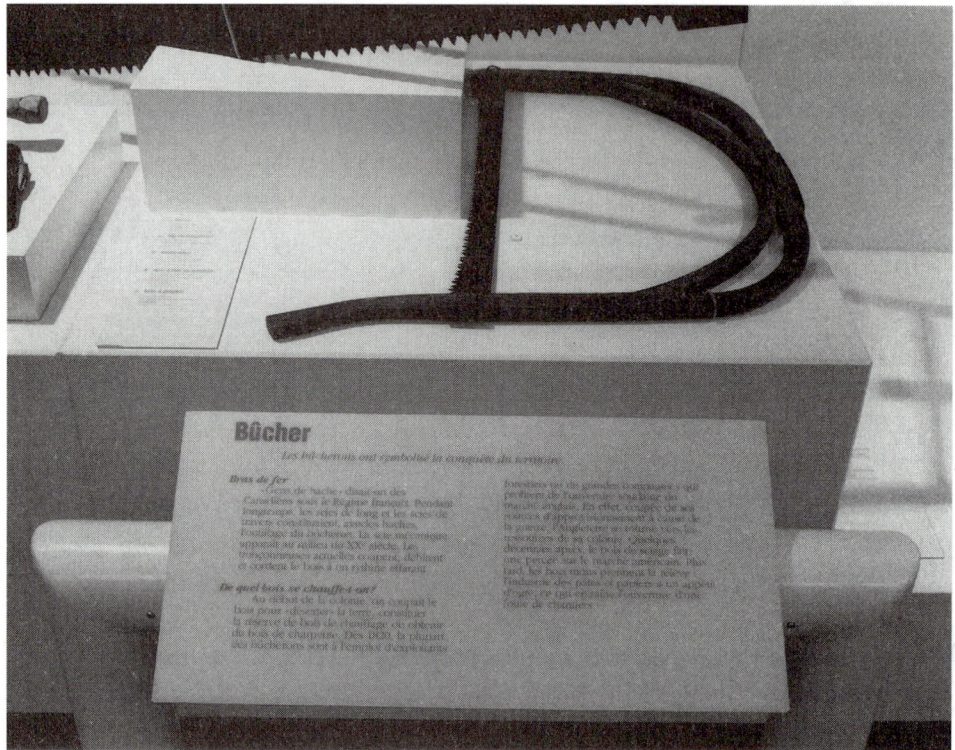

Memories exhibition, Musée de la civilisation, Québec City
(Photo: Pierre Soulard)

Small-scale scriptovisual message

It should be noted that a text classified as micro-scale will not necessarily be less frequently read than a larger-scale text. In some instances, the position of a text and its relationship to an object or a component of the exhibition cause a small-format text to have almost as much chance of being read as a large-scale one.

VISION, MATERIAL AND KNOWLEDGE

The scriptovisual message in space

First criterion:
The positioning of the scriptovisual message in space in relation to the visitor's eyes

The relationship between the visitor's eyes and a scriptovisual message positioned in an exhibition is entirely different from that between the reader's eyes and a page of a newspaper or magazine. The conceptual approach is radically different, given that the text is positioned in space, not on a two-dimensional page that remains a constant distance from the eyes of the reader.

Ideally, a scriptovisual message should fall within the visitor's normal field of vision, i.e. at eye level. However, this rule is impracticable because visitors are not all the same height. For this reason, the message should ideally be placed at different heights.

Like furniture design, exhibition design must from the outset take into account the same constraint, i.e., people come in different sizes, and a common denominator must be sought that satisfies the majority.

Working in an exhibition space means that each decision about the positioning of a scriptovisual message must be geared to a specific volume of space.

To simplify matters, we can say that the text should be located on a flat surface facing the visitor, between 1 m and 2 m in height. If a vertical surface roughly 1 m high is tilted downward, the relationship between the eye and the support surface is altered, to create a relationship that is just as suitable as the previous one.

In a pinch, the surface supporting the text could be positioned horizontally and visitors given an opportunity to look down at it. The visibility of the text would still be entirely acceptable.

The text could also be placed above the visitors' heads, although the greater the effort to raise the head, the harder it is to read. Consequently, the scriptovisual message should be placed clearly above the line of vision only in exceptional circumstances, in order to create a special effect.

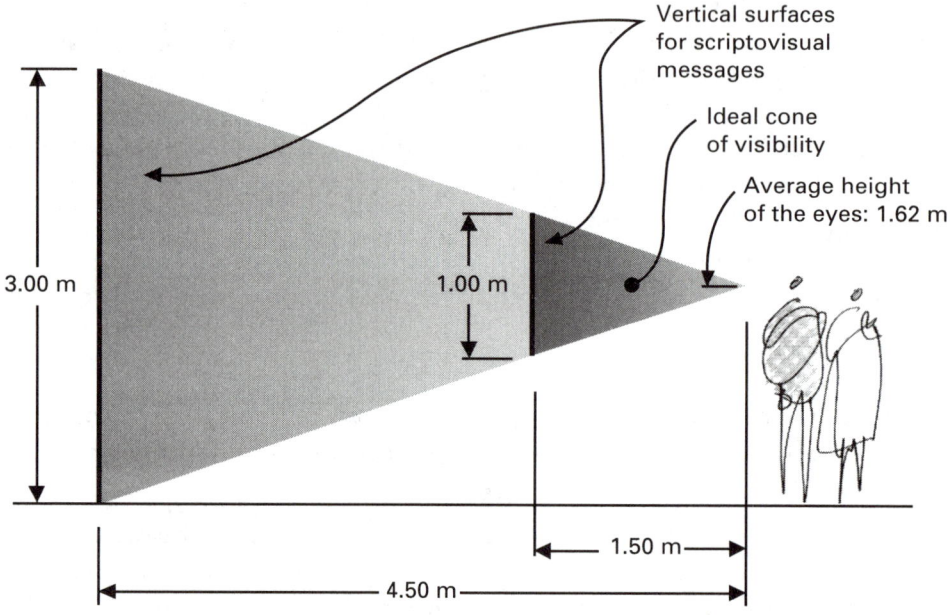

GSM Design

Optimum cone of visibility for a scriptovisual message located on a vertical surface

The area below the normal line of vision is much more natural, given that it is always easier to lower the head than to raise it.

What is most important is the position of the plane on which the scriptovisual message is presented, in relation to the eye. Ideally, the closer the surface is to being perpendicular to the floor the better, and, when the message is on a horizontal support, the closer it is to being parallel to the plane of the floor the better.

When the message lies outside visitors' normal line of sight as they move in a normal direction along the exhibition itinerary, it may well not be noticed at all.

The distance between the eye and the scriptovisual message

Second criterion:
The relationship between the visitor's eyes and the scriptovisual message as regards the reading distance

The cone of visibility widens as the distance from the object viewed increases. A scriptovisual message could be positioned at a height of 3 m provided it is sufficiently far away from the visitor.

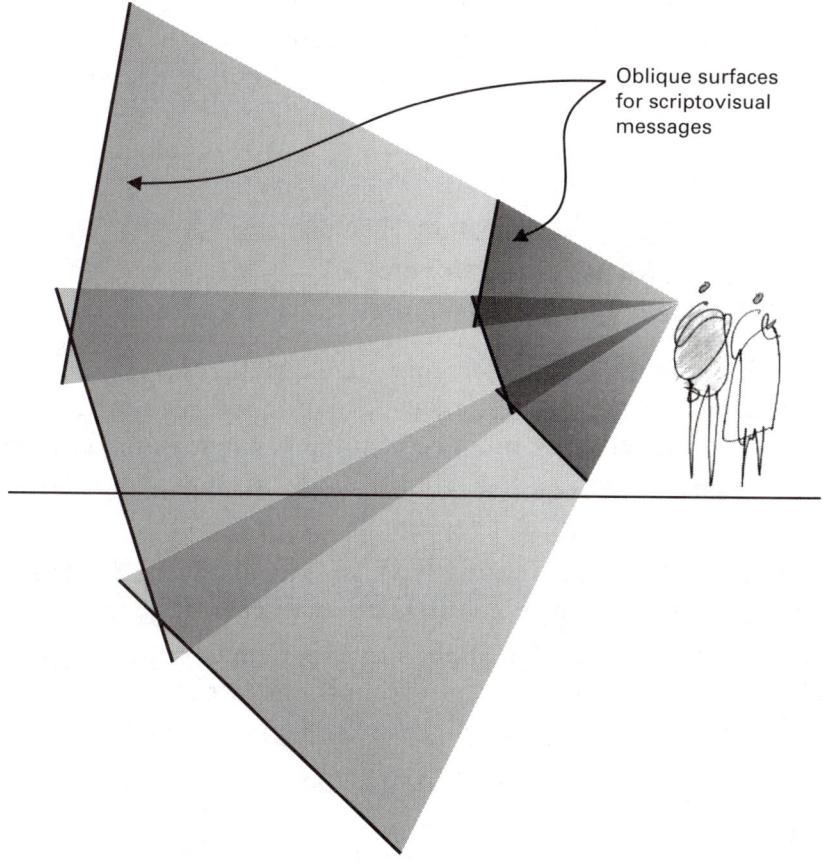

Oblique surfaces
for scriptovisual
messages

GSM Design

Optimal displacement of the visual cone upward and downward for a scriptovisual message

In this way, scriptovisual messages can suddenly take on a dimension in space that creates a volume entirely different from that of a page in a newspaper.

Imagine a visitor in the middle of a sphere made up of numerous small facets, each one at right angles to his eyes. Regardless of where the visitor looks, his eye perceives an ideal surface. In other words, the position of the scriptovisual message must be thought out according to the position of the visitor during his visit and designed to take advantage of the most appropriate time for looking at and reading the message.

Visitors at an exhibition move around. A hierarchical order in the positioning of messages must be adopted in light of the visitors' movements.

The scale of the message

Third criterion:
The scale of the message in relation
to the spatial reading conditions

To attain legibility, there is one basic, incontrovertible rule, again related to the fact that the scriptovisual message exists in a three-dimensional exhibition: the size of lettering must be adapted to the reading distance.

In each case, it is essential to accurately establish the desired position of the visitor for optimal reading of a scriptovisual message.

Instead of a pat formula linking type size and distance, it is best to carry out practical experiments based on the actual scale of the exhibition.

This recommendation also applies to experienced museographers who decide to stray from the beaten path and innovate.

The relevance of the choice of medium
for the scriptovisual message

Fourth criterion:
Choosing materials or reproduction techniques
in relation to the museum theme, while ensuring
adequate legibility

Decisions must be made on colours, materials and lighting.

Each of the three factors will alter the image of the scriptovisual message and confer on it a particular evocative power.

Text in black letters on a white background has been acknowledged once and for all as theoretically the ideal text presentation medium. However, the actual functional limitations of the black and white presentation can be overcome through the use of colour, different materials or finishes and lighting.

In principle, a wide array of supports for scriptovisual messages can be chosen to maintain a sufficiently high contrast between the lettering and the background to ensure the desired legibility under the conditions prevailing at a given moment along the exhibition itinerary.

While experience shows that the sharper the contrast, the more effective the reading, it should also be noted that colour, light and special materials also contribute to subliminal communication, whose impact should be weighed against the degree of legibility of the message.

The degree of legibility can also be weighed against various conditions affecting reading, e.g. positioning, lighting intensity, and shock value versus sobriety. In many instances, a subtle contrast between the colour of the lettering and the background will be more of an incentive to read the text than a sharp contrast.

Providing a visual change of scenery is another important facet of the use of colour, materials and lighting. The objective of disorientation or contextualization in space is achieved primarily by means of the shift from an anonymous typography to an expressive typography. From this standpoint, scriptovisual messages must be regarded as an integral part of the creation of an all-encompassing controlled environment. Such messages must be functional in terms of their legibility and the subliminal transmission of the intended message.

Going beyond the application of knowledge

Fifth criterion:
Using your knowledge of the basic rules in order to break them

This final criterion is important inasmuch as the designer must always enjoy sufficient leeway to innovate.

Scriptovisual messages can be used for purposes other than communicating content. For example, such messages can be used to guide, attract, intrigue or, even, shock visitors.

The communication of content, the primary raison d'être of a scriptovisual message, could be relegated to the background in favour of influencing the impact of the visit, creating a special visual environment, or even mystifying visitors.

If we take for granted that, in a conventionally designed exhibition, the use of scriptovisual messages is geared to the notion of the ideal position of the visitor, it is possible to imagine positioning the message in an unusual, unexpected, shocking or intriguing manner in order to influence the visitors' perception of it. In this case, the message has a motive force and is not confined solely to transmitting meaning.

Similarly, the incongruous position of a message may affect the visitor's attitude to reading a text. The creation of an unexpected, unusual situation implicitly creates another means of visual communication. However, the basic rules governing the organic relationship between the visitor's eyes and the message can only be broken if we know why and how to break the rules, which implies being thoroughly conversant with them.

SUPPORTS FOR SCRIPTOVISUAL MESSAGES

Once the structure of the scriptovisual messages has been established, their position and dimensions set, their design and execution determined, there remains the choice of treatment and of the supports on which they will be printed, applied or installed.

The Automobile exhibition, Musée de la civilisation, Québec City
(Photo: Pierre Soulard)

Emphasis through lighting

While the design process proceeds step by step, the choice of the materials on which scriptovisual messages are presented is an integral part of the development of the basic exhibition concept. The choice cannot be dissociated from the rest of the creative process. For example, the decision to use raised lettering or lettering on clear glass has a direct impact on the treatment of the backgrounds against which such lettering appears.

Two- or three-dimensional treatment

Three-dimensional typography reflects the very nature of the exhibition room. It is eye-catching and surprising to the visitor, as it is rarely used in the museum setting.

Special lighting can be used with three-dimensional lettering to heighten the effect of volume, thus creating varied, visually striking communications.

Obviously, most scriptovisual messages will continue to be two-dimensional for reasons of convenience and in light of production costs. A two-dimensional scriptovisual message can be enhanced by placing it on a transparent material such as glass.

Support surfaces

Support surfaces fall, broadly speaking, into three categories:
- The scriptovisual message is integrated into a two- or three-dimensional component of the exhibition;
- The scriptovisual message is mounted on a two- or three-dimensional surface, which is then incorporated into a three-dimensional component;
- The scriptovisual message appears on a freestanding support.

These categories apply both to small and large-scale messages.

The initial exhibition concept must guide the choice of support surfaces. Is the scriptovisual message to be read as a voluntary addition to a given surface or environment or is it to be wholly integrated into a surface that is markedly bigger than what is required for the message's installation?

The simplest example is the description of an object, which can easily be printed directly on the wall beside the object or on a two- or three-dimensional label placed near the object. It is entirely feasible to combine these approaches, printing some texts directly on the surfaces of an exhibition fixture and mounting other texts on autonomous surfaces, to be read separately.

The Automobile exhibition, Musée de la civilisation, Québec City
(Photo: Pierre Soulard)

**Scriptovisual messages on two-dimensional supports incorporated into
a three-dimensional exhibition fixture**

Support materials

Any material can, in principle, serve as a support, as long as it provides
contrast and its finish, colour and volume ensure the desired legibility.
For example, letters cut out of wood could be set on sand, or glass letters
could be mounted in concrete, metal or composite stone.

Aside from these unusual materials, there is a wide range of
conventional materials such as wood, plastic, metal and acrylic, which
can be used in their natural state, dyed or painted.

In addition to the foregoing materials, mention should be made of
less common, more delicate materials such as fabric and scrims, as well
as paper and cardboard, which can be coated with transparent protective
coverings.

These materials can be used in an infinite variety of ways. Letters can be made of small mosaic cubes or metal rods. It should be remembered that the choice of materials and the style of lettering will affect the general atmosphere of the exhibition and is directly related to the exhibition theme and the objects displayed.

Silkscreen printing on the basic materials discussed above will continue to be one of the surest and most elegant and accurate methods of reproducing a scriptovisual message.

The use of light

Light is the ultimate means of emphasizing a scriptovisual message. Whether backlighting or frontlighting is used to highlight the message, or the latter is projected on slides, the use of lighting to define the shape of the typography or the zone in which a message appears helps emphasize the area, make the space livelier and, when coloured lighting is used, change the underlying ambience.

An exhibition plan that fails to adapt the lighting to the scriptovisual messages presented is missing one of its most vital components.

This is especially true because a text, by its nature, has inherently less power to attract than an image. Sudden alternation of light and darkness, or gradual brightening and dimming can give a text a "feel" that it would otherwise lack.

It is even possible to display scriptovisual messages on electronic signboards, where they are in constant motion. However, the sense of movement tends to be obviated by the repetitiveness of such systems.

PRACTICAL EXPERIMENTATION

Organizing an exhibition space means understanding the eye and the volume of space in which it moves around.

Exhibition designers have at their disposal a remarkably accurate tool to verify the validity of their conceptual choices: practical experimentation.

Experience can of course be extremely helpful, but nothing can replace reproducing the actual conditions under which the scriptovisual messages are read.

The best way to assess the validity of the concept and the degree of legibility of the message is to build a rough, full-scale prototype and study it under the anticipated reading conditions.

This is especially true because practical experimentation enables the exhibition designer to validate or invalidate once and for all a given approach to visual communications. Experimentation makes it possible to check whether each factor that contributes to effective communication of a scriptovisual messages has been considered, and, more importantly, whether the various factors have been properly balanced.

Ultimately, the solution adopted will reflect a shifting balance among these criteria. Experimentation must focus on the positioning of the scriptovisual messages in relation to the visitor's eyes, the scale of the messages, the relationship between messages, the use of colour and the materials used to produce the messages.

In some instances, reproducing the lighting conditions is as important a part of verification as the visual impact of the overall design and the typography chosen.

Summary   Rock Anctil

Typographic Legibility: Definition and Field of Application in Exhibitions

Typography is one of the visual elements of an exhibition. It is a communications and creative tool. It does much more than simply set off or emphasize, its purpose is to make visitors as receptive as possible. This essay focuses on the study of typographic signs, with particular emphasis on factors that contribute to their legibility. The author examines microtypography and macrotypography. Microtypography encompasses, among other things, the appearance of characters, variations in letters, tools and systems for measuring letters and their environment, and typographic ornaments. Macrotypography refers to the manner in which readers perceive typographic signs. Using comparative tables, the author illustrates the key factors that affect the legibility of signs, i.e. serif and sans-serif typefaces, black type on a white background or the reverse, height of the characters, spacing and so on. Numerous factors can also guide readers or capture their attention, such as varied weights, rules, colours and initial capitals. To achieve maximum reading comfort, it is essential to ensure that typographic organization is clear. Without denying the importance of going by the rules, the author encourages designers to be audacious and avoid underestimating the reception skills of museum visitors who, after all, also belong to the generation of the media and the image. After this discussion of typographic legibility, Antoine Del Busso examines the different stages in the revision of texts.

Typographic Legibility: Definition and Field of Application in Exhibitions

Rock Anctil

Graphic Arts Designer
and Partner, Marinelli/Anctil
Art & design, lecturer
at the Collège de Sherbrooke

Which word is out of place in the following sentence?

"How would you like to go read an exhibition this weekend?"

In fact, it is not exactly reading that draws us to a museum. Under the circumstances, it is important to make the visitor as receptive as possible. Typography must be regarded as a key component of a visual system that serves effective communications. Images, sounds, colours, artifacts, movements and so on all attract the visitor's attention. To integrate a component does not imply camouflaging, making anonymous or hiding. If typography is presented as a necessary evil, then the text has failed to meet its objective. This essay focuses on the component parts of typography: the letter, the word, the sentence, the paragraph, the text, and the layout are discussed to enable readers to understand what enhances or impairs the visibility of texts in the realm of graphic communications and, in particular, in the museum environment.

MICROTYPOGRAPHY

Microtypography deals with the myriad details that make up the world of typography. More specifically, the "micro" analysis looks individually at various factors that do not converge at this stage. It is not involved with the relationships created between the different typographic elements as they appear in the general context of layout.

In this essay, I will examine the typographic character from the standpoint of its appearance, structure and other factors. Other terms will also be examined, notably classifications and measurements. I will try to establish a basic vocabulary to enable designers to make enlightened choices.

The appearance and structure of letters

Physical traits of letters

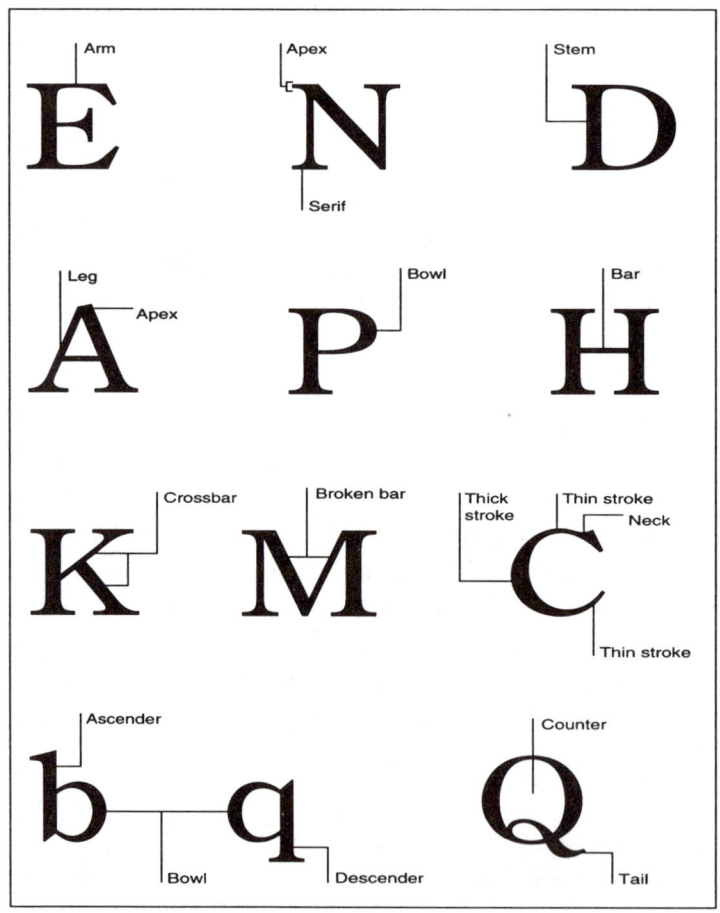

In typography, the word "character" is used to describe a letter or other alphabetical sign. It should be noted that the vocabulary used harkens back to the invention of letterpress printing, despite the generations of technological development that have led to computer graphics.

Characters have numerous distinctive traits, several of which are illustrated in the foregoing table.

Typographic classification and types of serifs

In order to create a reference system to indicate the distinctive traits of characters, it was necessary to select a trait by which they could be classified, i.e. the serif, or more specifically, its presence and forms or its absence (serif or sans-serif).

The systems used to classify characters are essentially conventions established at a given moment by a given authority, with a view to grouping together the characters according to their origin, style or design. There are several classifications based on different classification structures, which have become the very foundation of the system. Some are categorized according to period (Thibaudeau, American Type Founders), while others are based on the shape and style of the characters (Codex, Vox. A. Typ. 1962). Each of these systems establishes classes of characters that are denoted differently. There are numerous groupings, which are clearly indicated in the "Typographic Classifications" table. Each named class has attached to it numerous fonts or type families.[1]

Variations concerning the shape of the serifs correspond to the classifications defined in the "Parameters of a Letter" table, which illustrates the variety of classes of characters that may be denoted differently according to the system used.

At the microtypography stage, it is more important to define the classes of characters than the fonts.

---

1. Classification system: American Type Founders; class: Roman; font or family: Times, Baskerville; and so on.

Typographic classifications

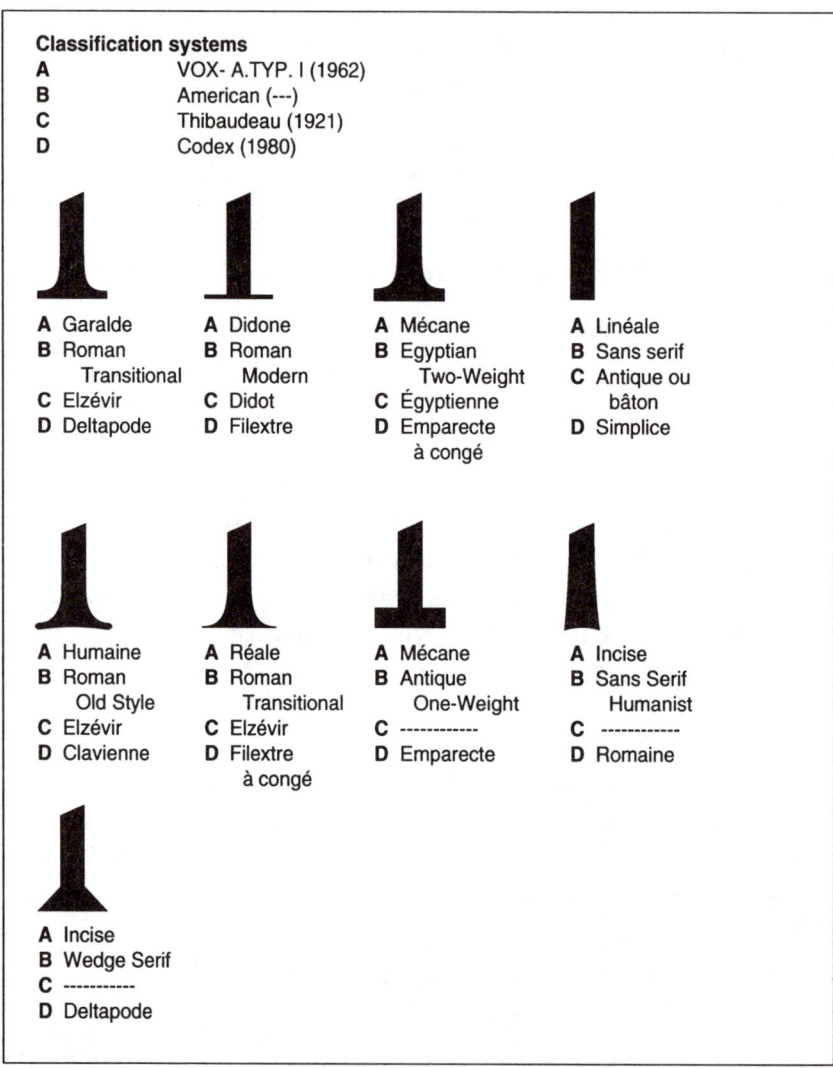

Classification systems
A   VOX- A.TYP. I (1962)
B   American (---)
C   Thibaudeau (1921)
D   Codex (1980)

A Garalde
B Roman
    Transitional
C Elzévir
D Deltapode

A Didone
B Roman
    Modern
C Didot
D Filextre

A Mécane
B Egyptian
    Two-Weight
C Égyptienne
D Emparecte
    à congé

A Linéale
B Sans serif
C Antique ou
    bâton
D Simplice

A Humaine
B Roman
    Old Style
C Elzévir
D Clavienne

A Réale
B Roman
    Transitional
C Elzévir
D Filextre
    à congé

A Mécane
B Antique
    One-Weight
C ------------
D Emparecte

A Incise
B Sans Serif
    Humanist
C ------------
D Romaine

A Incise
B Wedge Serif
C ------------
D Deltapode

Parameters of a letter (variations)

When a typographic composition is qualified, it is the factors that are described. Will the text be in boldface, lightface, italics, upper case or lower case, condensed and in what point size? Here are the principal factors.

Parameters of a letter

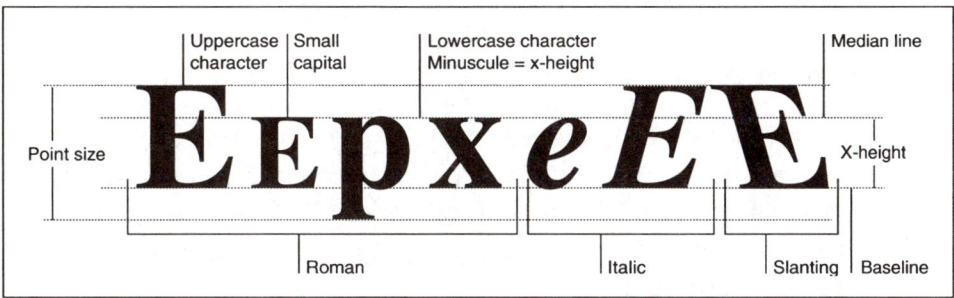

The face

The face of a letter is the visible sign on the printed surface, i.e. the letter itself as we read it. This term encompasses uppercase characters (capital letters), small capitals[2], minuscules (or lowercase characters), which in turn include ascenders (b, d, f, h, l...), short letters (a, c, e, m, n, o, x...), and descenders (g, j, p, q...). It should be noted that, for a given point size (14 points), the face of a letter may vary depending on the font.

Weight

Weight

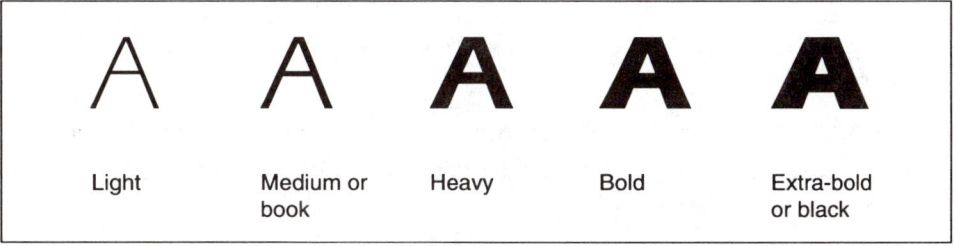

---

2. Small capitals generally have the same characteristics as uppercase characters, but are similar in height to lowercase characters.

The weight of a letter corresponds to its darkness or blackness, which can be accented or diminished depending on the effect sought. The terms "light", "heavy" or "bold" are used to qualify the thickness of the stroke.

Set-width

The set-width of a letter is the horizontal space it occupies: an "m" has a greater set-width than an "l". It is possible to alter the set-width of a given character (cf. condensed, normal, extended). Moreover, the set-width varies from one character to the next and from one family to the next at a given point size.

Set-width and several variations

Height

Height is the vertical measurement of the face of letters. It can vary markedly from one family to another.

Body size

Body size is expressed in points. Contrary to the face, these measurements are constant and are not affected by type styles or families. An equal body size does not necessarily mean an equal face.

Theoretically, the point size of a composition corresponds to the distance separating one line of text from the following line without line spacing or solid composition, i.e. 12/12 points.

Point size

Garamond corps 14   14pts Univers

Garamond corps 18   18pts Univers

ond corps 28   28pts Unive

corps 42   42pts U

Modification

Letters can be transformed in an infinite number of ways, usually for the purpose of decorating all or part of a text. Such modifications can emphasize the beginning of a paragraph or set off a title or a sentence.

Modified letters

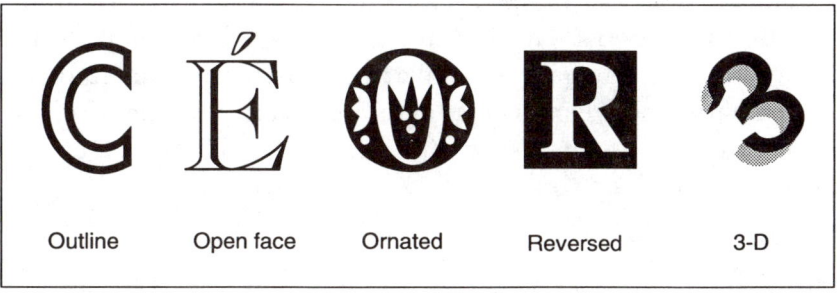

Outline   Open face   Ornated   Reversed   3-D

Typographic measurements

It is important to be familiar with typographic measurements and the reference points of the letter itself or its face, i.e. point size, set-width, cap height and x-height, before tackling measurements related to the environment of the letter, such as fit, word spacing, line spacing and justification.

Tools and systems for measuring a letter and its environment

A typometer is a device used to measure in points and in multiples of points, in picas and in agate lines. It is a steel or opaque plastic ruler graduated on both sides. Another model, shown below, gives examples of characters varying from 4 to 72 points. Because this ruler is printed on a transparent backing, it is especially effective for ascertaining the height and line spacing of existing texts.

TABLE OF THE SYSTEM USED IN NORTH AMERICA	
1 point =	1/12 pica or 1/72 inch
6 points =	1/2 pica or 1/12 inch
12 points =	1 pica or 1/6 inch or 4.511 mm
72 points =	6 picas or 1 inch

Measurements in the environment of the letter

The judicious choice of typefaces and the decision about their size are often made to the detriment of a number of equally important factors. The following factors warrant special attention: kerning and letterspacing (the lateral space between type characters); word spacing (the distance between words); line spacing (the varying amount of blank space between the lines of a text); and line length.

Kerning

Kerning is the lateral space needed between two printed letters in a given word to prevent them from touching.

Different letters of the alphabet do not automatically pair up with other letters at the same distance. If they did, white spaces or black spots would appear in titles and texts. Several factors affect kerning, such as reproduction processes, print or presentation surfaces, methods of dissemination and the distance between the text and the reader.

There is a risk of affecting the crispness of the type when silkscreen printing is carried out on porous or uneven surfaces. When the appropriate kerning value is adopted between the letters, they tend not to overlap. The luminosity of television screens often makes letters blur and dissolve into each other, especially when white letters appear on a black background, if the kerning is too close. Panels lighted from inside also affect the legibility of letters. A halo may make them seem thicker than they really are.

Letterspacing

Letterspacing is different from kerning in that the space between letters is adapted differently depending on the length of the lines in the text, especially when columns are justified. It should be noted that the more space is added between the letters, the more space must be added between the words.

Kerning and spacing values

Espace entre les lettres et les mots
Espace entre les lettres et les mots
Espace entre les lettres et les mots
Espace entre les lettres et les mots

Spacing

Spacing is the distance between words. If the reader can simultaneously grasp three or four words, it means the spacing is properly adjusted. Comfortable spacing enables the words to maintain their individual identity. However, excessively wide spacing breaks the reading rhythm. Make sure that the spacing is not greater than the line spacing. A condensed character does not require as much spacing as an extended character.

Line spacing

Line spacing is a variable blank space between the lines of a text or between a title and the text. In addition to individual tastes and those imposed by current fashion, other basic factors can serve as a guideline in determining line spacing. Among other things, mention should be made of the height of the characters (especially the x-height), their appearance (boldness of the vertical design of the letter, serif or sans-serif), and even the length of the lines.

Overly wide line spacing gives the impression that the lines are independent from each other and the text loses its unity.

Factors to be considered in deciding on line spacing

Lorem ipsum dolor sit amet, consectetuer adipiscing elit, sed diam nonummy nibh euismod tincidunt ut laoreet dolore magna aliquam erat volutpat. Ut wisi enim ad minim veniam, quis nostrud smod.

When the lines are long,
wider line spacing makes for easier reading.

Lorem ipsum dolor sit amet, consectetuer adipiscing elit, sed diam nonummy nibh euismod tincidunt ut laoreet dolore amy magna aliquam erat volutpat. wisi enim ad minim veniam, quis nostrud exerci tatio ullamcorper suscipit lobortis nisl ut aliquip ex ea commodo consequat.

Lorem ipsum dolor sit amet, consectetuer adipiscing elit, sed diam nonummy nibh euismoduer tincidunt ut laoreet dolore magna aliquam erat volutpat. wisi enim ad minim veniam.Unt nostrud exerci tation

Characters with strong vertical lines, like this Bodoni,
require wider line spacing.

Lorem ipsum dolor sit amet, consectetuer adipiscing elit, sed et dolo diam nonummy nibh euismod tincidunt ut laoreet dolore magna aliquam erat volutpat. Ut wisi enim ad minim veniam, quis nostrud oret

Lorem ipsum dolor sit amet, consectetuer adipiscing elit, sed diam nonummy nibh euismod tincidunt ut laoreet dolore magna aliquam erat volutpat. Ut wisi enim

It is preferable to use wider line spacing with sans-serif characters.

Adjustment and optical calibration of line spacing

La construction   La reconstruction
des ateliers en   des ateliers entre
1823   1971 et 1973

Regular line spacing

To calibrate the blank space between
these three lines, the line space of the
numbers has been deliberately increased.

The interplay of line spacing changes the appearance of a given character.

Line length

If visitors move their heads from left to right while reading, it means that the line of text is too long, making it hard to find the beginning of the next line. Overly short lines preserve the integrity of the words but make the reading rhythm jerkier. The result is a visual fatigue that impairs readers' retention of a panel's contents. A line 65 characters long,counting the spaces between the words, consists of between 8 and 10 words and is equivalent to a comfortable reading standard. In the case of labels and legends, lines of text between five and eight words long produce a reading rhythm with greater immediacy, appropriate for factual material.

Optical illusions

The alphabet consists by and large of horizontal, vertical and diagonal lines and curves. The combination of these elements produces geometric figures that warrant special attention when typographic characters are designed. There are no mathematical rules to optically establish the height, width and weight of the various shapes in relation to one another. Only the visual appearance and seasoned judgment count. However, it is useful to observe certain factors and be aware of when and why cheating is permissible when a typography is developed or used.

The three shapes below are of the same height and width and are equidistant from each other.

Geometric shapes compared with letter shapes

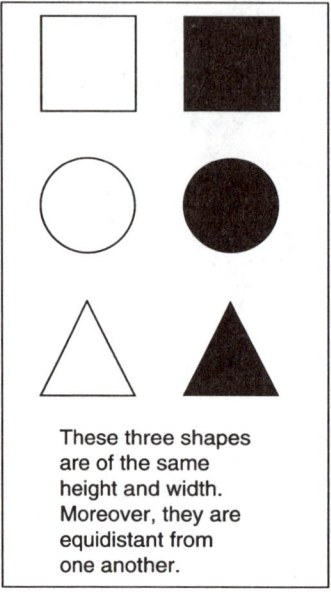

These three shapes are of the same height and width. Moreover, they are equidistant from one another.

Adjustment of the height of letters

Height adjusted optically

HOEA

HOEA

Height adjusted mechanically

In order to appear the same height, curved and pointed characters must extend slightly above and below straight-line characters.

Adjustment of the width of letters

Adjustment of the weight of letters

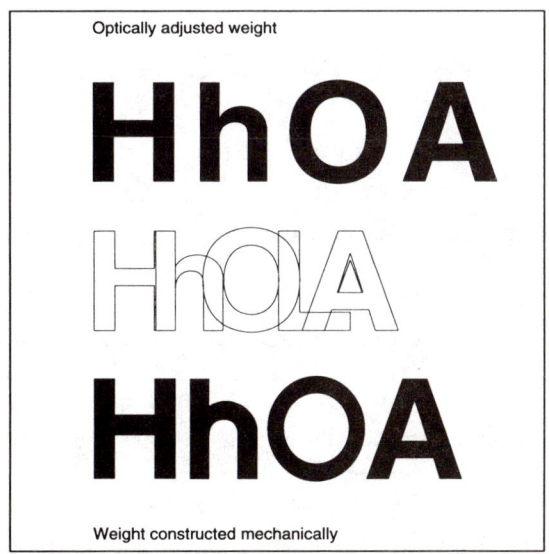

Adjustment diagram: Mechanical alignment of straight lines and curves.

If all letters were the same width, some would seem too narrow and others too wide. The weight of the letters is another factor to be considered. If the horizontal, vertical, diagonal and rounded portions were of the same thickness, certain letters would seem heavier than others.

MACROTYPOGRAPHY

Macrotypography focuses on the assembling of the elements of microtypography for a given purpose, e.g. the theme of an exhibition or the nature of a printed document. All of the various components are assembled at this stage. Proper control will make it possible to heighten visitors' receptiveness and, consequently, their retention of the message. The key factors are legibility and layout.

Legibility and reading habits

Shape of words and legibility

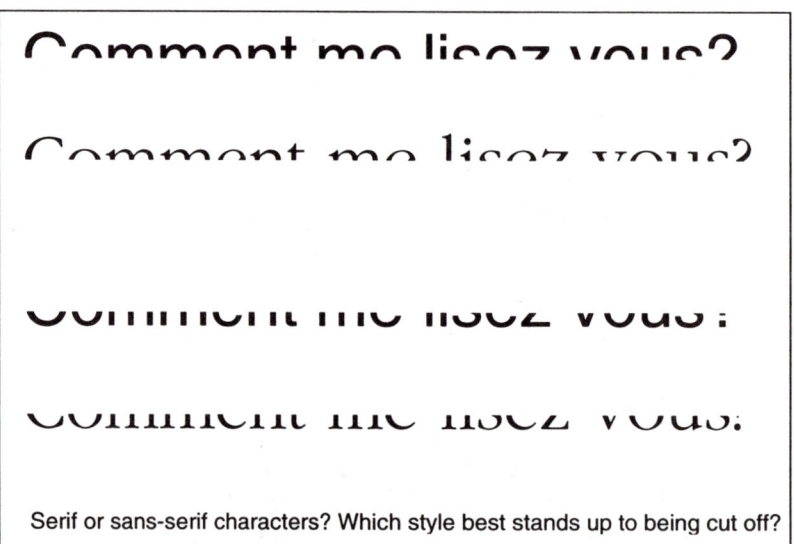

Serif or sans-serif characters? Which style best stands up to being cut off?

There was a time, in the 14th and 15th centuries, when Gothic writing was the typographic standard. Would a newspaper publisher consider using this typeface today? It would be virtually unreadable. However, when type families such as Baskerville or Helvetica appeared, people were alarmed and claimed never before to have seen such ugly characters. Today, they are regarded as among the most neutral typefaces. Aside from typefaces, other factors affect reading habits, notably the characteristic shapes of letters and words.

It is fairly easy to read the upper portion of letters. Reading the lower portion is much less common. When we skim through a text, our eyes focus on the upper portion of the letters and photograph the shape of the words in 1/3 or 1/4 of a second. It is not the letters in the words that we pick up, but their general shape. Even a word containing a typographical error is recognized and read in its entirety.

The irregular contours of lowercase characters confer a more distinctive form on words, making them more readily recognizable and easier to read. Words written in uppercase characters have an unbroken contour without distinctive features.

Perception of words by their contours

TYPO: READING HABITS

Typo: Reading habits

Which of the two blocks of text is easier to read?

Typefaces with and without serifs

Two arguments are put forward to justify the use of typefaces with or without serifs. According to François Richaudeau, there is no significant difference in reading speed between various styles using characters with or without serifs. An exhibition does not expose us to a great deal of text compared with a 400-page book. In *Designing with Type*, James Craig shows that we are more comfortable reading a text set in a serifed typeface. "Not only do serifs guide the eye in horizontal movements and the letters, but they all have a distinct shape, however small. Stick letters are more geometric and, therefore, more anonymous."[3]

Style of composition and prolonged reading

"LETTERS ARE LEGIBLE. IF SOME THINGS ARE NOT LEGIBLE, THEN THEY ARE NOT LETTERS. ILLEGIBILITY DOES NOT EXIST."
PETER MERTENS

"STUDIES HAVE SHOWN THAT READERS READ BEST WHAT THEY READ MOST. LEGIBILITY IS ALSO A DYNAMIC PROCESS, AS READERS' HABITS ARE EVERCHANGING."
ZUZANA LICKO

"Letters are legible. If some things are not legible, then they are not letters. Illegibility does not exist."
Peter Mertens

"Studies have shown that readers read best what they read most. Legibility is also a dynamic process, as readers' habits are everchanging."
Zuzana Licko

Do you find it easier to read UPPERCASE or lowercase characters?

Legibility and perception

Black on white or white on black?

Black type on a white background is easier to read than white type on a black background, although the latter procedure is not prohibited. In long texts, white type on a black background is too diffuse and quickly becomes irritating to read. To highlight 20 or so words or emphasize headings and subheadings, reversed type should be considered.

---

3. James Craig, *Designing with Type. A Basic Course in Typography* (New York: Watson-Guptil Publications, 1980), p. 123.

Reading regular and reversed type

Lorem ipsum dolor sit
amet, consectetuer
adipiscing elit, sed diam
nonummy nibh
euismod tincidunt ut
laoreet dolore magna
aliquam erat volutpat.
Ut wisi enim. **Adminim
veniam**, quis nostrud
exerci tation

Lorem ipsum dolor sit
amet, consectetuer
adipiscing elit, sed diam
nonummy nibh
euismod tincidunt ut
laoreet dolore magna
aliquam erat volutpat.
Ut wisi enim. **Adminim
veniam**, quis nostrud
exerci tation

Reversed type should be set in a sans-serif character. Choose a typography that is neither too thin nor too thick since overly thick characters tend to blur against a black background, while overly thin ones can be overwhelmed by it.

Typography and colours

Visibility does not automatically mean legibility. Schoolbus-yellow type set on a fluorescent fuchsia background is certainly very visible and may well lend itself to a whimsical theme. However, beyond five to eight words, legibility may suffer. Colour is not solely a decoration. It is expressive, communicative and evocative. Through the associations it engenders, it arouses sensations, feelings and recollections. Colour enhances the legibility of a name, a text or a message.

FIRST COLOR: **LETTERS** CLASSIFICATION		SECOND COLOR: **BACKGROUND** DAYLIGHT	ARTIFICIAL LIGHT
black on yellow	1	1.31	1.33
yellow on black	2	1.34	1.40
green on white	3	1.35	1.30
red on white	4	1.36	1.26
black on white	5	1.36	1.32
white on blue	6	1.36	1.37
blue on yellow	7	1.36	1.39
blue on white	8	1.37	1.35
white on black	9	1.40	1.35
green on yellow	10	1.40	1.38
black on orange	11	1.40	1.40
red on yellow	12	1.41	1.38
orange on black	13	1.41	1.40
yellow on blue	14	1.41	1.42
white on green	15	1.41	1.45
black on red	16	1.42	1.45
blue on orange	17	1.42	1.45
yellow on green	18	1.42	1.46
blue on red	19	1.43	1.40
yellow on red	20	1.44	1.50
white on red	21	1.47	1.43
red on black	22	1.48	1.43
white on orange	23	1.48	1.45
black on green	24	1.48	1.54
orange on white	25	1.50	1.50
orange on blue	26	1.52	1.60
yellow on orange	27	1.52	1.62
red on orange	28	1.54	1.64
red on green	29	1.57	1.50
green on orange	30	1.58	1.47

The foregoing findings are drawn from a table by Karl Borgräfe[4] that provides information on the legibility of coloured letters on coloured backgrounds. The ranking was established on the basis of reading 10 cm × 25 cm cards printed with letters 1.5 cm high. A tachistoscope was used to accurately measure reading time. For example, 1.31 means that a single exposure to the text was almost sufficient to allow the reader to

---

4. Jean-Paul Favre and André Novembre, *Color and Communication* (Zurich: Édition ABC, 1981), p. 50.

completely decipher it, as only a fraction (0.31) of an additional reading was needed for the complete reading of the letters in question.

Character height and legibility

Below 14 points, exhibition texts are hard to read. However, it is untrue that bigger point sizes facilitate reading. If the eye is unable to photograph more than three or four words at a time, prolonged reading becomes complex and tiring. In the reading itinerary of an exhibition, it is essential to consider the relationship between reading distance, lighting and character height in order to establish the maximum and minimum height of panels and labels.

Weight and legibility

Graphic designers can choose from light, medium, bold or extra-bold weights. The use of a particular weight depends, among other things, on the context and the message to be transmitted. Bold characters very effectively emphasize a title or portion of a text, but too much of it can make the text heavy.

Alignment

Types of alignment

On one line   Lorem ipsum dolor sit amet, consectetuer adipiscing elit, sed

Flush left
Lorem ipsum dolor
sit amet,nummy
consectetuer et
adipiscing elit, sed
diam nonummy nibh
euismod tincidunt.

Centred
Lorem ium dolor sit
amet, conecteter
adipiscing elit, sed
diam nonummy nibh
euismodincidunt
laoreet dolore

Justified
adipiscing   elit,
Loremipsum   dolor
sitadipiscing elit, sed
amet,consect etuer
adipiscing   elit, sed
diam nonummy nibh

Example of
river of white

Flush right
Lorem ipsum dolor
            sit amet,
      consectetuer
adipiscing elit, sed
diam nonummy nibh
euismod tincidunt ut

Asymmetric
      Dolorsit orem
consectetuert am
remagnaqi

                    Ut
minim
      ismod sum

Left-aligned text is entirely functional. It allows for a good reading rhythm and facilitates the movement of the eyes to subsequent lines by virtually eliminating the use of hyphens. It also allows for consistent letter spacing. More specifically, the text must be aligned optically and not mechanically at the left margin, and curved or angular letters must extend slightly beyond the overhang line. The same is true of right-aligned and justified text.

Centring lends a certain cachet to a text. However, it is harder to locate the beginnings of lines. Consequently, centring should be avoided in long texts. If it is used, it is preferable not to centre the text mechanically.

Justified text has an authoritative, objective look and is imperative, for example in newspapers. This type of composition is especially vulnerable and demands a thorough mastery of kerning, letterspacing and word spacing, otherwise there is a risk of creating rivers of white in the text. Because the lines are of equal length, it is almost inevitable to find more hyphenated words than in a left-aligned or right-aligned text. Spacing is, of necessity, irregular from one line to the next. Punctuation is placed outside the optical alignment lines, with the result that there are no blank spaces at the beginnings and ends of lines.

Right-aligned text is more demanding. Moreover, the line breaks conflict with our reading habits. Not more than three or four lines should be printed flush right.

Text is arranged in a random or asymmetrical manner in order to wrap it around a silhouette, a photograph or an illustration.

Layout

All of the elements of an exhibition coalesce in the layout, i.e. texts, headings, photographs, graphics and so on. Graphic artists must use their imagination to organize and emphasize the logic of the theme imposed on them.

Hierarchical arrangement of information

Hierarchical arrangement of information consists in respecting the organizational structure of the content of a given subject and clearly delineating its logic. The essence of a message can be effectively delivered through clever graphic and typographic tricks.

Clear typographic organization guides the reader

No newspaper is read in its entirety, and the same is true of an exhibition. To enable visitors to readily make use of their reading strategies, the mass of information presented must be structured by means of white spaces, rules, colour, and larger, bolder or italicized characters. The entire range of typographic parameters are adjuncts that make the content stand out and visually organize it. As Marshall McLuhan said, "The medium is the message."

Various kinds of typographic organization

Lorem ipsum dolor sit amet,tincid smod consect etu ersed adipiscing elit, diam nonummy nibh euismod tincidunt ut laoreet dolore magna aliquam erat	**Lorem ipsum dolor** Sit amet,nonumbh consectetuer adipiscing elit, sed diam nonummy nibh euismod tincidunt ut laoreet dolore magna	**Lorem ipsum dolor** Sit amet,nonumbh consect etuer adipiscing elit, sed diam nonummy ni. Euismod tincidunt ut laoreet dolore mag.
Lorem ipsum dolor *sit amet,* consectetuerdip isg adipiscing elit, sed *diam* nonummy euismod tinci *dunt* ut laoreet dolore magna	Lorem ipsum dolor sit amet,dipiscing consectetuer adipiscing elit, sed diam nonummy nibh euismod tincidunt ut laoreet dolore magna aliquam erat	*Lorem ipsum dolor sit amet,od consectetuer adipiscingreelit, sed diam nonummy nibh euismod tincidunt ut laoreet dolore magna aliquam erat volutpat.*

The same text printed six different ways

Striking facets of the image blending or contrasted with the typography

There are two approaches, either of which is justifiable, depending on the context. The first approach is based on the harmonization of the typographic forms with various components of the image, i.e. the lines of force, their importance and their direction. To some extent, the typography imitates the image, according to the theme and the environment. The second approach consists in contrasting the typography with the formal structure of the images or artifacts. For example, in a series of photographs devoted to the history of a factory, the compositions and objects are rigid and geometrical. To achieve contrast in this context, the typography is light, serifed characters are used and the titles are italicized.

Structures of the image

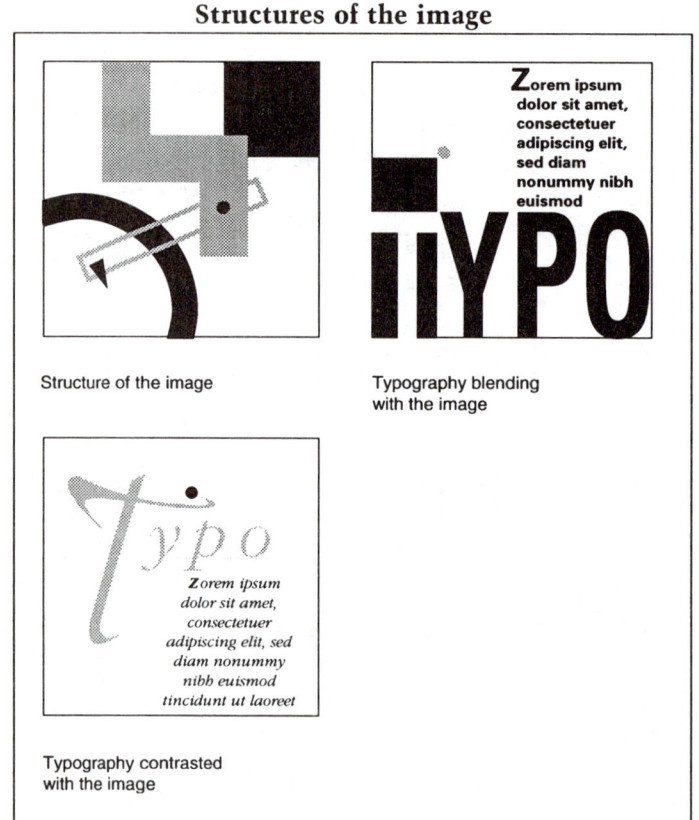

Structure of the image

Typography blending
with the image

Typography contrasted
with the image

In an exhibition, clearly display your intentions and do not attempt to integrate harmony and contrast. The effect of the two characteristics will be diminished and the message will be confused.

Typographic treatment in bilingual exhibitions

Typographic parameters make perfect instruments for combining two languages in the same exhibition. To clearly and subtly distinguish the two languages, it is essential to establish a clear, consistent code. The choice of parameters is vast.

TYPE OF COMPOSITION	LANGUAGE A	LANGUAGE B
Style	Roman	Italic
Weight	Bold	Light
Height	Body x	Body y
Characters	Serif	Sans-serif
Alignment	Flush left	Centred
Columns	Horizontal	Vertical
Contrast	Regular typography	Reversed typography
Position	Top	Bottom
	Left	Right
Other	On panels	In a companion booklet if there are more than two languages

Factors and strategies designed to capture and maintain attention

Large initial capitals at the beginning of a text are more inviting than a grey, compact, monotonous block of text. The initial capital can serve as a backdrop for the text. Pull quotes punctuate the text and spur the reader to continue reading. Paul Rand has demonstrated the virtues of numbers and punctuation marks.

The number as a means of expression possesses much of the same qualities as the letter. It may also be the graphic symbol for time,

273

space, position, direction, and quantity. [...] Punctuation marks as emotive, plastic symbols have served the artist as a means of expression in paintings as well as in the applied arts. Miro and Klee are notable examples.[5]

The sonority of a language or voice and "the sounds of silence" transposed to typographic language

As is the case in television advertising, we can suggest a particular voice in written messages. The unlimited choice of characters and weights, the use of uppercase and lowercase characters, italics and different spacings can replace a voice extolling the virtues of a laundry soap or another one encouraging us to drive more slowly. Make your own associations of timbre and voice.

Sonority of characters

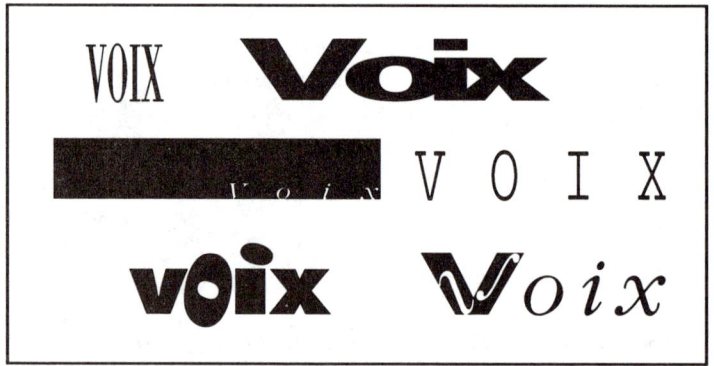

*

Do not over-design panels. You do not have to use everything you know in every project. Rules are made to be broken. If your compositions are governed by a strict, logical grid, find subtle means and slight exceptions to deviate from the structure. The presentations will be

---

5. Paul Rand, *Thoughts on Design* (New York: Wittenborn & Company, 1952), p. 156.

livelier. Oversimplifying or stating the obvious can make the presentation banal. Fortunately, not all of your work will consist in designing highway signs or instructions for lawnmowers. Do not underestimate the intelligence and receptiveness of your audience. Museum-goers are part of the media and image generation. Seek inspiration in the work of the pioneers you admire. Experiment, instead of simply accepting the default options that your computer software offers. "An airplane flies better if it is beautiful to look at."[6] The main rule in typography echoes the remark by Raymond Loewy: "What is beautiful works better."

6. Raymond Loewy, *La laideur se vend mal* (Paris: Gallimard, 1952), p. 220.

Bibliography

Aldersey-William, Hugh. *Cranbrook Design. The New Discourse*, Cranbrook Academy of Art, Bloomfield, Michigan. New York: Rizzoli, 1990, 208 pages.

Bitgood, Stephen C. *Design and Evaluation of Exhibit Labels.* Jacksonville: Center for Social Design, 1986, 9 pages.

Craig, James. *Designing with Type. A Basic Course in Typography.* New York: Watson-Guptil Publications, 1980, 176 pages.

Dreyfus, John; Richaudeau, François. *La chose imprimée. Histoire, techniques, esthétique et réalisation de l'imprimé*, Les encyclopédies du savoir. Paris: Retz-C.E.P.L., 1977, 640 pages.

Favre, Jean-Paul; Novembre, André. *Color and Communication.* Zurich: Édition ABC, 1981, 241 pages.

Klein, Larry. *Exhibits: Planning and Design.* New York: Madison Square Press.

Loewy, Raymond. *La laideur se vend mal.* Paris: Gallimard, 1952, 414 pages.

M et H ltée Montréal. *Choix de caractères typographiques disponibles à la titreuse*, 13th edition. New York: Visual Graphic Corporation, 484 pages.

Ramat, A. *Grammaire typographique*, 4th edition. Aurel Ramat, publisher, 1989, 96 pages.

Rand, Paul. *A Designer's Art.* New Haven: Yale University Press, 1985, 239 pages.

_____. *Thoughts on Design.* New York: Wittenborn & Company, 1952, 159 pages.

Rehe, Rolf. *Typography: How to Make it Most Legible.* Carmel, Indiana: Design Research International, 1976, 79 pages.

Rosen, Ben. *Type and Typography. The Designer's Type Book.* New York: Van Nostrand Reinhold, 1963, 9 pages.

Ruder, Emil. *Typography.* New York: Hasting House, Publisher Inc., 1981, 220 pages.

Serrell, Beverly. *Making Exhibit Labels. A Step-by-Step Guide.* Nashville: American Association for State and Local History, 1985, 199 pages.

Vermeil, François. *L'image des mots.* Paris: Centre Georges-Pompidou, 1985, 143 pages.

Reviews and other publications

Baseline, International Typographic Journal, London.

Emegre, Sacramento: Rudy Vanderlans, publisher.

Eye, The International Review of Graphic Design. London: Rick Poynor, publisher.

Font and Function, The Adobe Type Catalog. Mountain View, California: Adobe Systems Incorporated.

I.D., The International Design Magazine, Des Moines, Iowa.

Print, America's Graphic Design Magazine, New York.

"U and L C. Upper and Lower Case", *The International Journal of Type and Graphic Design.* New York: International Typeface Corporation.

Summary   Antoine Del Busso

Editing Texts for Scriptovisual Panels

The author summarizes, by means of practical guidelines, the essence of good editing, from the initial reading to the verification of the layout. However, even before texts are read, it is important ascertain their role in the exhibition, the manner in which they will be read and by what kinds of visitors. It may also prove useful to know who the editor is, in order to establish whether the form or the content should be subject to special scrutiny. For the first reading, the editor should keep in mind the nature of the exhibition and the target public. Are the tone adopted and the degree to which the texts are general in line with chosen objectives? Once these questions have been verified, the actual revision begins, described here in two stages. The first stage centres on the correction of basic mistakes. The second more complex stage focuses above all on style, vocabulary and the development of ideas. In all instances, the reviser should opt for simplicity and clarity, bearing in mind that the texts must be readily accessible to visitors. The same rule applies to graphs and histograms, which must be readable at a glance. Proofreading consists not only in eliminating all errors from the text, but in ensuring that it makes sense. The typography and layout must also be rigorously verified, as the legibility of graphic signs is just as important as correct usage. In the following essay, Dyane Plourde and Jean Michaud examine in detail the question of printing, the next step in the preparation of an exhibition text.

Editing Texts for Scriptovisual Panels

Antoine Del Busso

Director General, Éditions Fides,
Montréal

Generally speaking, good editing demands not only a thorough knowledge of the manuscript, but a very clear notion of the context in which it is prepared. For this reason, the work can be said to begin even before the text is read. For example, an experienced editor could conceivably feel the need to shorten paragraphs, simplify sentences and clarify certain terms while reading a description of a North American forest. The same editor would be ridiculed if he made such warranted changes without knowing that he was editing a text selected from the works of Susanna Moodie.

In order to edit a text for a scriptovisual panel properly, it is also important to be especially aware of the place and role of the text in a museum exhibition. Before focusing on the revision of the manuscript and proofreading, there are a number of more general considerations that should be examined.

PRELIMINARY STEPS

Before the editor reads the texts, it is useful to bear the following questions in mind:

- What role is the text to play in relation to all the supports used in the exhibition?

- Under what physical conditions and by what methods are the texts likely to be read?
- To what extent should the texts be general in light of the target clientele?

The answers to these questions will help place the texts in the proper perspective. However, the changes made to the texts will also depend on other factors, the first one perhaps being the identity of the editor. Two markedly different situations arise, depending on whether the texts are written by a freelancer or by the exhibition designer. In the first instance, there is perhaps good reason to pay close attention to the content and technical data while, in the second, it is the form that must be monitored.

In other words, it may be very useful to get to know the author of the texts, if only during a brief working session, to assess his particular qualifications. Is the writer an important scientist who has trouble communicating knowledge or an excellent communicator whose technical knowledge may be lacking? Obviously, it is essential to be thoroughly aware of the exhibition's objectives.

In what way will the texts be edited? This will depend on whether the editor is the director of the museum, the exhibition designer or an outside collaborator.

REVISING THE MANUSCRIPT

The importance of carefully reading all the texts at the outset cannot be overemphasized. While each scriptovisual panel has particular objectives, the panels are interrelated and are linked to other components in the exhibition. Each text must be read separately, and as part of a whole.

The reviser's role is crucial in that his reading is the only one that will focus on the texts overall and on specific details. No one else, not even the author, will read the texts as attentively and as critically.

During the first reading, three viewpoints should be kept in mind, i.e. that of the exhibition, that of the visitor and that of the author.

First, consider the nature of the exhibition and its objectives. Second, bear in mind the visitors who will read the panels. Even when the exhibition is aimed at a cultured, informed public, it is important to remember that visitors usually have little time to read and do not have a dictionary at hand. Check the tone adopted to transmit the spirit of the exhibition and the extent to which the level is general. Has the author succeeded in harmoniously integrating these elements? Once the first reading is finished, the actual revision begins and is performed in two stages.

THE TWO MAIN PHASES OF REVISION

The first, fairly simple phase consists in ensuring that the text is free of common errors such as misprints, incorrect spellings, incorrect grammar, faulty punctuation, and so on. Obviously, the editor's task demands excellent language training and good reference books. It would be unrealistic to attempt to point out the main difficulties encountered at this stage. Two pieces of advice often prove very useful: (1) When confronted with two turns of phrase, always chose the simpler; (2) When the rules of writing are not entirely clear and well established, choose one rule and stick to it.

It should also be noted that revision requires a very sharp eye and an unfailingly critical sense that even the most demanding readers rarely exercise. Normally, when we read for pleasure and personal interest, we automatically correct mistakes that appear in a printed text. An editor who lets down his guard and relies on this well known reflex is in trouble.

The second phase of revision is more complex and subtle. It is at this stage that the concern and responsibility to write for the public come into play. Usually, the editor will be forced to decry the sometimes yawning gap between theory and practice. How can the two concerns be reconciled? The question is a daunting one. Account must be taken of questions of style, tone, level of language, and the harmonious development of the texts. The rules in these fields are not quite as solid. However, there are a few guidelines to bear in mind.

First and foremost, a text intended for a scriptovisual panel must be clear and readily accessible to exhibition visitors. By definition, such a text is explanatory or descriptive. It must be self-contained and not rely on devices such as parenthetical explanations or infrapaginal notes.

To achieve clarity, steer clear of overly long sentences, e.g. those containing more than one subordinate clause, and complex formulations such as double negatives or inversions.

Do not hesitate to number each item in an enumeration and visually emphasize the items in relation to the rest of the text.

Similarly, a quotation will be all the more striking if it is short and clearly set off from the main text, unencumbered by a lengthy preamble and simply followed by the author's name.

Graphics, histograms and statistical tables should be treated in the same manner. They can serve as valuable pedagogical tools, provided of course that the reader can grasp them at a glance and that they are self-explanatory. If explanations are required, there is every reason to question whether the author has carefully considered the matter. It is always better to replace a hazy graph with a clear, precise paragraph of text.

PROOFREADING

People often speak, quite wrongly, of "reading" the proofs rather than "correcting" them. While it is obvious that, to correct the proofs, it is essential to read them, this type of reading has little in common with ordinary reading. In some respects, proofreading might be deemed a form of "anti-reading", in that our usual reflexes are suppressed by the need for rigorous observation of individual signs.

In some leading US publishing houses, proofreaders are asked to work line by line from the bottom of the page to the top, undoubtedly a somewhat radical way of focusing the proofreader's attention. It is tantamount to enunciating each syllable in a conversation and separately pronouncing each word. What is gained in precision and clarity is perhaps lost in meaning and interest.

To proofread a text also means to ensure that the text is meaningful. Once the pages have been examined one by one, the tree and, possibly, the forest must also take shape. It is this aspect of the task that makes proofreading so demanding. Essentially, it entails great precision and simple common sense.

CLARITY

For this reason, it is useful to broach the question from several standpoints. Not only must the language be correct (all errors must be eliminated), but the message must be clear and the graphic signs legible. In addition to revising the words and sentences, the reviser must also correct the typography and the layout.

All too often, editors tend to take the visual presentation of the text for granted. This aspect should be scrutinized as closely as the rest. Is the text legible from a reasonable distance? Is the line spacing sufficient to enable readers to easily see the end of one line and the beginning of the next? Is the text column properly proportioned in relation to the typographic character size? Are italics, boldface and capital letters over-used? The effectiveness of these typographic signs is inversely proportional to their frequency of use.

All the questions raised about proofreading must be considered simultaneously. Only an experienced proofreader can successfully perform the task. For this reason, it is often preferable for texts to be revised and proofread by two different people. Be that as it may, the exercise demands a sharp wit and a sharp eye.

*

Bibliography

Bouvaist, J.-M. *Pratiques et métiers de l'édition.* Paris: Éditions du Cercle de la librairie, 1991.

Tackels, S. *Typographie et terminologie.* Québec City: Les Publications du Québec, 1990.

Van Leunen, M.-C. *A Handbook for Scholars.* New York: Oxford University Press, 1992.

The Chicago Manual of Style. Chicago: The University of Chicago Press, 1993.

Summary   Dyane Plourde
                                                     Jean Michaud

From Photocopy to Data Bank

Printing, the final stage in the production of texts, is the last topic in this series of essays. The authors review all possible methods of reproducing texts, with particular emphasis on their advantages and disadvantages. They first examine high- and low-resolution black and white or colour photocopying on supple media such as paper, film or self-adhesive film. This category also includes backlit text on a transparent backing and text photographed using a multichrome process dubbed "colour velox". The second category encompasses texts integrated into the support, such as exhibition fixtures or even a wall. In this instance, the text can be reproduced on the surface, raised or engraved, or silkscreened. Despite its relatively high cost, the latter process is the method of printing par excellence. The third category includes texts reproduced on computer media. The authors cite the example of an exhibition held at the Musée du Québec in which information covering the principal themes was compiled in data banks. Only the main headings, brief introductory texts and the labels were reproduced by conventional means. Depending on the level of knowledge visitors wished to acquire, they could question the data bank or simply read the scriptovisual panels along the exhibition itinerary.

From Photocopy to Data Bank

Dyane Plourde

Graphic Designer,
Senior Associate,
Mauve design graphique

Jean Michaud

Graphic Designer

This essay is by no means exhaustive, but provides an overview of the methods used to reproduce texts. The reproduction of images is mentioned when it can be included in the text reproduction process. For this reason, we do not discuss photography.

We have also confined our remarks to those methods of reproduction whose visual and functional aspects we have been able to assess directly or indirectly. Rapidly changing technology imposes the mention of new processes that have yet to prove themselves.

Between the time the presentation sketches, which enable the client to visualize the conceptual approach, are reproduced and the approval tests are carried out by the suppliers, the graphic designer must produce all the basic documents (colouration, layout, cropping, camera-ready material[1] and films used for reproduction, cost estimates and

---

1. Camera-ready material is the form in which the document is submitted to the supplier for reproduction. The quality of the finished product depends on that of the camera-ready material. The supplier receives all the instructions needed to carry out the work: enlargement factor, number of colours, print run, type of support on which the material must be reproduced, positioning and so on.

mock-ups needed) to install the two-dimensional[2] components of the exhibition.

Several criteria govern the production of these components. Budgetary considerations, whether the exhibition is held in one location or will travel, the scope of the exhibition, duration (short-term, temporary, permanent) and the proximity of suppliers are all factors to be considered in the choice of scriptovisual reproduction methods.

It should be noted that printing processes used in publishing, such as four-colour process printing, letterpress printing and heliography, are not suited to exhibitions as they are intended for the mass reproduction of one message on a given support. An exhibition generally requires a unique method of reproduction on an array of supports.

REPRODUCTION ON SUPPLE MEDIA: PAPER, FILM, OR SELF-ADHESIVE FILM

Paper, film and self-adhesive film are fragile. Consequently, they must be mounted on rigid supports and laminated, especially when they are for lengthy or travelling exhibitions. However, care must be taken to avoid creasing large sheets of paper when they are mounted. The suppleness of paper lends itself to shaping, folding, cutting out or curling, so that objects can be made whose shapes amplify the exhibition's content.

Films must be inserted between two sheets of acrylic.

Photocopies

Texts and images can be photocopied on supple media in black and white or colour in formats that are now, or will soon be, useful to exhibitions. However, the competence of suppliers and the quality of the services offered vary widely from one reprographic printing firm to the next.

---

2. Two-dimensional refers to the images and texts reproduced on the supports selected, as opposed to various exhibition fixtures, artifacts or other accessories, which are deemed to be three-dimensional.

Black and white

High-contrast texts and images[3] or low-ruling[4] halftones[5] (65 l/inch) are reproduced on smooth paper with grammage[6] that satisfies the specifications of the photocopier.

Musée Bon-Pasteur, Québec City (Photo: Louise Leblanc)

Alabaster Virgin

---

3. A high-contrast image is one in which all shades of grey, i.e. any colour between white and black, have been eliminated.
4. The ruling indicates the fineness of the screen, i.e. the number of lines of dots per inch, expressed in lines per inch (l/inch).
5. A halftone is a screened image, i.e. one in which greys are represented by fairly large black or coloured dots that are fairly close together.
6. Grammage indicates the weight of the paper and is usually expressed in pounds per 1000 sheets, i.e. an 80-lb paper means that 1000 sheets of the paper in a given format weigh 80 pounds.

Advantages

- Fast, simple and inexpensive
- Large format, 36" × 500'.

An enlargement can produce a striking effect by eliminating details and creating a different texture. However, the result must be an integral part of the concept.

Disadvantages

- Reproduction quality is poor and the process creates black patches, so it is essential to supply an original with perfect blacks. This process is not very useful for texts unless an original that is at least 50 percent of the final format is supplied, which considerably increases costs.

Colour

A conventional continuous tone laser colour photocopier reproduces illustrations, texts, photographs, slides and camera-ready material in which the colours can be assigned to clearly demarcated surfaces that do not touch each other.

Advantages

- Rapid process
- Average cost.

When it is connected to a microcomputer, this photocopier can reproduce the contents of a document on diskette, which reduces the risk of errors that occur when the text is altered.

Disadvantages

- Only small standard formats are available: 81/2" × 11", 81/2" × 14" and 11" × 17", including from a minimum margin all around the printed area
- Blended colours[7] are to be avoided in colour photocopiers

---

7. A blended colour is one to which white or black has been added. The opposite of a blended colour is a saturated colour.

- Precision and the number of colours in a given reproduction are limited.

Oversize colour reproduction

It has been possible for some time to make oversize colour reproductions, although the disadvantages of the process (unusable small basic documents, only one type of paper available, poor value for the money) far outweigh the advantages.

A new process, however, has promising potential for exhibitions. The reproduction, at a resolution[8] of 400 dots per inch (d.p.i.), displays a blurred point that produces a grain similar to that resulting from airbrushing.

This new device makes it possible to reproduce all of the foregoing documents, including those on diskette, on an even wider range of supple media in formats up to 52" wide and 500' long. The quality-price ratio appears to be unbeatable. The process is worth trying, without a doubt. In the spring of 1993, the oversize "Québec Expérience" poster was produced by means of this process.

In-house low-resolution output

Black and white

Every agency and virtually every graphic artist now own computer equipment, including a laser printer. Such printers use 81/2" × 11", 81/2" × 14" or 11" × 17" paper and can print at resolutions of 300 d.p.i., 600 d.p.i. and even 1200 d.p.i.

Advantages

- Inexpensive
- Allows for the combination of texture and text on the same support

---

8. The resolution or definition of an image refers to the number of black dots per square inch of image and is expressed in dots per inch (d.p.i.). The higher the number of dots, the higher the resolution of the image and the more it can be enlarged without jagged edges appearing in diagonal lines.

- Facilitates the correction of errors.

Disadvantages

- Large formats are not available
- Black must be taken into account when the graphic concept is developed
- Definition is inadequate for quality enlargements, at least at 300 d.p.i.

SUGGESTION

Why not split up the text and print it on papers of different colours, to achieve an overall effect *à la Mondrian*? The idea is simple, effective and economical.

Regardless of the scope of the exhibition, the process can be used to produce labels, whose content is often finalized at the last minute when the exhibition is being mounted.

Colour

Desktop laser printers are available, although output is printed in standard formats. Colour printing can also be done by reprographic printing firms at reasonable cost.

High-resolution output

Very high resolution output, between 1270 d.p.i. and 3000 d.p.i., and the varied supports on which it can be produced (photographic paper, film, self-adhesive film), make it a worthwhile option when black and white printing is required.

Advantages

- Output is more durable as it is printed on photographic paper, which may save the cost of lamination, depending on the presentation's context.
- Because text is being reproduced, the format of the surface to be printed is fully usable in a context adapted to the

exhibition, i.e. 17.5" × the maximum height corresponds to that of the software used to produce the basic document. There is no limit to the length of paper. A 300-percent enlargement of a 5.75" × 48" document on diskette could produce high-resolution output measuring 17.25" × 144".

Disadvantages

- Available only in black and white
- The paper may discolour over time.

Backlit text

High-resolution output mounted on a transparent support is arresting. Light boxes can be used to display the text, provided it covers the full width of the support (18").

SUGGESTION

Why not take advantage of the support's transparency and make its presence more discreet? Mounted between two sheets of clear acrylic, it can be suspended or placed in front of an object or an image, or in a window. A word of caution: the background must be homogeneous and contrast consistently with the text.

A word of warning

A luminous surface is very taxing for the eye, as is the reading of a backlit text.

Backlit texts, especially those with certain letters illuminated instead of the entire background, are even more tiring for the reader.

Self-adhesive film

High-resolution output can also be reproduced on transparent self-adhesive film.

Advantages

- Affordable, fairly easy to install, more discreet support.

Disadvantages

- Not particularly interesting visually: the support quickly turns yellow, and dust and air bubbles are inevitable
- Reproduction quality poorer than in other processes
- Maximum surface: 81/2" × 11"
- Once installed, the film can pull paint or other finishes off the background surface; corrections are hard to make.

Photographed text

Oversize colour velox reproduction offers a product of excellent quality on photographic paper or translucent film. The use of screens to reproduce images allows for the smooth integration of text and image.

Photographed text is much appreciated in exhibition booths and backlit advertisements, and has its place in the museum environment. Everything depends on needs.

Advantages

- The maximum size of reproductions is 47" × 95"
- The output is of high quality provided the initial document is fairly large and contains screens with high rulings
- Photographs can be reproduced with continuous tones, i.e. without having to be screened
- Costs are lower than in the case of silkscreen printing, provided all or part of the content is reproduced only once.

Disadvantages

- It is hard to reproduce certain colours accurately
- To keep down costs, the final films must not exceed 11" × 16". A word of warning about enlargements: a 600-percent enlargement (to attain the maximum dimensions, for example) will reduce both the resolution of the text and the screen of images
- Unlike silkscreen printing, colour velox requires a paper backing, which is mounted on a rigid surface.

TEXT INTEGRATED INTO THE SUPPORT

Text engraved or embossed on the support differs from the preceding types of reproduction in terms of the support on which the message is reproduced. Paper or film are no longer necessary. Exhibition fixtures and even the walls can serve as supports. The text becomes an integral part of the whole.

Surface text: transfer text

This process, called "INT" or "Chromatec" by the initiated, is similar to transfer lettering, although the text is transferred in blocks or sections. How well the text adheres to the support depends on the smoothness of the support's finish.

Advantages

- Can be produced in an infinite range of colours drawn from the Pantone matching system[9]
- On-the-spot installation is quick and easy. With very little practice, museum staff can transfer the text to the support.

Disadvantages

- Surfaces are fairly small, i.e. 11.5" × 16.5"
- The product is very fragile prior to installation. Extra words should be made to replace materials damaged during handling. Once installed, the transfer text is stronger, but can easily be scratched very easily
- Not suited to travelling exhibitions or locations where visitors will brush against the text. Does not have a very long useful life
- No screen can be reproduced by means of this process.

---

9. The Pantone matching system is a reference guide for colour printing. The composition of printing inks corresponds to the composition of the colours in the chart. Because it is widely used, the Pantone chart is the main reference tool for silkscreen printing and other means of reproduction, even though the composition of inks and pigments varies. Any good graphic design supply store carries the charts.

Dear Love exhibition, Musée de la civilisation, Québec City (Designer: Louise Bélanger; graphic artist: Dyane Plourde; manufacturer: Gérald Turcotte)

Application on a curved wall

Surface text: vinyl

This method of reproduction is widely used in signposting and is useful for titles or short texts in big letters in short-term exhibitions. From a diskette or a visual element that the supplier digitizes, a computer transmits the information to a cutting table. The cut out self-adhesive letters are transferred to a pick up tape for precise, rapid mounting.

Advantages

- A wide array of characters are available
- Through digitization, it is now possible to reproduce graphic signs such as pictograms, symbols and so on.

Disadvantages

- Not suited to continuous text: characters must be at least1/2″ to 3/4″ high
- Screens cannot be reproduced

- Colours are limited to those of the vinyl; the finish may peel when it is painted or silkscreened
- Vinyl letters should be placed out of reach as they can be removed with a fingernail.

SUGGESTION
Vinyl letters are ideal for curved surfaces.

Raised letters

This text reproduction method is well suited to titles, as the letters must be at least one inch high. Materials such as metal, acrylic, beadboard and particleboard can be used to make raised letters, which will vary in thickness. Materials less refined than metal are painted different, occasionally metallic, colours.

Cities of the World exhibition, Musée de la civilisation, Québec City (Designer: Louise Bélanger; graphic artist: Gilbert Bochenek; manufacturer: Plastiques Blais)

Raised letter process

297

A number of specialized suppliers offer sets of characters in standard colours.

Advantages

- Unquestionable visual impact
- Enhances a simple, inexpensive text presentation
- Gives the text a three-dimensional look.

Disdvantages:

- Fairly expensive to produce and install, but affordable if used solely for titles and made of a simple material
- Letters that are too thick cast a shadow that impairs legibility.

SUGGESTION

An image converted into simple geometric shapes can be created to accompany the title.

Engraved letters

Engraved letters, a variation of raised letters that can be used for the same purposes, are produced by engraving the support material with acid or a knife. They have the same advantages as raised letters.

Sport and the Olympic Movement exhibition, Musée de la civilisation, Québec City (Designer: Bernard, Bertrand; graphic artist: Dyane Plourde; manufacturer: Plastiques Blais)

Silkscreen printing

Silkscreen printing is the ultimate scriptovisual reproduction method. It offers the designer enormous freedom. However, the designer must bear in mind different factors to attain optimum quality:

- The basic document must be of very high quality, e.g. high-resolution output, otherwise, recourse to silkscreen printing is not warranted. No process can rectify the shortcomings of the basic document. For this reason, photocopies should be avoided

- The printing surface must be flat and smooth

- The ruling of the screen used to reproduce the images affects the quality of the silkscreened image, e.g. photograph, illustration, texture and so on. The finer the screen, the higher the quality of the silkscreened image. The 55 l/inch screen is widely used, although it can vary depending on the silkscreener, the support, the ink used and specific needs. Other types of screens can be used to reinforce the visual concept

- The fineness of the silk directly affects the quality of the silkscreened image and text. Silk with 305 threads per inch produces excellent results.

Advantages

- Strength, which depends on the type of ink used (the most durable is heat hardened epoxy ink);

- Versatility: text, textures, halftones (for photographs), flat surfaces[10] and colours ranging to four-colour process printing[11] all lend themselves to making silkscreen printing the perfect method of reproduction for combining images and text in the entire range of formats. However, it should be noted that most silkscreeners cannot silkscreen screen areas larger than

---

10. A flat surface is one which is printed without a screen or halftone.
11. Four-colour process printing makes it possible to print a full colour document using four basic colours, i.e. yellow, cyan, magenta and black.

48" × 72" without making a joint in the printing, which will be apparent to some degree, depending on the silkscreener's skill

- Silkscreening can be performed at the silkscreening studio or on the museum premises. Outside the studio, for example, on a wall, the process is subject to additional constraints. In this instance, it is better to opt for a simple concept, with a screen and superimposed colours.

Disadvantages

- Fairly expensive
- The use of several screens for a single image, in addition to the one produced by the silk used, can create a moiré effect
- Corrections are more or less impossible or always apparent
- Production time is longer than for other processes.

SUGGESTION

Silkscreen printing can be used to reproduce one or more copies of a given message or part of a message. The graphic artist has every interest in developing the exhibition concept with this criterion in mind, as it justifies the use of the process and makes it more cost-effective.

Silkscreen printing is one of the few processes that can reproduce a colour image on a transparent support – a striking use of large transparent surfaces.

Illuminated titles

It is possible to cut a shape out of a gobo,[12] provided it is made of metal, and attach it to a spotlight, or create a title by masking a glass plate. The product is made by a firm specializing in lighting accessories.

The dimension of the element projected on a wall or other surface will depend on the distance between the spotlight and the projection surface.

---

12. A gobo is a glass surface partially obstructed by paint, or a metal surface in which a shape has been cut out and which is placed in front of a light source.

Advantages

- Striking impact
- Does not require additional lighting.

Disadvantages

- Manufacturing cost, which varies with the type of spotlight used and the type of glass plate
- It takes three weeks to manufacture an illuminated title.

COMPUTER MEDIUM

SUGGESTION

It is not easy to read at an exhibition, and there is much to be said about the themes presented. Visitors also have varied expectations.

Why not simply reproduce the main headings, a brief introductory text on each of the themes and technical labels using one of the traditional reproduction methods mentioned earlier, and compile more subtle information in data banks on the exhibition's theme and sub-theme?

Computers can be leased for the duration of the exhibition and space can be provided for visitors to sit down and satisfy their curiosity. The Musée du Québec did just that at its *Calices et ciboires* exhibition mounted in 1993—a splendid initiative.

Advantages

- Creates an uncluttered exhibition environment
- Reduces costs appreciably
- Major institutions can easily share the data banks with smaller institutions.

Disadvantages

- A computer can be used only by up to three people at a time
- Computer equipment often breaks down at exhibitions, although this problem should be remedied over time
- The visual and functional aspects of computerized graphic design should not be overlooked.

Acknowledgments:

We are grateful to the following individuals, who shared their expertise with us:

Michel Lajoie, Copie de la Capitale, Québec City

Louis Parent, Repro-graphic, Québec City

Raymond Chartré, Cartier reproduction, Québec City

Claude Rondeau, Les laboratoires Prisma, Beauport, Québec

Summary Table 1

Reproduction method	Main use	Support	Maximum dimensions	Basic document to be supplied	Cost
Oversize black and white photocopy	High-contrast image	Paper or translucent polyester film of a weight accepted by the photocopier	36" × 500'	Photograph	$
Colour laser photocopy	Text and image combined or separated	Paper or translucent polyester film of a weight accepted by the photocopier	8 1/2" × 11" 11" × 17"	Camera-ready material or document digitized on diskette	$
Oversize colour photocopy	Text and image combined or separated N.B.: Text definition will depend on enlargement factor	Paper, transparent backing or other	52" × 500'	Camera-ready material, document digitized on diskette or photograph	$$
Colour velox	Full-colour text and image combined or separated	Photographic support: paper and "Duratrans" or "Duraflex" film	47" × 95"	Camera-ready material or colour-separation films (depending on supplier)	$$$$

Legend:
$ Among the least expensive
$$ Inexpensive
$$$ Average
$$$$ Most expensive

Summary Table 2

Reproduction method	Main use	Support	Maximum dimensions	Basic document to be supplied	Cost
Low-resolution laser printing, small format	Text and texture Ideal for small surfaces such as labels	Paper, acetate, self-adhesive film of a weight accepted by printer	Depends on the printer: 8 1/2" × 11" 11" × 17"	Obtained directly from a microcomputer or a diskette	$
Low-resolution laser printing, large format	Text and image combined or separated	Paper, acetate	3' × 24' long	Obtained directly from a microcomputer or a diskette	$
High-resolution output	Text and image Basic document for silkscreen printing or transfer text	Photographic paper, film, self-adhesive film	17 1/2" × length allowed by software used	Document on diskette	$$
Transfer text	Text only	Film on the walls of the exhibition room	12" × 18" sections	Camera-ready material or film negative	$$$
Vinyl letters	Text (mainly titles) Minimum height of characters: 1/2"	Film on the walls of the exhibition room	22" wide	Annotated document or digitized document on diskette	$$$

Legend:
$ Among the least expensive
$$ Inexpensive
$$$ Average
$$$$ Most expensive

Summary Table 3

Reproduction method	Main use	Support	Maximum dimensions	Basic document to be supplied	Cost
Raised or engraved letters	Titles, simple graphic forms	Any rigid support, exhibition fixtures or walls	Letters over 1" high	Annotated document or digitized document on diskette	$$$ to $$$$
Silkscreen printing	Text and image combined or separated	Supple or rigid, even the walls of the exhibition room if only one colour or colours that do not touch are used	Virtually limitless	Camera-ready material or final films	$$$$
Gobo	Titles, simple graphic forms	Walls or large surfaces of exhibition fixtures	Depends on distance between spotlight and lighted surface	Basic drawing and projection distance	$$$ or $$$$
Computer medium	Data bank	Computer screen	Dimensions of screen	Program	$$ to $$$$

Legend: $ Among the least expensive
$$ Inexpensive
$$$ Average
$$$$ Most expensive

CHAPTER 6

EVALUATING

Scriptovisual
Evaluation Grid

The evaluation grid can be used to check the content, layout and positioning of each type of text bearing in mind the message they transmit and their formal organization. The criteria listed in the grid should be analyzed and evaluated according to the typology of the texts established during the planning phase. Once the components of the typology have been evaluated, the coherence of the overall scriptovisual system can then be checked.

CRITERIA / TYPE OF TEXT	GENERAL	CONCEPTUAL	SPECIFIC	ILLUSTRATIVE
Content				
Attainment of communications objectives				
Nature of information versus type of text				
Level of information versus type of text				
Intelligibility and clarity of the message				
Balance of message in relation to the text overall				
Level of language (common words/neologisms)				
Redundancy				
Lexical ambiguity				
Sentence length (average: 15 words)				
Text length versus reading time				
Relevance of titles				
Coherence of paragraphs				
Relevance of literary genre				
Layout				
Choice of characters				
Point size of characters				
Line length				
Linespacing				

LEGEND: Poor 1/Acceptable 2/Good 3/Excellent 4

Criteria		
Choice of colours, content-form contrast		
Text-image balance		
Relevance of support and printing process		
Effectiveness of hierarchical ordering of content		
Balance of proportions		
Positioning		
Integration into overall exhibition itinerary		
Quality of lighting		
Location of text		
Height of support		
Ease with which visitors see text		
Proximity of text and object		
Visitor comfort (distance and reading angle)		
Overall effect		
Nature of discourse suited to subject (inform, analyze, argue, recount and so on)		
Power of attraction		
Ease of retention		
Typographic legibility		
Aesthetic originality		
Clear identification of typology		

LEGEND: Poor 1/Acceptable 2/Good 3/Excellent 4

The types of texts in this grid are drawn from the sample typology on page 170.

Conclusion

As the observations of the authors reveal, text plays an undeniable, but widely discussed, role in an exhibition. What is its role in general exhibition discourse? One answer to this question is that text is referential, i.e. the text and, implicitly, its author refer to the object or work of art. Thus, the information in the message is objective or scientifically verifiable. However, there is a shift in text in the museum environment from the strictly referential to the self-referential. A ray of transparency has penetrated the opaqueness of exhibition text, giving way to museum know-how. The text is no longer limited to describing, but now reflects the practice, of which it is the product, and reveals the underlying communication intention of that practice. Text is display and as a result, words are both shown and show. The text designates not only the objective fact, but also the point of view of the author, the exhibition theme and the spatial organization of the exhibition itinerary.

The exhibition text thus subtly reveals its self-referential function. However, it must not be concluded that it has fallen prey to pernicious narcissism. Instead, it has embarked upon a process of definition and introspection which, inevitably, makes it the object of its own analysis. Such a process has already been noted in other media-related practices, notably in television and radio.

The scriptovisual text has become an object displayed along the exhibition itinerary. What will become of its poetic function? Aside from the tone and style adopted, could exhibition texts be designed specifically for the aesthetic pleasure of language?

Andrée Blais

Works in the Muséo collection

Bernard Schiele, editor. *Faire voir, Faire savoir. La muséologie scientifique au présent*, 1989.

Michel Forest and Jacques Viens. *Le défi de l'exposition itinérante. Vue d'ensemble et expérience pratique*, 1990.

Michel Côté, editor. *Musées et gestion*, 1991.

André Bergeron, editor. *L'éclairage dans les institutions muséales*, 1992.

Annette Viel and Céline de Guise. *Muséo-séduction, Muséo-réflexion*, 1992.

Michel Côté, editor. *Les tendances de la muséologie au Québec*, 1992.

_____. *Museological Trends in Québec*, 1992.

Jean Davallon, Gérald Grandmont and Bernard Schiele. *The Rise of Environmentalism in Museums*, 1992.

Andrée Blais, editor. *L'écrit dans le média exposition*, 1993.

Andrée Gendreau, editor. *Le musée: lieu de partage des savoirs*, 1995.

_____. *Museums: Where Knowledge Is Shared*, 1995.

• Cap-Saint-Ignace
• Sainte-Marie (Beauce)
Québec, Canada
1995

«L'IMPRIMEUR»